I0822212

HEMINGWAY, RACE, AND ART

HEMINGWAY, RACE, AND ART

BLOODLINES AND THE COLOR LINE

MARC K. DUDLEY

THE KENT STATE UNIVERSITY PRESS KENT, OHIO

Library of Congress Catalog Card Number 2011030816
ISBN 978-1-60635-092-8
Manufactured in the United States of America

Library of Congress Cataloging-in-Publication Data
Dudley, Marc K., 1971–
Hemingway, race, and art : bloodlines and the color line / Marc K. Dudley.
p. cm.
Includes bibliographical references and index.
ISBN 978-1-60635-092-8 (hardcover : alk. paper) ∞
1. Hemingway, Ernest, 1899–1961—Criticism and interpretation. 2. Race in literature.
I. Title.
PS3515.E37Z58577 2011
813'.52—dc23
2011030816

British Library Cataloging-in-Publication data are available.

15 14 13 12 11 5 4 3 2 1

CONTENTS

INTRODUCTION

The Specter of Race in Hemingway's Grave New World

"Civilization's going to pieces," broke out Tom violently. "I've gotten to be a terrible pessimist about things. Have you read 'The Rise of the Colored Empires' by this man Goddard? . . .

"Well it's a fine book, and everybody ought to read it. The idea is if we don't look out the white race will be—will be utterly submerged. It's all scientific and stuff; it's been proved."

—F. Scott Fitzgerald, *The Great Gatsby*

The specter of race can be a wondrously terrifying thing. Ernest Hemingway certainly thought so, as did his friend F. Scott Fitzgerald. But you would not know that judging by the dearth of related critical material on each artist. Like a ghost, that dark specter played on their minds for years, and for Hemingway, especially, it was a lifelong psychic possession. The preceding excerpt from *The Great Gatsby,* in all its glorious brevity, captures that growing anxiety plaguing the American imagination in the twentieth century's dawning years. While the segment clearly mocks the irrationality of America's consciously hyper-nationalist Tom Buchanans, Fitzgerald simultaneously echoes W. E. B. Du Bois's 1903 proclamation that the "problem of the twentieth century" would most assuredly be that of the "color line." This single statement could not have been any truer had it been made just ten years ago, let alone a hundred. These assertions maintain their resonance and power a century later because of both the messengers and the message. Du Bois made his observations as a sociologist, and as a historian, but most importantly as a black man living in white America. Hemingway, as a student of history himself and a man reflective of his times, certainly heard Du Bois's declaration. As an artist, Hemingway recorded what he saw and heard and made mental notes for future reference.

These mental notes would prove instrumental as Hemingway reconstructed both the American and African landscapes in his fiction. Through these reconstructions, he exposes the color line and concepts of racial essentiality for what they are: products of racial mythmaking. This is a grand truth revealed time and again in his writings. Of American writers he tells us through Papa's voice in *Green Hills of Africa* that "we have had writers of rhetoric who had the good fortune to find a little, in a chronicle of another man and from voyaging, of how things, actual things, can be . . . and this knowledge is wrapped in the rhetoric like plums in a pudding. Occasionally it is there, alone, unwrapped in pudding, and it is good" (20). We do not find anything valuable in the rhetoric, Hemingway assures us; we find it in the conveyed reality. These valued plums are bits and pieces of truth—unvarnished, raw, and real.

In several of his American stories, Hemingway tells tales about the "other" America, allowing our nation's marginal figures, its racial phantoms, to speak—even if indirectly—on the true state of things in America. There is always an almost hyper-cognizance of the color line as fallacy. In the writings spawned by his final African safari, Hemingway demonstrates yet more possibilities inherent in identity's construction. In Africa, Hemingway makes race's malleability quite apparent, first in fortifying the color line (we see this in those first Africa-inspired texts), then (in the works springing from his last safari) in erasing and raising it at will, and seemingly always in the back of his mind was Du Bois's early twentieth-century admonition.

In his seminal essay collection of 1903, *The Souls of Black Folk,* Du Bois explores the ideas of blackness, specifically what it means to be black in America at the beginning of what was then a new century. Looking at himself through the lens of Du Bois's "double consciousness," the African American stands as a torn and tortured entity striving to craft himself in the mold of both his new and his old homelands, yet seeming to belong wholly to neither. The Emancipation Proclamation of 1862 left a people physically free but bereft of home, of livelihood, of the privileges of (political) voice and education; it also left them stripped of personal pride and, to a great degree, of hope. What to do became the quandary for both the white and the black, and the white man proclaimed it his burden. This also became the burgeoning century's greater problem of the color line, and this problem refused to be bound by the strictures of formal politics, forcing its way into both the science and art of the day.

Yet, relatively speaking, the white literary academy's members during Du Bois's day who addressed, let alone immersed themselves in, the politics and sociology of race were few. As an artist, Fitzgerald makes mention of race in *The Diamond as Big as the Ritz* and *The Great Gatsby,* but he certainly does not make its exploration his central mission. Perhaps more than any other twentieth-century canonical representative, William Faulkner immerses himself in the issues of biology and ethnicity. *Light in August,* for example, is an attempt to exorcise the demons and defeatist sensibilities haunting an entire region generations after the actual sectional strife ceased, generations after its unconditional surrender. In fact, Faulkner's 1932 novel shows a remarkably heightened awareness of both racial epistemology and miscegenation's attendant horrors in the 1930s American South. Notions of race, power, and authority are foregrounded in Joe Christmas's own story and, arguably, the story of an entire region.[1]

But what of the rest of America? Surely the South was not alone in its angst. Tom Buchanan's imaginative ramblings—or, more correctly, Fitzgerald's—suggest otherwise. In fact, race consciousness and the ever-present color line even pervade the texts of the unlikeliest of America's so-called moderns, Ernest Hemingway. Not only was Hemingway aware of Du Bois's declaration that *the* defining problem of the twentieth century was that of the color line, but his lifelong engagement with race suggests that he believed it to be true.

Some of Hemingway's earliest writings are racially bound, and the author was never able to shake free of those tethers. We see this in Hemingway's fascination with and eventual push toward the African continent. Several of his later texts born of his safaris are a grand experiment meant to both placate and comfort his own psyche, and to challenge and unsettle it, too. Hemingway visited East Africa two times. His African travels, especially his first, were on one level a means of escaping the challenges to white privilege being mounted at home and, on another level, a way, he hoped, to clarify for himself increasingly muddied notions of racial identity and authority. With its clearly delineated social hierarchy, 1930s Africa became the white artist's true land of opportunity and, in some respects, the last good country. Yet the African safaris, especially his last, also stand as socio-aesthetic experiments that ultimately challenge notions of racial essentiality and what I will call absolute identity.[2] In fact, Hemingway's greater body of work, when examined in its totality, is a career-long experiment exploring a variety of identity issues, of which race is an integral part. Such is the legacy of a modern, but Hemingway's true modernity has, until now, been only partially recognized.

Suffice it to say that Hemingway talked about new things or, if not new things, new ideas in a burgeoning new century. And he certainly explored these ideas in a vernacular new to the scene. His contributions to this way of writing form the foundations of Hemingway critical scholarship. While mimicking the great artists of his day and before—the Cézannes, Matisses, and Picassos—Hemingway crafted a writing style whose syntax expanded the literary landscape and whose diction drew from imagination. Often he would work this magic without saying much.[3]

Hemingway's modernity, though, is equally present in his subject matter. Critics typically point to his skewed reflection of a nation bent on progress, yet still both visibly and invisibly reeling from the realities of war.[4] Hemingway was indeed very much the existentialist, and we get glimpses of this in the early stories of *In Our Time,* in Frederic Henry's soul searching in *A Farewell to Arms,* and in the wanderings of Jake Barnes and his not-so-merry band of wayward souls in *The Sun Also Rises.* In more recent years, just as Hemingway scholarship seemed to be running out of fuel, we experienced another marked critical shift, with gender explorations marking a return and resurgence for the author. But as we forge ahead into a new century, a new millennium even, a critical lack persists. Even as this new century seems to usher in a new day—with a black man acting as leader of the free world—the racial divide in America remains that untapped resource for scholars of both Hemingway and the American cultural scene.[5]

My interest in Hemingway and race actually arose years ago as I explored the texts produced from his first African sojourn, particularly his fictional memoir, *Green Hills of Africa.* My examination of *Green Hills* initially sprang from Toni Morrison's suggestion that much of America's literary canon necessarily depends on an unnamed, often unspecified, "marginal element" to forge and maintain its own sense of American-ness. She specifically names that site the "Africanist presence," but her template works with an expanded racial circle as well. In the years since Hemingway's latest critical resurgence, Morrison's *Playing in the Dark: Whiteness and the Literary Imagination* has become a staple point of reference for scholars intent on engaging the canonical (read: *white*) text for its racial investment, although such critical readings are relatively few, and those prescriptively reading Hemingway even fewer.[6] My own investigation is no different, insofar as it acknowledges a debt to Morrison's book, a work that spawned what surely were then not wholly new ideas, but certainly boldly ventured and impeccably timed ones. In the postcolonial era, Morrison's work clearly pays homage to Edward Said's orientalist textual prescription, but, I would argue, Morrison's work goes a step further. It contextualizes such a reading for an American audience still haunted by its own racial ghosts.

What better time to exorcise and interrogate this presence than in the years immediately following the last of Hemingway's posthumous publications—the substantially abridged *True at First Light* or its more complete iteration, *Under Kilimanjaro,* works inspired by his final African safari in 1953–54?[7] When placed alongside his other race-centered texts, Hemingway's later African stories, particularly his safari books, become an answer to the earlier Nick Adams–centered American tales. This juxtaposition prompts several questions: Can we connect Hemingway's African stories to the American tales that precede them? More appropriately, should we? What function does race play in the early tales? What role does it play in any of the texts, for that matter? Put another way, what is race's purpose for Hemingway, someone with *seemingly* little to no real investment in the game of acculturation?

But American culture was very much Hemingway's concern. Hemingway is a product of his times, and his interest in race, outside any personal connection to the Native American community or Africa as that grand abstraction he had chased since boyhood, is tied to a national anxiety over a changing American racial landscape. That being said, each of his individual works becomes a treatment and expression of that collective (white) American angst. Hemingway's modernity is thus in his recognition of race as *the* pervasive issue for a progressive nation defining itself in a burgeoning century. While his works may lack the apparent complexity of William Faulkner's, they share Faulkner's concerns with race and take them well beyond the bounds of the South and extend them to the rest of the nation. Hemingway's treatment is an American treatment, his body of work a lifelong exploration of national (racial) identity, in letters.

Hemingway stepped onto the literary scene and spoke to his country, his generation, with provocative narratives. In *The Sun Also Rises* (published in 1926) and *A Farewell to Arms* (published in 1929), Hemingway asks, among other things, what it means to be a man and, more specifically, what it means to be an American man. World war prompted the existentialist scramble for meaning as old values were obliterated; similarly, warring racial realities and ideals prompted a comparable scramble for meaning. Why not then transfer this inquiry to the realm of race? Is race of the blood, essential? What necessarily is blackness? What is whiteness? Does anything separate one from the other? Further, what would a blurring of that all-important color line do to an understanding of racial identity, if anything at all? Hemingway's modernity lies in his early recognition of race's flexibility, its malleability, and ultimately its artificiality.

Hemingway's body of work suggests that as we shift the dividing line between the races, between (white) self and racial "other," difference disappears. Moreover, imagined difference must be amplified to maintain any sense of "true" selfhood. Hemingway demonstrates early on that racial configuration is just that: a configuration, a construct, an idea whose days seemingly are numbered. Today, several generations later, the essentialist-constructivist argument regarding racial definition rages on unabated.[8] Hemingway's real modernity thus lies in his recognition of racial "truths" at a time when few other canonical artists were expressly addressing them. And such a cognizance empowers the artist bent on experimentation.

At first glance, Hemingway's racial investment seems specious at best. Epithets color the text more than do actual people of color. In some instances, the minority presence is seemingly nonexistent. However, it is there; one just has to be willing to see it. And entangled with the phantom racial presence is that love for Africa. The key to seeing, if not understanding Hemingway's strategy, is in a more comprehensive recognition and appreciation of his work's collective. When joined together, the race-centered texts—those texts, both long and short, featuring an important minority presence—stridently push toward Africa, a space that occupied the author's mind even in his youth. Hemingway's landing on the "dark continent," his repeated literal and metaphoric return to it, and his profound fascination and love for it then should come as no surprise.[9] But one question remains: why Africa?

Like the man himself, the answer to that question is complex, Hemingway's fervor complicated by fear. Fear of a lost dominion drove many to the green hills of Africa during the new century's dawning years. Although even in his most conservative moments Hemingway pushed the aesthetic envelope, in truth, (self-)preservation was the first order of business in his trek to the African continent. The African sojourn was as much a flight of fear as it was a flight of fancy. Truthfully, his recollected forays into the African wilderness (in 1933 and again in 1953) were in part an attempt to stave off impending change. On a very basic level, the collected safari fiction becomes an attempt to preserve some semblance of the known (white) order; it is a means of negotiating—as only an artist can—racial issues that would dog the writer throughout much of his career. With a once-clearly delineated color line blurring on the home front, with the old racial power differential in a state of constant flux, Africa ultimately provided the perfect locus within which to both reflect and reaffirm: there, with added distance, the white man could properly reflect upon this inconstancy. There too he could reaffirm those once-reliable racial tenets entrenched in the mythos of white superiority.

Yet however entrenched the author was in this mythology, one fact remains: this very act of (white) reaffirmation also becomes the ultimate aesthetic experiment for a writer bold enough to try it. White reconstitution, Hemingway shows us, is itself an active, deliberate, and grand exercise in identity construction. However, raising whiteness was only part of the exercise; razing the color line was the other.[10] The African space also provided for the writer a sanctum of uninhibited creation. Here, again with the benefit of distance, the white male idol could transcend the strictures and expectations of celebrity (and race) binding him at home and transgress the color line with all the fervor that artistic license would allow. And noting the quickly changing cultural landscape around him, a young and impressionable Hemingway had been engaged in the grand experiment from an early age.

Young Hemingway's America, most especially in the first decades of the new century, shook with the rumblings of a nation not only at war with others abroad but at war with itself domestically; "foreign" elements at home ensured this. And writhing under the dominant culture's boot, struggling for some semblance of agency, that nebulous racial other threatened to destroy the bedrock of difference upon which much of white American identity rested; it threatened to expose the mythological behind so-called established truth and thereby undermine Anglo claims to power. Early twentieth-century America was still clearly attempting to fashion a future for itself from a past steeped in lore, loss, and lies.

We see that bedrock's bricks laid bare in the era's Native American trading cards, in its fascination with Wild West shows, and in a resurgent Ku Klux Klan. For years, the racial propaganda of Thomas Dixon, author of *The Clansman* and *The Leopard's Spots,* transcended the literary realm and held sway over much of popular culture. Dixon's novels inspired the emerging cinema; his romantic spirit inhabits the body of W. D. Griffith's 1915 landmark film *Birth of a Nation,* a film that captivated a country by openly playing on racial stereotype and its attendant fears. So visceral was its initial cultural impact that President Woodrow Wilson declared admiringly that *Birth* was "history writ with lightning." More importantly, it was a film and a history with which Hemingway was very familiar.[11]

Recall also that, particularly in the South, in the waning decades of the nineteenth century, writers like Thomas N. Page, the author of *In Ole Virginia,* sold many a book touting the virtues of the plantation tradition, a tradition glorifying the Old South and defending established racial order and white privilege. Turn-of-the-century America experienced great growing pains and the dominant culture made frantic attempts to make necessary adjustments. It was an era of reconstruction, reevaluation, and redefinition. What exactly was the "authentic American self" of which Ralph Waldo Emerson and others had spoken just a generation or two before? Often the easy answer lay in the negative; aptly, in the new century's dawning years, many Americans answered in terms of what America was *not* or what it did not wish to become.

Throughout this mutable era, white America actively engaged in a campaign of differentiation, seeking to recraft itself in light of the other, and this meant accentuating the interracial divide wherever and whenever possible. That negative space became the "un-American" home to a myriad of racist ideological varieties perpetuated well into the new century. Conversely, the dominant culture assured itself of its promised progress, seizing upon Darwinian principles to define it; this often meant using so-called science to explain societal and, more specifically, racial difference. Race and genetics, then, accounted for a shared—whether ascending or descending—cultural trajectory.

Science would certainly explain much to mainstream America during those formative years. However, artists were not exempt from such racial cognizance and wholesale propagandist strategies. Extending this line of thought to the literature of the day, a few of Hemingway's earliest short stories point to the prospects of a blurred color line and to the inherent horrors of a destiny shared by whites and racial others. Carl Eby rightly posits that Hemingway, as an artist, came to represent the "psychosocial dilemmas of his age—an age in which many of his white male compatriots felt challenged by the rising power of racial and sexual 'others'" (166). For many whites then, the mere prospect of a shared moral depravity made pure definition and clear dividing lines all the more critical to maintaining a valid claim to ultimate social authority. Simply put, the racial totem depended upon difference for its very survival. And Hemingway's recognition of this fact was unparalleled.

Hemingway's acclaim as modern thus stems from his very unapologetic exploitation of this racial dynamic. Upon closer examination, an apparent device quickly becomes an equally important part of Hemingway's overall narrative strategy. While the Fitzgerald example at the beginning of this chapter clearly pokes fun at Tom Buchanan for his markedly unsophisticated world reading, many of Fitzgerald's contemporaries were clearly disturbed by what they saw as a trend toward social devolution. Hemingway too noted this anxiety, and he seized upon it in his own storytelling. Clearly, for the artist, life and art spoke in tandem. The "Goddard" of Tom's verbal misstep is a very real person. In actuality, he is Lothrop Stoddard, whose work *The Rising Tide of Color,* along with several other similar works, was sanctioned by academics and laymen alike as scholarly. In it, Stoddard rails against a perceived encroachment by the rapidly multiplying colored peoples from Asia and Africa. The raw numbers did not lie, and the fears, on a very fundamental level, were steeped in quantifiable fact.

A marked immigrant influx during the new century's first decade helped foster a strong and (un)healthy hysteria and xenophobia; between 1900 and the end of the First World War, over seventeen million foreigners (mostly of European descent) immigrated to the United States, and in the years following the Great War, various acts of legislation seeking to limit and control immigration became the establishment's response (see Divine, Breen, Fredrickson, and Williams). These sentiments become haunts of sorts, echoes of utterances from a previous decade when the works of social spokesmen like B. L. Putnam Weale held sway. Weale's 1910 work *The Conflict of Colour* was one of several early twentieth-century sociological works promoted by critics as scientific scholarship. It was also one of many to engage the notion of a shrinking white dominion. Within this worldview, whites were quickly losing ground in an increasingly hostile world.

Additional works like Madison Grant's *The Passing of the Great Race,* reprinted several times in the years following its original 1916 publication, demonstrate the issue's pervasiveness and its continued resonance with the reading public.[12] Such books were read widely and sold well. These publications surely were part of Hemingway's consciousness—much in the same way a young Ernest drank in the skewed spectacle of Griffith's *Birth of a Nation* as a teen. Such early influences would play on his imagination for years and would play themselves out in his early fictionalized interactions with both Native and African Americans, and later in the works born of his first African safari in 1933–34.[13] These works in particular show us a young writer very much at the top of his aesthetic game; more importantly, they show us a man very much informed by history, both past and in the making.

By the end of the nineteenth century, America had witnessed a westward expansion that seemed without bounds. With the subsequent closing of the great frontier, enthusiasm for international expansion grew exponentially, extending America's Manifest Destiny and its romance with the quest in perpetuity.[14] All the while, the dominant culture actively engaged a racial mythology, one entrenched in crafted difference and notions of white superiority. Appropriately, Indian captivity narratives, a staple of seventeenth- and eighteenth-century American historical documentation, saw a revival in the nineteenth century. Furthermore, Wild West shows re-created scenes of a dying white American glory, strategically pitting white sacrifice and valor against Native American savagery and cruelty. This was not simply happenstance; local historians fought hard to preserve and redefine their part in America's glorious development (see Derounian-Stodola and Levernier).

Still, American racial politics could also show a subtler hand. The day's consciously racial politics assumed more innocuous forms in the less incendiary but equally powerful consumer marketplace. Marketing campaigns became ways of further dealing with the second of the so-called white man's burdens. For example, manufacturers strategically planted in bread packages and rice boxes trading cards revisiting yesteryear's cowboy-and-Indian motif or else romancing the red man in commune with nature. These proved subtle ways to re-create and reclaim as American images of a not-so-distant past. Contemporary magazine advertisements also "innocently" played on the age-old Janus typology inherent in the word "Indian": to a culture craving myth, he was both the noble savage and the beastly degenerate. No matter what the product, the propagandist agenda was unmistakable: reclaim history, or altogether recast it in the crafting of a national mythology. As S. Elizabeth Bird posits in her *Dressing in Feathers,* re-created mythology became a way to "explain to whites their right to be here and help deal with lingering guilt about the displacement of the Native inhabitants—after all, the 'good' Indians helped us out and recognized the inevitability of white conquest" (2). Most important here is the correct assertion that white hands ultimately retain conceptual power. Furthermore, that power, we must remember, is a crafted power. Hemingway recognized this truth, and his early tales reflect his cognizance.

Hemingway's Native American stories, the subject of the first two chapters, represent the author's earliest explorations of and confrontations with America's racial demons. In these tales, we witness a doe-eyed Nick Adams's initiation into the world of "otherness." To be sure, Nick's baptism occurs during a pivotal time in our nation's evolution, a time when the very social foundations upon which the Adams family and so many others rested increasingly showed their cracks and fissures. Each of Hemingway's Indian stories works as a complement to the others in exposing these fallibilities and in showing national and cultural identities for what they are: constructs.

The collected Indian stories are, on the one hand, an author's conscious reconstruction of a seemingly shattered essential bedrock. Joel Williamson calls this primal push "the rage to order"; when juxtaposed with red decadence, white, in one sense, reads as "right." On the other hand, though, these tales are an expression of collective (white) American guilt for past wrongs. They are also an inquisition of whiteness itself and the notion of racial essentiality.[15] We see Williamson's ordering process in the dominant culture's mythmaking, in its deliberate attempts to reestablish and sustain at least some semblance of white authoritarian control. In the end, though, Hemingway recognizes the folly inherent in such mythmaking. He also quite deftly suggests that racial difference and therefore the authority and agency predicated on such difference is the true myth here. His crafted American reality bears this out wonderfully.

Hemingway begins razing the American race mythology in his early storytelling. In "Indian Camp" and "The Doctor and the Doctor's Wife," two works from his first acclaimed story collection, *In Our Time* (published in 1924), and the focus of the first chapter, he crafts a diametric diorama, taking us along with young Nick Adams and his father into the woods, where the wild things are, or where we expect them to be. But Hemingway subverts reader expectation and gives us a white protagonist who is expressly labeled a "great man," but whose greatness is questionable.

In "Indian Camp," Dr. Adams is masterful with fishing twine but arguably socially inept as he proudly performs an impromptu cesarean section on an ailing Native American woman, all the while deaf to the woman's cries, because, he assures young Nick, they are "not important." In "The Doctor and the Doctor's Wife," Hemingway revisits the "great man" as he tangles with Dick Boulton, a Native American man who occasionally does cleanup work for the Adams clan. Rumored to be part white, Boulton's true racial makeup is a bit nebulous, and so, much to the chagrin of the doctor, is the color line separating the two men. Unwilling to play the part assigned to him by (white) society, Boulton shrewdly sees through the doctor's apparent thievery (he lays claim to wood washed onto his beach from an upstream company), deftly parses his words, and boldly calls him on his malfeasance. Once more, Hemingway turns conventional knowledge on its ear as he transposes the civilized and the savage and skillfully shifts the color line.

In the stories that move beyond the Indian camp, Hemingway seemingly highlights native debauchery at every turn in telling the tale of a community's decline. I examine three such stories in the second chapter: "Ten Indians," "Fathers and

Sons," and "The Indians Went Away." In "Fathers and Sons," sex is Hemingway's vice of choice as a mature Nick Adams recounts his childhood encounters with Trudy, a young and apparently less-than-pure Native American girl instrumental in Nick's own sexual awakening. Fittingly, in this tale Hemingway also explores miscegenation's horrific prospects.

Published in 1933, "Fathers and Sons," a story not typically labeled one of Hemingway's Indian stories, is perhaps the author's most forceful expression of this latent racial anxiety. In it, Hemingway's literary imagination violently confronts the prospects of miscegenation, the ultimate blurring of racial lines in actual, real terms. Here, an older Nick Adams, his son in tow, remembers his own father. Metaphorically, Dr. Adams becomes the great (white) father to both his son and the inhabitants of the nearby Native American camps. His own personal history and hunting prowess are nearly legendary. Channeling his past ghosts, Nick conjures images of his first sexual exploits: the nearby camp, a Native American girl, and lessons passed down by his father. The warm memories, however, belie an anxiety both pervasive and potent.

Hemingway's purpose is clear as he deliberately juxtaposes Nick's sexual "taking" of young Trudy Gilby (in the memories of experimental play) with his later, quite violent defense of his own sister's maidenhood from Eddie Gilby (Trudy's half-brother). Implication alone draws from young Nick the most extreme of racial epithets and the starkest, most violent of images, including threats of scalping. The key issue again is (white) control and the threat of its loss; circumstances force Nick into the role of spectator from that of actor, defender from that of offender, savage from that of civilized. In each instance, Hemingway suggests, the line separating white from red is illusory at best. Once more the phantom presence (here it is racialized memory) speaks from the darkness (the recesses of Nick's mind); Nick's memory and conscience are a national memory and conscience wrestling with its racial demons.

In the other two stories, drink saturates the narrative as both a commonplace Native diversion and apparently the root cause of a community's decline. "Ten Indians" is an enumeration of (ethnic) debauchery. In it, a young Nick Adams makes his way through both memories of his first sexual experiences—again with a young Indian girl (Prudy here)—and a sea of prostrate and inebriated dark bodies. "The Indians Went Away," a fragmentary but equally salient piece, emphatically marks the end of the Indian's downward slide in the Nick Adams collective. In this piece, the Native American community is a shell of its former self, more spooky than organic. Alcohol has reduced its people to pandering and recollected smells, sights, and haunting memories. The story's closing words, "Now no good," are a marked exclamation point ending the sad tale of a people's demise, and this becomes an important subtext to the life and times of Nick Adams, American ascendant.

Alcohol's decimation of Native American tribal communities is well documented and real; Hemingway's historical record is accurate. Where the writer takes artistic license is in the hyperactive system of binary oppositions he crafts with his narrative. Perpetually, he enlists the aid of a panoply of separators to divide white from nonwhite, civilized from savage. In doing so, he gives us a narrative that emphatically and very deliberately underscores difference, and difference here serves a very definite purpose: to underscore and make natural ideas of essentiality and the racial totem. Exaggerated dividing lines reify preconceptions. Hemingway's differential narrative strategy is to remind a contemporary audience of the coexistence of two worlds torn apart by an artificial totem, one world doomed to dwell in the shadows. And like Gilbert and Gubar's madwoman in the attic, Hemingway's phantoms lurk in and eventually speak from that profound darkness.

Tapping into an American psyche laden with all the guilt inherent in a complex and conflicted national history, Hemingway writes his own American Gothic. The author borrows freely from the Gothic tradition in exploring an American conscience wrestling with itself. While not steeped in the supernatural, the author's racial narratives are instead appropriately grotesque at times and cast in both literal and metaphoric darkness. These narratives and their grotesques belie a shocking new truth suggesting, among other things, the possibility of white culpability in Native decadence and a very real fallibility. In turn, a fallible, imperfect whiteness suggests an impermanent, if not mutable, color line. Thus, Hemingway seems to suggest, a race-based (read: *red*) natural proclivity toward self-destruction may in fact not be an exclusively Indian problem. Hemingway's white subject aptly asks, "What if he and I aren't so different after all?"

Surprisingly, this question also sits at the heart of Hemingway's satirical send-up of Sherwood Anderson's Chicago school of literature, *The Torrents of Spring*. I say *surprisingly* because one would hardly expect to find profundity in a work written intentionally to be bad, written, by the author's own account, in a matter of days. Because of spatial constraints, my treatment of the parody is brief. I merely wish to underscore Hemingway's deliberateness in crafting his earliest professional writing. This often overlooked but potent little text anticipates quite nicely his career-long racial inquiry. Published in 1926, partly as a means to escape his contractual obligations to Boni and Liveright, the novella lampoons the Chicago school of literature in its heavy-handed, hyper-expressive, introspective style. But it does something more: it mocks both contemporary (white) xenophobia and the essentialist racial argument being levied in professional and lay circles alike.[16]

Not simply just another example of style over substance, his small compendium of laughs succinctly encapsulates, in its roughly ninety pages, one of the primary working theses of Hemingway's career: much of American identity is inherently racial. In *Torrents,* we find the same drunken Indian trope he makes good use of in "Ten Indians" as Yogi Johnson, a war veteran and pump-factory worker and one of the story's two principal (white) players (the other being Scripps O'Neil), waxes philosophic to two strangers he meets on the street on such topics as war. The two men listen, as a captive audience is apt to do. For their time, they each receive, appropriately, cigarettes and alcohol (as per their requests). The two strangers are Indian. Instinctively, the two look to Yogi Johnson for direction and he becomes their sage, their "white chief." After all, as one of the Indians aptly asserts in stereotypically broken English, "White chief nature's nobleman" and "educated like hell" (75).

Torrents also gives us Bruce, an African American cook who says very little and appears to be even less. He is an uncomplicated Bugs from "The Battler": he is all acquiescence, all service, all smiles, with a laugh that echoes throughout the text from beginning to end. But even Bruce, the quintessential "happy darky," has a smile that belies, like Bugs's smile, a secret knowledge. Like Bruce, the other stock types that people the landscape also, invariably, lead our protagonists to a secret knowledge.

The two Indians with Yogi Johnson—one appropriately missing both arms and wearing prosthetics—unwittingly lead the white man to a form of self-revelation. Herein, we once more see Hemingway's enduring homage to Gothic convention. The grotesque becomes instrumental here and on more than one occasion in Hemingway's racial storytelling and truth-seeking. Ultimately, the author gives us the essentialist's story only to subvert it in the end. He too conveys a coveted knowledge, and while it may offer no real prescription for an ailing national psyche, at the very least, *Torrents of Spring* underscores the author's cognizance of the ailment. It also demonstrates the potency and place in Hemingway's imagination that race would hold for years.

To be sure, Hemingway's racial cognizance and America's channeled angst were not confined to the Indian camp. While Hemingway's inclusion of Native Americans in several of his earliest stories is, arguably, an homage of sorts to his own experiences with the Ojibwa of Michigan, simply explaining away his ardent interest in blackness and his persistent employment of African American figures in his work becomes much more of a challenge. To be sure, blackness figured prominently in his imagination for good reason. In the third and fourth chapters, I demonstrate how a national anxiety manifested itself in Hemingway's depiction of his countrymen's negotiation with their black brethren. All three stories discussed in these chapters expose a newly awakened national discomfort. More specifically, they become metaphors for an early twentieth-century white American male reacting adversely to a shifting social climate.

The new century's first two decades bore witness to the Great Migration of African Americans from small southern towns to the cities of the North. Almost two million blacks would make the trip northward during those years, for various reasons, including the promise of economic and educational opportunities not afforded them in the South. Chicago alone, a city Hemingway knew all too well, saw its numbers begin to swell by the tens of thousands in 1916. Whatever their reasons, for most, the migration became in and of itself a grand act of self-assertion, something reenacted time and again in towns and cities across America, and black self-assertion becomes that "unspeakable thing unspoken," the latent specter in several of Hemingway's stories.[17]

White America's fear of its vocal black brethren and its consequent grappling for authority are most pronounced in what I will call Hemingway's black-and-white stories. The racial prism through which we view his Native American stories becomes an equally viable tool here as well. Three tales in particular prove most useful as we examine Hemingway's negotiation of race and authority: "The Battler," the more obscure "The Light of the World," and the all-but-unknown fragmentary tale "The Porter." In these black-and-white stories, Hemingway expands the bounds of the inquiry he established early on in the Indian stories. In those works, he pointed to difference and its effectiveness as a tool in maintaining the color line; here, he does something similar but complicates the equation a bit with an additional component. In the black-and-white stories, he suggests that violence is the unspoken component necessary for both the color line's maintenance and its erasure. In the Indian stories, Dick Boulton in "The Doctor and the Doctor's Wife" and young Nick Adams in "Fathers and Sons" are the closest expressions of this new truth, and Boulton's insolence as red man is exceptional. Also new to the equation, says Hemingway, is a black cognizance of this very fact.

In the third chapter, I purposefully conjoin the first two of the black-and-white stories, "The Battler" and "The Light of the World," because of a commonly employed trope. In both, boxing serves as *the* key subtext. In the former tale, Hemingway explores the unconventional relationship between two road comrades, a white champion fighter turned convict turned vagabond and his former prison-mate turned caretaker. The former fighter is white; his companion is African American. The black man is also, most importantly, the story's ultimate authority figure.

In the latter story, the action centers on an argument between two white prostitutes over a boxer's heart. This fighter is a complex amalgam of sorts: great lover that he is, he is the object of both their affections, but he is also notorious for dirty tricks in the ring. Most importantly, though, he is white. We discern from their disagreement that this former heavyweight contender loses to Jack Johnson, the first black man to hold the championship belt. My interest in this story lies not in the featured relationships but in Hemingway's deliberate manipulation of contemporary history. With it, Hemingway does more than craft effect here; he challenges conventional thinking. The prostitutes' shared reverence for all things white in this tale becomes an absurdity; here, the Anglo figures themselves become grotesques, each with his or her own version of a shared racial truth. And Hemingway embodies that truth in the heavyweight champion, the black man, whose absence from the fictional landscape is very pronounced and very deliberate.

Each story's revelatory kernel has, at its heart, the truth about whiteness's imperfection, if not its fallibility, and Hemingway knows full well that this is a truth, in an age of progress and eugenics, that runs counter to much of the day's scholarship and popular thinking. Quite notably, in both stories, the white figure's glory is a past glory as he stands in the shadow of the other, defeated. Also, in both stories, Hemingway weds a tempered violence with both that shadowed self and white defeat. Hemingway crafts defiant minority characters and a world that openly challenges stereotype, whiteness, and the racial totem. In this world, notions of civilization and the primitive conflate, and labels become just that: labels.

Hemingway steps outside the boxing ring's confines altogether to continue his exploration of America's racial mythos and the great (white) man in the third of the black-and-white tales. Juxtaposed with his pugilistic stories is the fragment "The Porter." This text, incomplete as it may seem, warrants thorough examination and thus is the entire subject of the fourth chapter. It is a provocative text whose import cannot be overstated. In this narrative, Hemingway chronicles the growth of a young boy but steps outside the Nick Adams saga to do so. "The Porter" follows young Jimmy Breen's initiation into a treacherous world imbued with new racial realities. In this narrative in particular, Hemingway perpetuates stereotype and racial mythos—as he has done in each of the other race tales—and again ups the ante in his inquiry. "The Porter" is a direct questioning of white authority's validity, but also the totem's strength and stability. In this piece, through George the porter, Hemingway not only questions the color line but also expressly questions the right of white America to draw it. For this reason alone, I include "The Porter" as a centerpiece of sorts in my examination. This work stands as Hemingway's most deliberate expression of black America's own self-awareness and its (self-)consciously stifled volition standing in the shadows of whiteness.

Jimmy's experience is early twentieth-century white America's experience. From the outset, the young boy's narrative is unconsciously lined with racial epithets; typology constricts and skews our conception of the African American, particularly George the porter, whose name already aligns him with the "happy darky" type. Hemingway initially paints him as lackey content with drink, cards, and an unquestioning service to whites. In Hemingway's deft hands, George is seemingly a Tom-like caretaker, something Toni Morrison in *Playing in the Dark* calls a "nurse" figure and critic Kenneth Lynn in *Hemingway* labels the "dark mother" character. He is the great paradox, both childlike and subject to vice, and an entrusted manservant who, like Bugs in "The Battler," takes the narrative's protagonist under his wing to teach him a life lesson. However, trust notwithstanding, Hemingway's man-child actually has an agenda all his own; as he does with his dark mother's lessons in "The Battler," Hemingway heavily invests his porter's pedagogy with a streetwise savvy and violence.

Unlike the boxing stories, particularly "The Light of the World," where the ring becomes the site of a sanctioned square-off between the races, "The Porter" pushes the possibility of a race war beyond the confines of rope and canvas and out into the streets. In "The Battler," Hemingway places Bugs in the privileged position as he looms literally and figuratively over his white confidant; however, George's lesson in "The Porter" on the nuances of razor fighting goes a step beyond Bugs's cognizance in demonstrating black awareness and self-actualization. Hemingway gives us a black man who recognizes the color line's illusory nature, and once more history informs the author's narrative.

Race riots were a prominent new reality for many in Wilmington, North Carolina; Tulsa, Oklahoma; Atlanta, Georgia; Chicago, Illinois, and other cities all across America during the new century's first decades. The worst of it played out in Hemingway's own backyard—Chicago's 1919 riot was among the most disastrous, claiming almost forty lives and leaving a great metropolis shaken to the core.[18] When coupled with New York City's silent soldier march (protesting rampant racism greeting black servicemen returning home after the First World War) of the same year, and the insistence by "radicals" Marcus Garvey and W. E. B. Du Bois that American blacks were entitled to so much more, the viral unrest of these events suggests a people struggling to emancipate themselves from the cultural yoke of type. Images of the dark predatory beast, the incompetent fool, the petulant coward, the apolitical and antisocial underling dominated the contemporary white imagination and suggested a template for reading the nonwhite. While acceptable to the majority, this protocol invited open challenge by the minority—and challenge they did. Again we return to the notion of reconstituting definition and reassigning ultimate authority; again, we return to Hemingway.

The lessons of "The Porter" seem to wager that violence of the strategic and controlled variety could easily undo the knot in the black man's noose, and this fear played on the white imagination. As George Fredrickson asserts in *The Black Image in the White Mind,* "Like so many other elements in the racist rhetoric and imagery of 1900, [the image of the Negro] had its origins in the proslavery imagination, which had conceived of the black man as having a dual nature—he was docile and amiable when enslaved, ferocious and murderous when free" (276). Hemingway uses this imagined duality to great effect in crafting George's public and private personas; his porter is a wonderful amalgam of all things (conceptualized as) black. Our author relishes the ambiguity and seems to suggest that, like the Wilmington riot of 1898, Jimmy's momentary fear watching the black man wield his razor may be no aberration. The new century brought with it new questions that simply refused to go away: Where do authoritarian lines begin and end? What do historical events suggest about the racial totem? How much deeper than the epidermis does the blood of race truly flow? Clearly, such great questions warrant answers, and these questions haunted Hemingway for years. No longer a young boy in 1933, he carried these questions with him to the African continent, his imagination clearly wrestling with much more than big game while on safari, and this is the object of my inquiry in chapter 5.

Real-world issues, both social and political, took precedence over aesthetics for the author in the months and years leading up to and immediately following his safari of 1933–34. During those years, the dark politics of the Third Reich began to cast a long shadow well beyond German borders. The crippling ripples of racial politics and a growing eugenics movement were felt across the ocean as ideology took both a national and international stage. Franklin Roosevelt may have brought with him to the White House all the hope and promise of the New Deal, but the special amalgam of science and politics ushered in a new day for age-old prejudices both at home and abroad. The cauldron had, however, been boiling already for decades.

As an introduction of things to come, London had played host to scholars the world over at the first of the International Eugenics Conferences in 1912. New York would do the honors for both the second and third in the series in each of the following decades (in 1921 and 1932, respectively). Meanwhile, closer to home for Hemingway, the Race Betterment Foundation of Battle Creek, Michigan, hosted three national conferences (1914, 1915, and 1928) promoting eugenics as the new era's defining ideology. Even little Oak Park, Illinois, was not immune to the fever; like so many other communities in small-town America trying to connect with something larger than themselves, Hemingway's hometown hosted lectures and banged the eugenics drum as part of local celebrations.

As the ideology's popularity grew, so did its proponents' credibility. Supporters along the way included renowned eugenicist Lothrop Stoddard and respected psychologist Henry H. Goddard. Early on, the movement's growing list of proponents also included one of America's true captains of industry, steel magnate Andrew Carnegie, who would also add philanthropist and idealist to a growing list of descriptive titles; his financial contributions to the eugenics movement have been well documented. However, his investment in the movement went beyond the financial; the Carnegie Institution of Washington acted as an official think tank of sorts and played host to the Eugenics Record Office (see Daniel Kevles, *In the Name of Eugenics*, 55). Even Hemingway's boyhood hero, Theodore Roosevelt, waved the eugenics flag for white America.

Appropriately, at its apex in the 1920s, the movement's biggest advocate was government. So, as jazz music triumphed and American optimism flowered, in its blatant and warped attempt to "preserve a more perfect union," Congress passed the Racial Integrity Act of 1924, initiating a set of constrictions to limit immigration and (as many saw it) stay the flood of foreign blood tainting American purity. New and newly enforced state laws forbidding interracial marriage—laws particular to the South—further pushed the eugenics agenda, an agenda propelled by so-called science and fear.

What we see unfolding during the 1930s in America is the culmination of scholarship and policy making that had been in the works for decades. Moreover, the phenomenon of racial "passing"—blacks actively passing themselves off as white, infiltrating and encroaching upon white circles—did little to assuage white fears.[19]

Those fears manifested themselves most prominently in the laws of the land. As the critic Robert Farnsworth suggests of turn-of-the-century American social justice—both legal and illegal—and the color line, "Jim Crow laws had been entered on the books in many states, and rigid social segregation was turning the dreams and ambitions of Reconstruction into bitter gall for those 'tainted' by black blood. Lynch law was bearing an increasing harvest of strange fruit." Strictly enforced marriage codes in Virginia and South Carolina had particular bite as whites sought to preserve Anglo stock by stamping out miscegenation altogether; state statutes also pushed for genealogical searches in the hopes of more fully defining whiteness. Louisiana had struck preemptively years before (1911) with its own set of race codes bent on halting incursions across the color line. Such was the day's political agenda.

This prompted the code's critics to ask the ultimate question, which became an actual newspaper headline: "When is a Caucasian not a Caucasian?"[20] Conversely, one may ask, then, when *is* a Caucasian a Caucasian? Hemingway certainly had these questions in mind as he ventured to Africa's green hills in the winter of 1933. His sojourn to the African continent allowed him—at least for the moment—to leave behind Eddie Gilby, threats to white maidenhood, and young Nicky's angst explored in "Fathers and Sons" earlier that year. Answering the din of the drum with the African material engendered from this trip, Hemingway shows himself to be a man at least half-believing the rhetoric of the day. Following the lead of local and national politics, he appears to be a man with a renewed commitment to reconfiguring whiteness and a fast-fading color line; however, he does all this with the license and fervor of an artist, so to the sharp aesthetic eye, his sins are forgivable. In one sense, the path traveled was familiar. Hemingway had explored the complexities of identity in *A Farewell to Arms* just a few years before in 1929: Frederic Henry's quest is in part one of national investment as he struggles with his American-ness. Before that, and more germane to our inquiry, Robert Cohn, as character and conceit, had, in *The Sun Also Rises,* allowed Hemingway to examine the racial totem's intricacies and its potency (for example, Hemingway emphasizes Cohn's Jewishness as yet another space of otherness and as a liability) in 1926. But these were the dark days of Hitler's Aryan superman; the world had changed, and as a man of his times, Hemingway had changed with it, and the day's politics were palpably mean. However, while the social climate was perhaps a bit different in 1933, Hemingway, as public figure and as artist, remained unchanged in one sense: as a middle-aged man, he was still very much an ardent believer in the crafting of individuality and the art(fullness) of identity; he continued to push the same aesthetic boundaries with which he had wrangled years before. His own racial politics and ideological designs while on safari, his insistence on rhetorically reassembling that shattered white body made small by "alien" inroads, tells us so.

In "The Snows of Kilimanjaro," "The Short Happy Life of Francis Macomber," and *Green Hills of Africa* especially—the works born of his first African safari—Hemingway re-entrenches himself in white mythos, fully intent on crafting his own brand of it. I explore this re-entrenchment and the works documenting it in chapter 5. To be sure, he expressly tells us that these works are narrative experiments that explore new imaginative territory, and they are. But in them, Hemingway treads familiar ground. In these first African works, he walks in the shadows of familiar literary and historical luminaries, stalwart figures of safari fiction. *Green Hills* perhaps best exemplifies Hemingway's engagement with the genre. In it, we see a writer perpetuating the same typologies and employing the same literary strategies crafted and exploited by Lord Stanley years before him. Closer to home, and closer to his heart, Theodore Roosevelt—rough rider, slayer of beasts, childhood hero—spoke with a contemporary voice, and he demonstrates Hemingway's place within this long-standing tradition of the great white hunter on safari.[21]

Hemingway's own library demonstrates more than a casual interest in Africa and the celebration of the white African hunting experience.[22] The author knew well the path trod by his predecessors. Those texts and their authors share a common agenda: within the safari text, beast, land, and ultimately people all fall prey to the colonial gaze. The most glaring of the tradition's tropes is the self-reflective, almost narcissistic narrator whose self-aggrandizement aligns itself with an amalgam of whiteness and greatness. His is also a literary imagination actively engaging racial difference whenever and wherever possible. While Hemingway does promote aspects of social egalitarianism at times, and while he does temporarily mitigate difference, in the end, difference and a reconstituted color line dominate his early African texts, particularly *Green Hills.*

In these writings, *Green Hills* especially, Hemingway vacillates between embracing Africa's countrymen as kindred spirits and surveying the country as Occidental tourist; to be sure, his surveillance time in this narrative far outweighs that spent in active embrace. The short fiction engendered from that first safari is no different. Ultimately, Harry's story in "The Snows of Kilimanjaro," Francis Macomber's story in "The Short Happy Life of Francis Macomber," and Papa's story in *Green Hills* are, on one level, the same story: they are the story of white competition, completion, and reconstitution; Harry *is* Macomber *is* Papa. And irrespective of the texts' panoply of characters peopling the landscape, the African excursion ultimately becomes Hemingway's alone. By extension, Hemingway's African experience becomes the white masculine experience, and in the process, it becomes Hemingway's most express form of identity formation.

Unlike the boxing ring, or even America's wilds, featured so prominently in Hemingway's black-and-white stories, Africa, for a time, offered racial stasis to Americans feeling displaced at home in the twentieth century's dawning years. Here the white could stave off, at least temporarily, the rising tide of colored people threatening stability at home. During the first decades of the new century, Africa, unlike America, was a space wherein the lines of racial demarcation were still clearly drawn, even as empire crumbled all around. In colonial Africa, white greatness, theoretically at least, went unquestioned. So while in America, Dr. Adams can only watch as the Native American freely and openly crosses all lines of formality in addressing his "superiors," in colonial Africa, Harry, Macomber, and Papa all share the respected title of Bwana ("master" or "father" in Swahili). Thus, as something to be tamed and possessed, and as something particularly gendered, Africa expressly and fittingly becomes Hemingway's woman of choice during these very tenuous years.[23] Simultaneously offering him both novelty and excitement and familiarity and comfort, Africa was still very much his safe space.

But even in his unabashed reversion to things once known, Hemingway's cognizance of race as artifice is clear. Most importantly, throughout this racial reconstruction, Hemingway is markedly aware of himself as an artist; in each instance, he shows us race's malleable quality in the artist's hands. We see this reflective experimentation played out to a much greater degree in the years following his second African safari as a more mature, more self-assured Hemingway embraces, more than ever, his own ambivalence about the color line.

In the final chapter, I explore this racial ambivalence in light of Hemingway's loftier aesthetic goals and his grander vision going into his second African safari. By 1953, the year of his final visit to Africa, Nazi Germany's prejudiced propaganda and the "science" of eugenics were a fading memory and Africa was a part of his very being, infusing his every thought and fully commanding his imagination. To that end, he spent the better part of his life's last seven years writing about her and chasing the possibility she seemed to embody. As such, his relationship with the African continent could easily be labeled a full-blown love affair. As his mistress, Africa placed few constraints on him. Unlike a fickle reading public, she was understanding, open, and forgiving. She allowed him to be whatever he wished to be. In 1953, Hemingway wanted to be many things, it seems; and in Africa, Hemingway seems to suggest, all things could be true.

After all, even during the 1930s, Africa allowed Hemingway to assume—if only briefly—the role of brother to M'Cola (his personal tracker) and other local tribesmen. In 1953, he would relish that moment a bit longer, a bit more overtly. Here too, on his second trip to the motherland, he immersed himself in Wakamba culture and boasted a second wife in the form of a local tribeswoman. But the compulsions of self-reification and the expectation attached to celebrity were there too. Africa is also where Hemingway, on both occasions, all too easily donned the garb of great white hunter, of Bwana, an incarnation of the ruling white patriarchy. One could be a king in Africa, and celebrity culture expected a reappearance of the great white hero. Only in Africa, it seems, is it possible to be both, and as an artist, Hemingway relished both the ambiguity and the opportunity inherent in the creative process. One could make allowances for both in Africa.

In the twenty years since his first sojourn, Hemingway had learned much, and his last writings bear this out nicely. However, critics all too easily point to the author in his later years and suggest he had become a caricature of sorts. They label him an old man ensnared by his own celebrity, sapped of creative spirit, and wallowing in self-parody. To be sure, some of that criticism is certainly merited; however, the short fable "The Good Lion," written before his final safari, and the sprawling fictionalized memoirs that spring from it, *True at First Light* and the more comprehensive *Under Kilimanjaro* (often called his "African journal"), perhaps Hemingway's final posthumous gift to us, give us hints of brilliance. Both works show a writer almost gleefully exploiting those racial truths he exposed so long ago. They show us an artist bent on pushing the aesthetic envelope one last time, and that daring push began in the years before that final fated safari.

"The Good Lion" was spawned years before Hemingway set foot onto African soil again. Hemingway wrote it in anticipation of his 1953–54 trip, and although the short piece is light and whimsical, it fits nicely within our critical framework. The work's terseness and apparent levity make it a deceptively easy read, and that may account for readers' perceptions of it as generally innocuous and its relatively unheralded status through the years. However, perhaps more than any of his other published pieces, this work demonstrates both Hemingway's lifelong ambivalence about race and his keen awareness of racial construction, and the author works the material deftly, without the slightest mention of race.

In "The Good Lion," gone is the seemingly refined binary model; gone is the color line separating white from black, civilized from savage. Instead, Hemingway paints a complicated Manichean portrait of not black and white but gray. A young lion is a cultural pariah in his own African community because of his unique genetic mixture (he is part eagle) and his ability to fly, and because of his very refined, very European sensibilities. Like Dick Boulton in "The Doctor and the Doctor's Wife," he is this tale's cultural "half-breed," both African and European yet fully neither, and this apparent difference ultimately drives him away from his community. In the end, though, Hemingway gives us a "good" lion not much different from that community and arguably no better than the ravenous, flesh-craving pride members he chooses to leave behind. In the end, Africa, it seems, is in his blood.

Through a fanciful tale about *place,* Hemingway pushes the aesthetic envelope and slyly explores racial construction and mythmaking. From its inception, Hemingway conflates good and evil, civilized and savage, and asks, "What if?" What if we blur the differential line? "The Good Lion" anticipates beautifully Hemingway's personal exploration of his own savage holiday, his own immersion in Native culture, just a few years later. The author revisits and documents this transgressive watershed moment in the manuscript that would be published posthumously as *True at First Light* and *Under Kilimanjaro.* Hemingway proclaimed *Green Hills* his grand literary experiment in 1935, but we could just as easily apply that proclamation to his second safari book.

While much of the bravado of the great white hunter—seen so prominently in *Green Hills* a generation before—remains in that final safari book, some of it is fairly tempered by an egalitarianism that this time around seems truer than anything he gave us in the years following his 1933 trip. Back then, he simply, quite easily, proclaimed himself a brother to the Natives serving him, but the cultural melding seems to begin and end with the proclamation. This time around, Hemingway purportedly takes a black bride and even inhabits the skin, if only temporarily, of his darker brethren. During that final safari, he does not simply live among the Wakamba; he *becomes* Wakamba, briefly jettisoning his whiteness and his totemic privilege and erasing the color line.

Africa becomes, then, for Hemingway the nexus of possibility, where ideas regarding racial formation and authority are negotiable. There, racial lines can be transgressed freely, without stricture or reservation. Whereas in *Green Hills,* a young Hemingway worked hard to maintain the strictures of race, in *True at First Light / Under Kilimanjaro,* the elder statesman, perhaps wiser with experience and with tricks to spare, works hard to demonstrate race's fluidity. In each instance, race is a construct. *True at First Light / Under Kilimanjaro* documents Hemingway's grand experiment, and to be sure, on one level, it is grand. Largely working without the safety net of more purely fictionalized tangential characters—there is no Bugs, no Dick Boulton, no George here—Hemingway himself freely assumes the role of racial transgressor in his final fictionalized memoir. We see this in the friendships he forges as he becomes brother-in-arms to local Natives. We see it too in his temporary but total assumption of Wakamba identity and in his African "wife." Indeed, the possibilities appear endless as Hemingway becomes a racial shape-shifter of sorts in the green hills of Africa.

Always, though, Hemingway transgresses with the relative luxury and security provided by his own white skin. Well into the twentieth century, throughout most of Africa, erasure and reinscription of the color line remained almost exclusively a white prerogative, and that is where Hemingway's literal and metaphorical sojourn ultimately ends: with a return to himself and a reconstituted whiteness. Like the fable, but unlike his previous African treatments, Hemingway's second African book, at least at times, dares to erase divisional lines, blending black and white. Unlike the fable, though, the memoir ultimately corrects its transgressions and ends with a return to the boundaries set by the color line.

But why the apparent regression in the midst of such grand experimentation? To simply discount Hemingway's conservative behavior as the product of old age alone would be facile; the author appears more steeped in conservatism as a middle-aged man of thirty-five in the wake of his first African trip than he does at fifty-five. If anything, in those early African writings, Hemingway bolsters the existing totem and transgresses few, if any, racial lines. In the later African writings, more specifically *True at First Light / Under Kilimanjaro,* and unlike those early episodes featuring Nick and his American encounters with men both red and black, moments of racial transgression in the African space are unilateral. In them, an older Hemingway tempers the experiment and reverts to old-world politics, ultimately choosing to maintain the racial totem without the accompanying doubts, anxieties, and prospective horror. Still, though, the true thrill is in the experiment itself. And experiment he did. In Africa, Hemingway could be what he wanted. As a man trapped by his own cult of personality, Hemingway needed the far-off foreign space of the African bush to try on new skin, free of criticism, to deconstruct and reconstruct the great (white) man.

The African safari thus becomes the best of both worlds, providing Hemingway with the perfect opportunity to don simultaneously the garb of brother-in-arms and great white father. Most importantly, Africa becomes the site within which he can control the color line's placement, demarcation, and enforcement.

Simply put, he draws, places, and erases the color line at will. Unlike America, an Africa still steeped in colonial dictates provides the perfect nexus wherein the extent of racial interaction and ultimately questions of agency and authority remain unquestionably within the white purview. However, as Hemingway himself recounts in his final safari book, even the security inherent in this apparent white bastion was dissipating—former European colonial strongholds fast became sites of a fading color line, internal strife, and realized violence and revolution. In the end, then, for the author, the text becomes the ultimate means by which to both explore the space between the races and still preserve and perpetuate that long-sought-after racial order.

We saw Hemingway re-entrench and reinscribe himself within the white mythos some twenty years earlier in *Green Hills,* but even then, with relatively few lines being crossed, Hemingway's cognizance of identity construction was keen. For even in the act of reinscribing marginal lines, Hemingway demonstrates race's artifice; and in daring to cross those lines in his later years, even if that transgression is only temporary, he demonstrates race's fluidity and identity's tenuous nature. In this way, Hemingway's grand experiment ultimately proves successful, and it is something the author seems to have known all along.

CHAPTER ONE

"Indian Camp" and "The Doctor and the Doctor's Wife"

Deconstructing the Great (White) Man

Let him think I am more than I am and I will be so.

—Ernest Hemingway, *The Old Man and the Sea*

Hemingway's inquisitive ways were with him since youth. The spaces in and around the Indian camp captured and held the author's imagination throughout his life, and appropriately, they make up an extensive part of his ethnic writing for much of his early career. He had begun exploring these wild (imaginary) spaces as a youth, drawing on his own experiences and observations in and around his family summer getaway at northern Michigan's Walloon Lake.[1] As several of his biographers demonstrate, the connection between the Hemingway family and the Native American people in and around the lake was strong, something indicated in the affectionate nickname given to his father by the Ojibwa and the occasional claims to Indian blood made by young Ernest himself. Race, Hemingway observed, was complicated, and he turned his keen eye toward racial matters early on, using skin color as a convenient trope in his stories "A Matter of Colour" (a boxing story with cheating and blackness at its center) and "Sepi Jingan," a tale whose subject matter a young Hemingway clearly mined from his own memories and experiences with the Ojibwa. The seeds sown during those formative years ensured his imagination's growth and fecundity for decades.

The people, places, and, at least in part, memories come directly from these experiences. Billy Tabeshaw and Prudence Boulton were real individuals in young Hemingway's early life. But that is only partly the point. In his racialized stories, Hemingway transcribes truth and, as per artistic license, he turns this truth into something more. That something more is an active exploration of race, something that becomes quite clear when we begin piecing together the minimalist's meager words.

So, I begin my treatment with the Indian stories because these tales account for a relatively small but certainly significant portion of Ernest Hemingway's initial short-story output. More to the point, these short stories and several others ("The Light of the World," "Fathers and Sons," "The Battler," and "The Killers," to greater and lesser degrees) are bold explorations of race and marginalization in early twentieth-century America. In them, we see Hemingway's own ambivalence toward the Indian and matters of color in general but, significantly, Hemingway's inquest comes at a time when relatively few others were driven across the color line by curiosity, let alone politics.

Aside from a few pieces of literature of the era, the Native voice was all but silent in the early decades of the century.[2] Governmental efforts like Franklin Roosevelt's Works Project Administration of the 1930s, established at least in part to promote minority employment and interests, simultaneously divested the Native of his own history. Projects like the writing of the state travel guide often reduced the Native American to promotional conceit and device, making him nothing more than a product pitchman (see Isernhagen). Such large-scale (re)presentational initiatives effectively silenced a people. Hartwig Isernhagen claims that the "dominant interest of the project lay in solving the urgent questions of the present, and that The Indian was not one of them" (176). Contrary to what the initiatives seem to suggest, though, racial authority *was* an "urgent" question of the day, and, at the very least, Hemingway recognized its import, and even his ambivalence (in print) helped break the silence.

The author's questioning of the color line and his exploration of the gray spaces in between black and white underscore his established reputation as modern. His modernity further lay, partly, in his recognition of the unrecognized, and his Indian stories are great examples of a renewed American Gothic sensibility forging its way into (and forcing a renewed reading of) his oeuvre. In *Gothic America: Narrative History and Nation,* Teresa Goddu argues that "American gothic literature criticizes America's national myth of new-world innocence by voicing the cultural contradictions that undermine the nation's claim to purity and equality" (10).[3] Goddu specifically has slavery in mind as chief among the "cultural contradictions" haunting the American conscience; however, white America's tragic relationship with its red brethren is yet another such contradiction, another story stifled by mythology. Gothic literature seeks to expose these historicized contradictions while simultaneously allowing for their perpetuation; this is the Gothic paradox.

If we suggest that often part of the Gothic's purpose is to translate the unspoken, the quiet and latent, then reading the Gothic in Hemingway's Indian story becomes easy enough for the critical reader. Further, if we suggest that the Gothic is, in part, a tradition that, for its own realization, necessarily relies on divisional markers to ultimately explore and expose what Toni Morrison has called an "unspeakable thing unspoken" ("Unspeakable Things Unspoken"), then we can exorcise the specter haunting Hemingway's pages and expose the tradition at work in several of his most prominent pieces. Several of his stories fit nicely within this framework by doing just that: sometimes, even as they seek to question racial myth, they emphatically seize upon unspoken notions of difference and the horrors of color-line transgression. I see this transgression as miscegenation in its broadest sense. By this, I mean a highly intimate, although not necessarily sexual, commingling of the races. These particular stories make a very modern statement about the tenuous nature of America's racial divide: the lines that separate white from nonwhite are forged and—most importantly—they are quite erasable.

Hemingway shows us the pure invention of race as identity marker in the first of his Indian stories, "Indian Camp," and racial ambiguity figures prominently in "The Doctor and the Doctor's Wife," one of his more popular tales. Daphne Lamothe posits in her essay "*Cane:* Jean Toomer's Gothic Black Modernism" that "the most unsettling example of racial transgression proves to be the mulatto, whose existence acts as proof of miscegenation, the emblem of subversion of racial categories" (59). I would amend this statement and suggest that the mulatto's existence acts as *tangible* proof of miscegenation. But within my own very loose parameters, transgressive acts do not always garner such palpable evidence. I would also suggest that the mixed-race figure's nonexistence—his marked absence, in fact—in Hemingway's painted world (outside "The Doctor and the Doctor's Wife," the overtly insolent Dick Boulton figure is nowhere to be found) is a testament to the author's ambivalence toward the unspoken and unseen. However, while Hemingway fails to exploit the passing and tragic mulatto tropes popularized in the early century's literature, like a phantom, within and without his own writing, the *threat* of racial transgression looms large.

Published anonymously in 1912, James Weldon Johnson's *The Autobiography of an Ex-coloured Man* is a black-authored work that responds to this anxiety. And Johnson's national stature later on all but guarantees Hemingway's awareness of its existence. *The Autobiography of an Ex-coloured Man* stands as the epitome of defiance of the "order," with its protagonist flagrantly positing the ultimate "What if?" scenario to a wary (white) audience. In it, Johnson addresses ideas of racial identity as his narrator willfully and opportunistically creates his own racial space, both white and black, and in the process makes a mockery of the establishment. For many whites, the passing mulatto becomes *the* feared Gothic specter; a concealed blackness is that feared unseen quantity. And Hemingway's Gothic emblem—especially in his Indian stories—is America's silent shifting tide of racial authority.

"Indian Camp" provides us with a template for reading later works. This story functions as a foundational tale of discovery, as Hemingway initiates the young naïf Nick Adams into the adult world of sex, violence, and death. To this well-established paradigm I add the variables of race and difference. A narrative entrenched in difference lends itself nicely to colonial discourse, as Ania Loomba suggests in *Colonialism/Postcolonialism.* With a lineage firmly rooted in an orientalist tradition, Loomba demonstrates the necessity of polarity to Western ontology:

> Said shows that this opposition is crucial to European self-conception: if colonized people are irrational, Europeans are rational; if the former are barbaric, sensual, and lazy, Europe is civilization itself, with its sexual appetites under control and its dominant ethic that of hard work; if the Orient [i]s static, Europe can be seen as developing and marching ahead; the Orient has to be feminine so that Europe can be masculine. (47)

In Hemingway's model, the journey toward enlightenment means engaging spatial and linguistic separators; it means emphasizing racial difference, hyperbolizing a differential of which his audience would have been fully aware. To that end, Hemingway deftly plays the race card to his advantage then shockingly questions the accepted racial order. In other words, Hemingway's narrative actively and consistently constructs a paradigm of difference—playing to the audience and promoting latent anxiety—only to deliberately undermine it in the end. The subversion is often subtle, undetectable at first glance. The divisional tactic accounts for 90 percent of Hemingway's narrative iceberg below water. His initial efforts to divide become part of a grand exercise, Richard F. Berkhofer Jr. would argue, on the part of whites "to understand themselves, for the very attraction of the Indian to the White imagination rests upon the contrast that lies at the core of the idea" (111).[4] And deliberate contrasts mark Hemingway's text from beginning to end.

Mining from childhood memories of time spent on Walloon Lake, Hemingway manipulates reality to suit his purposes, as an artist is prone to do.

From its inception, "Indian Camp" crafts difference by exploiting a spatial divide: "At the lake shore there was another rowboat drawn up. The two Indians stood waiting" (67). The Indian camp is located "across the bay" from the white man, and implicitly away from "civilization." The "foreign" space itself has its own connotations, and Hemingway gives them to us freely. The doctor and crew "start off in the dark." Their trek toward the indefinable space of the Indian camp is a movement from lightness into a curious darkness. Nick speaks first, his questions emphasizing the mysterious: "Where are we going, Dad?" (67). These questions reverberate throughout the text as the party silently makes its way through the darkness toward the camp.

The camp dwellers have summoned the doctor to help an ailing woman have her baby; there have been complications. Again, Hemingway mines memory as he sets the scene, reflecting on his father as lone doctor in these wild parts. And again, the facts themselves are not quite as deserving of our attention as is their presentation. As the story opens, Dr. Adams, Nick, Uncle George, and their Indian guides are en route to the camp. This necessarily means a journey "across the bay," going "through a meadow that was soaking wet with dew," entering the woods, and "follow[ing] a trail that led to the logging road that ran back into the hills" (67). Through these various descriptions, Hemingway creates a vast narrative space separating white man from red. If, as Ruth Anolik suggests in *The Gothic Other,* both figurative and literal dividers drive the Gothic text, then this sequence itself becomes the first of several Gothic barriers implicitly emphasizing racial difference that we encounter. Greeting the white contingent of father, uncle, and son are stark scenes both primitive and savage: "They came around a bend and a dog came out barking. Ahead were the lights of the shanties where the Indian bark-peelers lived. More dogs rushed out at them. The two Indians sent them back to the shanties. In the shanty nearest the road there was a light in the window. An old woman stood in the doorway holding a lamp" (67). The doctor's entrance into the Indian camp is an entrance into a kind of narrative hell. Personal greetings and handshakes are in short supply as perpetual darkness and voracious barking dogs are the only things to welcome the familial party. The snarling beasts are reminiscent of Cerberus's multiple heads guarding Hades' gates (Strong, "Screaming through Silence"). However, setting is only the first of the narrative divisors Hemingway employs.

The author further emphasizes the chasm separating white from red in his usage of name. With name comes emotional investment of some kind, and Hemingway knows and exploits this basic human truth with the Adamses' entrance into the Indian world. While Hemingway allows us some degree of closeness to the principal white figures, he flatly denies us any closeness to the "other." From the outset, Hemingway jettisons name in his approach to the marginal figures peopling the landscape: perfunctory and ready to serve, "two Indians stood waiting" for the Adams contingent as guides and nothing more. Their existence is one of quiet acquiescence, anticipation (waiting for orders), and functionality (they are their occupations). Hemingway's narrative reduces a people to occupation as our author describes for us an Adams family in the darkness, among the barking dogs and the "shanties where the Indian bark-peelers lived."

We have at the story's core an anonymous laboring woman and her nameless husband, who agonizes along with her just feet away. Faceless old women trying to help their ailing peer are also present as the Adams family arrives. Nowhere is a name to be found. Boiling Dr. Adams's water is an unnamed Indian woman. In fact, Dr. Adams has at his disposal several subservient Native Americans, all nameless. The narrative distancing continues as the procedure begins and other anonymous community members actively restrain the now-irritable pregnant woman. Within this framework, deliberate namelessness works to foster an image of orientalist "otherness" steeped in mystery and *unknowableness.* And such unknowableness begs for translation from without.

Once Dr. Adams arrives, all the parties recede into the homogenous background, save Uncle George. As for the pregnant woman herself, while her story is so closely intertwined with that of doctor and son, she never becomes anything more than a plot device. She is, it seems, there for Dr. Adams's (self-) aggrandizement and Nick's initiation into the world of violence and death. While Dr. Adams initially calls her a "lady" as he relates her plight to his son, the respect proves specious as Hemingway quickly dismantles whatever stature she has. He immediately replaces the respectable title with the more generic label of "Indian woman," and during the scuffle with those restraining her, slur quickly supplants that label as "lady" becomes "squaw bitch." Hemingway intentionally leaves little room in the margin's recesses for names.

Hemingway closely aligns this very deliberate strategy of namelessness with the muted voice. It should be noted that none of the Native figures in this story ever speak. Hemingway grants all voice, and therefore all agency, to the story's prominent white male figure. He further circumscribes authority with racial prerogatives, and in the white figure, at this stage, these prerogatives go unquestioned. Doctor, uncle, and even young Nicky monopolize voice. Again, we begin with the myriad of references to the nameless Indian, an image that Hemingway begins to paint with the rowers bringing the Adamses to the camp: "The two Indians stood waiting." Neither says a word as the two row the party ashore, nor do they speak at any other point in the story. The Native American figures simply guide the Adamses through the woods, row the boats, and fend off stray dogs roaming the campsite, all without saying a word. Once at the camp, the Indian men "sit in the dark and smoke out of range of the noise" made by the Indian woman (68). Thus, Hemingway creates a world in which, within the Indian contingent, silence is pervasive.

In employing such strategies—crafting the spatial divide and most especially denying the Indian both name and voice—Hemingway assumes his place in a long tradition of (white) Western interpreters. As Kathryn Shanley argues, "A blindness to the exclusion of Indian voices perpetuates the idea that non-Indians can speak better for Indians than Indians can speak for themselves, perhaps because the raw pain of loss expected from Indians would be unpalatable" (40). Dr. Adams's speculation over the suicide at the end of the story stands as such a translation. With a little help from our author, the ailing husband conveniently leaves himself open to such interpretation; he suffers silently from an axe wound in the wooden bunk above his wife. He smokes his pipe and eventually slits his own throat (a point of some importance, I think, and something I will explore a bit later), leaving his story for the interpreters to translate and convey.

Taking this marked silence to another level are the story's many Indian women, cast by Hemingway in the roles of mute and mime. We never hear from the distressed woman herself regarding her fears, her frustration, her pain. In fact, as the least vocal of the story's principal players, the woman at the story's center is far from central. Feminine diminution begins as the community women converge on the pregnant woman's shanty to help her through the birthing process: "The woman in the kitchen motioned to the doctor that the water was hot" (68). This is the extent of the tale's feminine communication: voiceless gesticulation. Later, after the surgical procedure, an old nameless woman dutifully takes the baby from Dr. Adams's hands without saying a word. Further, while the women around the birth mother silently behold the spectacle that is the doctor's miracle medicine, Hemingway reduces the adoptive mother herself to animal stature. Cries that seem to fall on deaf ears (recall that the doctor tells his son that "her screams are not important" [68]) and savage bites become this primitive's only means of expression. Conversely, as the woman's screams reverberate throughout the camp, father and son engage in active dialogue; for his reading audience—an audience who he wagers is familiar with such a dialectic—Hemingway strategically juxtaposes the white's words with the red's crude pantomime and primal scream, and he does all this as a matter of pedagogy (for Nick on the simplest of levels, for the reader on another).

The entire session becomes a forum within which young Nick learns life lessons. And as the doctor speaks, we on the outside also learn lessons—the most important of which are about race. Here, Dr. Adams, namer of all things, gives voice to all things (including things unspoken by the voiceless). After performing a medical miracle of sorts, Dr. Adams "was feeling exalted and talkative as football players are in the dressing room after a game" (69). Ultimately, in homage to things said and written, Dr. Adams suggests to Uncle George that his backwoods ingenuity and surgical prowess merit documentation: "That's one for the medical journal, George" (69). Adams points to the written record as thought's paramount measure and validation.

Starkly opposing the doctor's moment of self-aggrandizement is the Indian's pronounced silence and degradation. Berkhofer, in his now-classic study *The White Man's Indian: Images of the American Indian from Columbus to the Present,* calls this diminished figure of the white imagination the "degraded or reservation Indian." He is a third-space entity standing between the classic models of the noble savage, or the acquiescent, peaceful, and simple Native we get in James Fenimore Cooper's Natty Bumppo, and the ignoble savage or the fierce, sexualized, and often brutally defiant man-beast haunting the plains of Western lore (30). The reservation Indian—as a morally depraved and often dependent type (alcohol often precipitates his descent)—becomes that third romantic Native American variety. Imbued with an Edenic fallen-ness, he garners not ire but pity. In "Indian Camp," Hemingway gives us an entire cast of such characters with no apparent means of expression and no equivalent mastery of anything. Instead, we have figures that mindlessly haunt the literal landscape and a people wholly unable to care for themselves. By juxtaposing primitive and civilized, dark and light, voicelessness and enunciation, Hemingway widens the Gothic divide between powerless and empowered, and just when that social gulf is seemingly at its widest, he subverts the model altogether.

Native incapacitation gives rise to the anxiety haunting young Hemingway's America. His is yet another iteration of the white man's guilt saddling the national consciousness, exposing the white mythos for what it is: imperfect. And further complicating matters is the perceived looming threat of racial corruption. But therein lies the paradox Hemingway seeks to exploit:

darkness emanates from the beacon of light. Corruptibility suggests fallibility. And for Hemingway, each story's ultimate horror is the prospect of racial corruption, and in each story, one figure comes forward to expose that horror. "Indian Camp" proves no different, and in it, that revelatory man is Uncle George. Through him, the doctor's foibles and folly and those of the (white) community at large come to light.

If the Gothic world seeks to express the inexpressible, and if it seeks to do so by way of shroud and divisor, then Uncle George becomes that medium of expression incarnate; he is the medium through which our ghosts speak. Further, Nick's initiation becomes George's initiation too as racial truths reveal themselves. George's baptism in the racial river is notable: "Later when he started to operate Uncle George and three Indian men held the woman still. She bit Uncle George on the arm and Uncle George said, 'Damn squaw bitch!' and the young Indian who had rowed Uncle George over laughed at him" (68). Here the imaginary other, in a moment of self-actualization, confronts Uncle George head-on. Further engaging the Gothic, Hemingway gives us the first of several grotesque moments over the course of his career as he pushes the racial envelope with a bizarre physical conflict between white and nonwhite: anxious to be heard, seen, felt, the Indian woman bites her white oppressor (who literally restrains the agonized woman) in a sequence that becomes a metaphor for an intra-national cultural clash. The bite is a marked movement for this nonentity, totally divorced of history, toward reification and confirmed existence. Like the title character in Ralph Ellison's *Invisible Man* some thirty years later, Hemingway's nameless racialized figure erupts violently against a world intent on ignoring her.

For both Uncle George and this woman, the bite itself becomes a site of self-confirmation and a lost moment. While he automatically reverts to a curse and racial pejorative, Uncle George becomes in that instant the liminal figure: a white man (consciously) without authority. The objectified other forces a reaction from the white man ("Damn squaw bitch!"). In the sequence's closing moments, the white man's cries draw laughter from the nameless Native ranks (we witness one "laugh[ing] *at* him") as an Indian boatman momentarily seizes control as he laughs at the expense of his white "superior." Uncle George's curse then becomes a weak attempt to reestablish order, but the bite and laughter are fair warning that this perceived order is tenuous at best. Just as quickly as Hemingway builds the racial paradigm of difference, he begins to erode and subvert it. While we get no actual physical intercession of race in this story, we do get the Gothic expression of prospective horror in Uncle George, whose part in the story is small but important as he becomes an unwitting purveyor of a new racial truth.

All of this makes the closing talk between father and son—the doctor's post-operative declarations and his explanation for the ailing husband's suicide at story's end—all the more significant. After enduring hours of his wife's screams, the nameless father abruptly slits his own throat. Dr. Adams's attempts to make sense of the senseless to his son is well worth noting:

> "Why did he kill himself, Daddy?"
> "I don't know, Nick. He couldn't stand things, I guess." (69)

The answer to Nick's question is noncommittal and deceptively simple. To just what "things" is Dr. Adams referring? One possible answer works well within our model and also explains Uncle George's sudden and inexplicable disappearance at story's end. The Indian's suicide comes as a result of his not being able to "stand things," but not the obvious things the narrative seems to suggest: his own pain and the perpetual screams of his ailing wife.

Hemingway would suggest looking beyond the tip of that iceberg. The husband's suicide comes on the heels of his wife's dehumanizing experience ("her screams are not important"), and, expanding the scope outward, the degradation of his people (they all dwell in shanties), and perhaps his own emasculation (*he* is powerless to help her). Arguably, the Indian's incapacitation drives him to take his own life. His physical condition becomes a metaphor for his psychic condition. After all, he endures days of protracted labor alongside his wife, unable to assist in any way, only to witness her salvation by the great white healer. And only Uncle George, as the sympathizer and third-space representative and purveyor of cigars at the story's inception, realizes the truth behind the Indian's action. But in the end, Hemingway lays this leaden truth in our laps, and George is nowhere to be found.

George's sudden disappearance is important. With no one able to explain either his flight or his whereabouts, Uncle George is once more aligned with the unknowable Indian. He too apparently finds it difficult to "stand things" as they are or have become. He discovers the very mutable line and law of race in the bite and the truth of it in the laughter he endures. And, perhaps most importantly, he sees it in the makeshift procedure performed on the Indian woman. Uncle George's reaction to his brother's self-aggrandizement bears out this reading: "Oh, you're a great man, all right." His words drip with sarcasm. Questioning his brother's greatness, Uncle George becomes the story's truly transgressive figure. At least momentarily, he sides with the Native. With the regressive surgery, and with his mockery at the hands of the other, the white doctor becomes the primitive one. Uncle George's quiet melting into the background at story's end nevertheless reverberates with Conradian force; in George's trailing footsteps, we can almost hear Kurtz's terrified refrain in *Heart of Darkness:* "The horror! The horror!" George's flight is white flight. Suddenly, the fear of "infection" from dark surroundings is realized as the self becomes the other. Through the eyes of Uncle George, we experience the prospective horrors of diluted racial purity and lost authority, and through Uncle George, Hemingway begins to chip away at the myth of white primacy. Further, he demonstrates to his (white) reading audience, in limited fashion, the performative quality of race.

Hemingway invites us to further compare and reconstruct the rapidly dissolving ordered white world in his complementary piece, "The Doctor and the Doctor's Wife." Like "Indian Camp," this story also follows my prescribed exploration of the space along the color line. Here, though, Hemingway does not venture into foreign territory, instead carrying out his examination and eventual assault on racial essentiality and whiteness on the home front. Our first glimpse of this principal tenet comes in the opening sequence, where we witness a "foreign" invasion of the Adams property:

> Dick Boulton came from the Indian camp to cut up logs for Nick's father. He brought his son Eddy and another Indian named Billy Tabeshaw with him. They came in through the back gate out of the woods, Eddy carrying the long cross-cut saw. It flopped over his shoulder and made a musical sound as he walked. Billy Tabeshaw carried two big cant-hooks. Dick had three axes under his arm. (73)

Hemingway immediately gives us the first of many inversions of the initial "Indian Camp" paradigm. Whereas in "Indian Camp" the doctor and company venture deep into wooded territory en route to the camp, here Dr. Adams ventures nowhere. *He* is the discovered territory—eventually exposed, by Dick Boulton, for what he is (or at least what Boulton would have him be): a thief, a liar, and a flawed man. Here, Hemingway directly inverts the prior story's principal structure as the band of Indian woodsmen take up arms (they carry saw, axe, and hook) and physically and symbolically infiltrate the white man's personal space. The configured "savage" world wills itself onto the good doctor's doorstep, so that this becomes more than a clash of class or of culture; it becomes a confrontation of races as well, as Hemingway once more begins with a Gothic engagement of sorts.

Lamothe suggests that in the Gothic universe, psychic angst is invested in the physical barrier, the ultimate guardian of preserved wholeness and defined order. Within this context, the gate dividing the Adams compound from the field and woods stands as the principal marker between inside and outside, civilized and wild. To be clear, the very notion of this inner-outer polarity exists only because of the gate's presence in the text, and Hemingway makes good use of it. The gate's initial symbolic significance is as guardian against transgression. In this case, the transgression becomes racialized. Note that Dick Boulton conspicuously leaves the gate ajar as he exits the Adams property. With the Indian's flouting of protocol, Hemingway's implications to the reader are bold and clear: Boulton is transgression incarnate. But again the superficial topical reading is where the narrative engages us first.

While this story's transgressor—unlike his "Indian Camp" counterparts—is given a name, Hemingway already mires him in typological trappings as he first enters the scene. We quickly learn that the doctor regularly recruits Dick Boulton, Boulton's son, and another Indian named Billy Tabeshaw to help clear what he describes as driftwood that washes upon his beachfront. We first glimpse Boulton coming, spook-like, from the wooded area adjacent to the Adams cottage. Hemingway is deft with his linkage of the primitive and the Indian figure's conjured emergence; he comes suddenly and without warning from the dark and mysterious depths of the woods. And all of "primitive" man's foibles follow him into the light.

Hemingway plays with the mysterious and primitive in his racial conceptions of this Indian laborer's character, more specifically his work ethic. As Valerie Babb suggests in *Whiteness Visible: The Meaning of Whiteness in American Literature and Culture,* the (mis)conception of the other greatly defines the subject in much of America's later cultural promulgation.[5] She bolsters this point with an in-depth examination of the literary memoir, which enjoyed great readership during the twentieth century's early years, and emphasizes its effectiveness in forging a sense of American-ness among newly arrived immigrants desperate for acceptance. An indulgence of the very American ideal of self-realization through diligence and industry becomes part and parcel of this accepted paradigm. In "The Doctor and the Doctor's Wife," Hemingway aptly tells us that "Dick was a half-breed and many of the farmers around the lake believed he was really a white man. He was very lazy but a great worker once he was started" (73). Boulton is simultaneously both a "lazy" man and "a great worker," a walking contradiction of sorts whose contradictory nature can be explained by race.

In this segment, Hemingway reduces the Indian to function and occupational performance. His very racial-ness (i.e., his color and culture) both relegates him to worker status and terminally brands him as lazy. We know that race is in fact a necessary connector here because the narrator prefaces any judgment with an express racial declaration ("Dick was a half-breed and many of the farmers around the lake believed he was really a white man"). Here Hemingway conceives of the self by redefining the other, an idea masterfully explored by Babb, who contends that through popular culture staples, America forged a stylized tapestry of selfhood closely yet inconspicuously aligned with whiteness as *the* racial aspiration. According to Babb, immigrants and other "outsiders" quickly learned from prescribed models—the regional fair, the boardinghouse, and the literary memoir—what precisely constituted American-ness. Hemingway, too, understood the prescription, and he exploits these same cultural associations in constructing Boulton's character.

To be sure, Dick Boulton is in one respect the embodiment of Americana: he is industrious, a hard worker, and the living representation of the Puritan work ethic. According to the traditional (Puritan) model, hard work garners reward, a notion the very secular Benjamin Franklin would eventually underscore and popularize for generations. Boulton's work ethic directly reflects the white blood coursing through his veins. But Hemingway complicates matters even as he simplifies this Indian. In Boulton, Hemingway constructs a walking complication; the worker is both red and white. Boulton's redness, however, necessarily subjects him to criticism and makes him worthless. While a great worker once pushed, Dick is implicitly "very lazy" *by nature*. Thus, the hyper-simplicity of the initial assessment belies Hemingway's greater strategy and the bloodline's actual complexity, a complexity Hemingway seems to relish. It also anticipates the potentially horrifying complications ahead for both Dr. Adams and the contemporary (read: *white*) reader. But payoff comes later, and in the interim, Hemingway provides his reader with a large comfort zone between red and white.

While the Adamses' gate serves its purpose as a symbolic wall preventing foreign encroachment, nebulous distances and unspecified points of origin work as equally effective separators. We saw Hemingway use it to great effect in "Indian Camp." As this story opens, we learn that Dick Boulton "comes from the Indian camp to cut up logs for Nick's father." Hemingway links race with function, service, and place. Dick comes from the Indian camp and stereotype completes the reader's knowledge. Soon after, the narration continues, "They came in through the back gate out of the woods, Eddy carrying the long cross-cut saw. . . . Billy Tabeshaw carried two big cant-hooks. Dick had three axes under his arm" (73). Hemingway's description forces the imaginative leap as his imagery forges links between Native man and wilderness. Hemingway gives us the savagery of primitive man as he connects the violent potential of the hand tool to the deep forest's latent mystery. The narrative reinforces these initial ideas throughout as we see the Native American as a figure of toil; images of physical labor and sweat litter the text. By contrast, the Adams cottage, images of the lake, and suggestions of a mill are all physical markers of progress, civilization, and warranted authority. Recurring images of Boulton's tobacco chewing and spitting do little to advance his case for gentility; instead they further underscore the divide between the primitive backwoodsman and the refined doctor.

The Adams cottage itself becomes the doctor's refuge after a verbal confrontation with the Indian (Boulton accuses his "superior" of thievery while Adams insists that his accusation is a diversion as the Indian reneges on moneys owed for medical services rendered); at least initially, it also underscores the chasm separating civilized man from savage. The cottage is the doctor's Eden in this fast-changing, devolving world. In fact, after the row with Boulton, the cottage is the first place to which he looks for solace, and at least initially, solace is what he finds in that symbol of things white. Twice in the story Hemingway elevates our plane of vision as he both figuratively and literally lifts the country doctor before our eyes. The narrator's repeated refrain underscores the importance of place for the author and, implicitly, for the (white) reader: "They all watched him walk up the hill and go inside the cottage" (74). The domestic space becomes his metaphorical City on the Hill as he walks *up* the hill, leaving the Indians *behind, below,* and psychically *beneath* him.

Even once inside the cottage, Dr. Adams looks to reinforce the old totemic order. Significantly, he chooses the bedroom over the kitchen (the room closest to him) as his contemplative space. As he surveys his private sphere, he sees "a pile of medical journals on the floor by the bureau. They were still in their wrappers unopened. It irritated him" (75). The room is replete with books, a bureau, and compendia of wisdom. Hemingway shrewdly juxtaposes the woodsman's saw, hook, and axe with the doctor's medical journal, bureau, and Bible (Mrs. Adams's constant reminder of temperance), all serving as markedly different sources of intellectual/spiritual sustenance for the white couple.

Hemingway implicitly illuminates the holy and the rational, even as the rest of the room goes dark, the windows closed and blinds drawn; these are literal beacons of light in the consuming darkness.[6] The bedroom also serves as a study, and it is a bastion of civilization amid the branch and brush of the savage Indian woods. The bureau is a physical manifestation of the intangibles promised to the reader, the writer, the thinker. And the medical journals, reminiscent of the doctor's self-congratulatory revelry in "Indian Camp," are a testament to the thinking man and progress. Just as the hook, the axe, and the saw are the points of definition for the toiling Indian, the books and related paraphernalia serve to situate the doctor within a world of literacy and psychic ownership.

Bolstering the narrative's seemingly progressive agenda are Mrs. Adams herself and her preoccupations with method and manner. The narrator's sparse wording has far-reaching implications: "She was a Christian Scientist. Her Bible, her copy of *Science and Health* and her *Quarterly* were on a table beside her bed in the darkened room" (75). Armed with these, Mrs. Adams reassures her husband of temperance's virtue. In light of his row with Boulton, she reminds her husband that "he who ruleth his spirit" is the mightier man. And here, clearly informed by scripture and text, the mightier man is white. Her spiritual admonishment, coupled with the Bible and Christian Science, works to underscore the philosophical and ideological foundation on which the Adamses of the world rest. Hemingway's attentive (mind's) eye is never keener.

The concluding exchange between husband and wife becomes grist for the racial purity mill. If we were supposed to sympathize with Adams in his confrontation with Dick Boulton as the story begins, then what transpires afterward is meant to make us question our initial allegiances. This segment arguably exposes the doctor as a liar and his questioning of Boulton as a possible deliberate fabrication of sorts. At the very least, Hemingway forces the reader to posit legitimate questions: Are the doctor's accusations true? Where is the evidence to suggest Boulton does have an ulterior motive? And, even if true, does any of it necessarily exonerate the doctor of the accusations levied against him? Dr. Adams seems to improvise when pushed by Boulton and pressed by his wife, leaving open the possibility that he is mustering false justifications for his behavior. His answer to his wife feels strained. If Adams tells the truth, the narrative's underlying tension goes away; on the other hand, if Adams is lying, his lies work masterfully within our paradigm. In any event, Hemingway seems to relish this ambiguity and imbues these accusations with associations of otherness.

When pressed by his wife to explain the row, Dr. Adams responds with an answer that is both provocative and seemingly disingenuous:

> "Tell me, Henry. Please don't try and keep anything from me. What was the trouble about?"
>
> "Well, Dick owes me a lot of money for pulling his squaw through pneumonia and I guess he wanted a row so he wouldn't have to take it out in work." (75)

Adams's story makes the Native seem petty, small, and un-American. He underscores this otherness with the pejorative he gives Boulton's wife ("squaw"). Flouting responsibility, the lazy Indian implicitly runs counter to an American ideal grounded in the Puritan ethos. Hemingway masterfully arms Dr. Adams with an ethical appeal and strips the Native of all integrity; Boulton, the doctor suggests, should feel indebted to the white man, whose previous exploits included miraculous work "for the medical journal." In accusations of his own, Adams turns the tables and implicates the Indian in a breech of basic human decency. And on that count, as if to guide the reader, Hemingway injects marked silence into the conversation as Mrs. Adams listens without saying a word. Coupled with subsequent questions—each uttered in seeming disbelief—her silence underscores the dubious nature of her husband's story and Hemingway's very deliberate push toward ambiguity.

Of course, the ultimate irony is a point of such importance that it colors the story's entirety. The work ethic featured so prominently at the tale's inception is almost immediately abandoned by *the doctor* himself. If Hemingway means for us to question the doctor's intentions, not Boulton's, then Mrs. Adams's implied criticism seems all the more reasonable and appropriate, and the diametric descriptions preceding the talk all the more artificial.

As the story opens, Hemingway tells us that Nick's father, one of the many white men around the lake, "hired the Indians to come down from the camp and cut the logs up with the cross-cut saw and split them with a wedge to make cord wood and chunks for the open fireplace" (73). Adams hires Boulton and his associates to do the work he refuses to do himself. Patricia Limerick posits in *The Legacy of Conquest: The Unbroken Past of the American West* that "Frontier opportunity was supposed to permit a kind of labor by which one simply gathered what nature produced. The laborer was to be self-employed; and the status of laborer was to be temporary, left behind when the profits made escape possible" (97). Adams goes beyond mere profiteering—within Limerick's Anglo capitalist model—in the hiring of these men to cut, remove, and deposit the wood for him. In taking what clearly does not belong to him, he implicitly takes the ultimate shortcut: thievery. Or at least this is Boulton's accusation. And, given the circumstances, the accusations are not wholly unreasonable.

While Mrs. Adams's response to her husband's answer applies a fair amount of good faith to the incident ("I can't really believe that any one would do a thing of that sort intentionally" [75]), Hemingway makes it increasingly clear that someone *would* do a thing like that, and that her husband is no exception. Uncle George's caustic sneer to his brother in "Indian Camp" reverberates here in both Boulton's accusation and the wife's vexing question. In them, Dr. Adams's character and his prospective greatness come under fire. For both the brother and the wife (and implicitly the reader), Adams's words become a matter of incredulity.

Philip Young would suggest that Mrs. Adams's doubts point to a woman who—like her young naive son—experiences a world initiation marked by harshness and cruelty. However, her questions also point to interrogation and, possibly, accusation. And the biblical allusion works to remind her disoriented husband of the principles that have theoretically fortified them both up to this point. Such a reading suggests an implosion of the doctor's psycho-spiritual fortification and a blurring of authoritarian lines; these sparse words do much not to heal but to exacerbate fresh psychic wounds. With Mrs. Adams questioning her husband's integrity, the power dynamic shifts from the manor's master to its mistress. Quite simply, even a limited implication in moral corruption draws the doctor closer to, not farther away from, the red man of imagination. With power markers blurred, Hemingway shows us that dividing lines of race conflate, and the two men—the doctor and his Indian laborer—become harder to differentiate.

In the end, Dr. Adams's answer to his wife rings hollow to both her (as evinced by her marked silence afterward) and him, and dissatisfaction eventually drives him from his private sanctum back into the woods. His own apparent culpability in the affair serves to affirm his wife's question; indeed, *he* would stoop to such lows, and the projected horror once associated with the other has come home to roost. Mrs. Adams's questions drive her husband from the house to the woods, and for Hemingway, this very questioning of racial essentiality drives the narrative itself. With tethers to the Gothic, the inquiry begins, appropriately enough, with the red man, who emerges from the woods.

Despite its title, the principal figure of "The Doctor and the Doctor's Wife" is not the doctor at all, nor is it his wife. Instead, Hemingway makes Dick

Boulton, as mystery man, central. The confrontational Indian becomes the story's first and most prominent marker of racial upheaval; defiant and mysterious, he is the work's primary signifier of racial transgression. We quickly see that he is also the character who in actuality comes closest to fulfilling definitional expectations of American-ness. From the beginning, the narrative paints him in mythic, almost Jay Gatsby–ish hues. Boulton is a man whose reputation precedes him, and that reputation—rumor, innuendo, the unknown itself—works to empower him (even before Hemingway gives us a proper introduction). Treading heavily on the white man's soil, both literally and figuratively, Boulton is the self-made man, as we soon see.

Further, the only concrete and therefore definable aspect of the Indian that Hemingway gives us is in scant physical description and in the argument levied against the doctor. Hemingway simply describes him as "a big man" (75). The author need not say much more. Our first glimpse of Boulton is as leader of a band of Indian woodsmen, tools in hand. While his son carries a singular saw, and his friend Billy Tabeshaw totes cant hooks, Boulton—"big man" that he is—effortlessly holds three axes under his arms. Later, in the row with Adams, the Indian's size becomes paramount in the doctor's retreat to the cottage. Hemingway juxtaposes the doctor's hollow threat ("I'll knock your eye teeth down your throat") with the very real damage potential inherent in Boulton's cruel body and curt retort ("Oh, no, you won't, Doc") to demonstrate the realities of a violent world and the shifting balance of power. This is where our true knowledge of Boulton ends: with the physical. Here is where Hemingway's narrative furtively plants its fearful seeds, and here is where notions of essentiality typically help quell such fears. We will hear echoes of the same fears replayed years later in "The Porter," where young Jimmy Breen is the fearful, wide-eyed spectator to his black porter's razor play. In that story, Hemingway temporarily quells such fears and ultimately stabilizes the shifting totem.

But Hemingway gives us no such stabilization in this situation. The Indian as man of mystery comes to the fore early in the narrative ("Dick was a half-breed and many of the farmers around the lake believed he was really a white man"). As the story progresses, questions only seem to multiply as race-defining truths wither and disappear. And they all begin with this enigmatic figure who is and can be either white or red, but not both—at least not within our prescribed binary system. Boulton becomes Hemingway's answer to the mulatto figure haunting many a turn-of-the-century narrative landscape. Yet unlike the tragic mulatto of a Charles Chesnutt or Nella Larson work, Dick Boulton's "half-breed" status is predicated on open defiance and a bold commandeering of power. Flaunting his own indeterminateness before a white audience (of one), Boulton is more like James Weldon Johnson's ex-colored man in the tale of the same name.[7] Therein lies the often inexpressible horror haunting the white psyche, and Hemingway parades it proudly before our eyes.

The question mark looming over Boulton is precisely what empowers him as he stands before the white man and an anxious (white) audience. Hemingway tells us that Boulton speaks in Ojibwa to his co-workers. This is his native tongue. Or *is* it? What seems to confound the doctor most are the Indian's bilingual abilities, and his amazing facility with English especially. However, the first time he speaks, we do not hear his voice—we hear neither what he says nor how he says it. An otherness seems to mark this relation. Yet the narrative subverts this conception immediately as a new power matrix develops, with Boulton assuming the dominant role, wielding agency, and giving orders to his crew. While Hemingway does not give us direct speech at this juncture, he does show us a crew silently acquiescing and dragging logs from the water at his command. This is the first of several clues the narrative gives us regarding Boulton's erosion of white power and his inversion of the racial totem; the exchange between white man and red marks the next in a series of subversive moments.

The verbal assault Adams endures is also noteworthy for an additional and equally salient reason: in a battle of wits, language—tool of the rational—fails George's "great man." One word from Boulton establishes a marked tonal shift, and it speaks volumes:

> Dick Boulton turned to Nick's father.
>
> "Well, Doc," he said, "that's a nice lot of timber you've stolen."
>
> "Don't talk that way, Dick," the doctor said. "It's driftwood." (74)

Here Boulton's agency expands beyond the limited prescriptive radius of the other. Unspoken rules of decorum become figurative lines in the sand dividing white from red. This makes Boulton's marked turn toward the doctor both willful and brash. In a grand irony, the Indian demonstrates his proficiency in the common tongue and bests his "superior" in the process.

Linguistic dexterity is yet another barrier meant to separate primitive from civilized. Recognizing Boulton's encroachment for what it is, the doctor meets the challenge, but weakly. Like the Indian's bloodline itself, Adams's admonition to the Indian not to "talk that way" is appropriately ambiguous. Certainly we can read it as a blatant violation of the understood protocol. Not only does Boulton dispense with the employee's formality, but he altogether jettisons respect and crosses an understood social boundary. Boulton's retort and tone are all wrong for a man bound by his skin's strictures. But Adams's own footing atop the racial mountain is tenuous at best, and his response to Boulton reads more like a plea than a reminder, an insistent *request* to maintain *established protocol,* and the liberties Boulton takes with the master('s) language stand as doubly insulting. After deciphering the log's half-covered inscription and identifying the wood's rightful owners, Boulton reads for himself the scenario for what it is.[8] He then employs the ruling order's own language against its standing representative, implicating the doctor in an act of wrongdoing. Hemingway effectively has servant informing, exposing, and chastising master. Such an unwarranted usurpation is enough to destabilize the order and send the doctor scrambling for solid ground.

This scramble begins in earnest anger as the doctor insists that the Indian cease his accusations and refrain from calling him "Doc." Again, most important here are language's seizure and the attached rights afforded by it. First, the uninvited nickname is an obviously unwelcome crossing of formal lines. And the appellation appears suddenly as an unexpected haunt, coloring the entire exchange. Second, the overly familiar address also subverts the proper name. Scripturally speaking, it is a perversion of the first order. The Indian renders Adam(s)—original progeny and first credited namer of all things—powerless as he turns the doctor's own name against him. Adams is defenseless as Boulton seizes agency and himself becomes the (re)namer of things.

The depth of the insult becomes more apparent as we examine Boulton's overt refusal to relent from his attack, and in the doctor's empty threat that closes the exchange:

> "If you call me Doc once again, I'll knock your eye teeth down your throat."
>
> "Oh, no, you won't, Doc." (74)

With that, the doctor silently and shamefully falls back to the cottage. Boulton's own veiled threat in the coda demonstrates his new position within the totem and the ease with which he takes over traditional roles of interrogator and antagonist. What is more, it further underscores the Indian's proficiency and mastery of both language and himself.

Linguistic prowess is a powerfully liberating tool, and Hemingway gives us an Indian character who understands this in Dick Boulton. Watching Adams's retreat, the Indian switches codes and speaks to his brethren in Ojibwa, again at the doctor's expense. Dr. Adams—himself now markedly colored, red with indignation and embarrassment—feels the eyes upon him as he retreats to the cabin: "Dick Boulton looked at the doctor. . . . They all watched him walk up the hill and go inside the cottage" (74). Spurred by Boulton's insolent glare, each crew member in turn watches the doctor's retreat to his safe house. Eddy responds accordingly, laughing aloud as the crew departs into the woods in ghostly fashion as quickly as it first appeared. Acting as an exclamation point to the Indian's brash verbal defiance is the open gate left in the row's wake. Boulton purposefully leaves the gate ajar as he and his men depart. The Indian's facility with language, his fluid transgression of traditional racial roles, and his seamless assumption of power all underscore a greater Hemingway statement regarding the performative nature of race: essentiality is an illusion. In the showdown between Adams and Boulton, the Indian shows us whiteness for what it truly is: a practiced art.

With his defiant look and insolent words, Boulton effectively snatches agency from the (white) hands holding it; showing white to be black or, more appropriately, white to be red, he inverts the accepted racial totem. With only a stare and a strategically directed comment, he erases generations of oppression, objectification, and intentional obfuscation. That erasure begins with the accusation of thievery. The assertion itself is bold and unprecedented, but so is the shift for the drama's principle players. White male subject stands accused of a crime, of lowliness formerly associated with the rogue, the "not me," the other. Dr. Adams reverts to the nonwhite's traditionally shiftless ways; he acts out in desperation much in the way the white frontiersman resorted to brutality in settling the West. In his assessment of frontier literature's brand of heroism and the hero's negotiation of savage and civilized, Berkhofer asserts that "all authors . . . recognized that this balance of good qualities from the two societies could be lost and the White turn into a savage" (94). We can easily apply Berkhofer's statement to Hemingway's story and Dr. Adams's own ethical breach. We will see this lapse again later in Nick's rage-tinged defense of his sister's honor in "Fathers and Sons." In the end, Hemingway shows the color line to be amorphous, temporal, fictional. For Adams, Boulton is the face of a changing social landscape.

Emasculated, forced to acknowledge his own inglorious nature, and confronted with new realities, the doctor seeks solace in what he *does* know. His retreat to the cottage is a retreat to the domestic sphere and a return to the comforts of civil familiarity. Crossing the threshold is a marked symbolic escape from perceived savagery. Represented in the bureau and medical journals at its feet are generations of knowledge and Western wisdom. Offering spiritual solace, a Bible looms large in the background. These texts are also self-congratulatory artifacts of exclusion; only those versed in the language may partake of the fruits of this knowledge tree. Yet Adams knows that the club's exclusivity is fast fading. Dick Boulton, master of multiple languages, just proved he is up to the challenge.

The biblical allusions painted into the scene are appropriate given Mrs. Adams's own entrenchment in another kind of knowledge. Hers is a scriptural knowledge. She too brandishes weapons against a perceived savagery and ignorance; the word (of God) is her weapon. The Holy Bible and a copy of *Science and Health* magazine seem to illuminate the shaded room, with Hemingway deftly underscoring the darkness of the remaining space as the doctor reflects on the strife outside.

But what transpires inside is of greatest importance here. Although she is limited to few words, Mrs. Adams's significance, like Uncle George's in "Indian Camp," cannot be overstated. Like Uncle George and Dick Boulton, she is a purveyor—even if indirectly—of Hemingway's new racial truth, and per our prescriptive Gothic paradigm, she appears and disappears with this truth in the darkness.

Hemingway tells us that Nick's mother is a Christian Scientist. We can easily transpose Philip Young's assertions in *Ernest Hemingway* about her and her relationship to the worldly—specifically, elements of prostitution, homosexuality, and adultery—to my examination. Young suggests that "Nick has been in close contact with things a young boy who had stayed at home would normally not meet—with things that the conventions governing the average boyhood do not define or present answers for, and that raise problems which the scripture-quoting Mrs. Adams would not even admit let alone deal with" (108). Armed with her own texts, Mrs. Adams, too, is the breathing amalgam of both Western theology and rational thinking. Young's claims of general initiation are also easily those of a father and son's baptism into the waters of culture, color, and race.

In light of Young's model of initiation, the post-squabble question-and-answer session between husband and wife gains special significance. She questions his conspicuous silence and general agitation as he enters the house. The advice she proffers, meant to offer him validation in his uncertainty, clearly frustrates him. Meant to reassure and assuage, her words are instead vexingly flaccid. Clearly Hemingway wants us to read his controlled spirit before Boulton as cowardice. His smoldering anger is evidence of his own self-awareness.

Further, the truths buried in her platitudes are emblematic of the texts by her side and become for the doctor, perhaps for the first time, more problematic than reassuring. With false pillars razed, Dr. Adams is no better than and no different from the primitive enigma emerging from the woods.

For his part, Boulton offers none of the stabilizing comforts inherent in racial label and type. As a physically imposing man and a threat to whiteness, Boulton is not the noble savage. Nor does he fit neatly within the parameters of the "ignoble savage" or the wild man of lore as he outwits and out-talks the doctor, using words as weapons in Richard Wright–like fashion. As Bonnie Duran posits in her "Indigenous versus Colonial Discourse: Alcohol and American Indian Identity," the conception of "the savage Wild Man allowed the comparison with a European civilization seen as the pinnacle of social evolution and provided the ideological foundation for the Christian 'civilizing' mission" (113). In the end, though, Dr. Adams recognizes a mission full of hypocrisy and a mission statement devoid of any real meaning. It is enough to push him outside once again.

However, his psychic retreat begins well before he physically leaves the room. In between Mrs. Adams's interrogative bullet points, only the mechanical action of the doctor's gun breaks the relative quiet: "His wife was silent. The doctor wiped his gun carefully with a rag. He pushed the shells back in against the spring of the magazine. He sat with the gun on his knees. He was very fond of it. Then he heard his wife's voice from the darkened room" (75). Only Mrs. Adams's voice draws her husband back to reality. Realizing the frailty inherent in the books lying around him—especially in light of the thinking brute clouding his black-and-white vision—Dr. Adams answers the barrage of questions with all the safety and predictability that alloyed steel and spring action can provide; confronted with the hollow rhetoric his wife recites from memory, the doctor cleans his gun. Mindless ritual provides a temporary comfort, but only momentarily. Effectively spooked by reminders of the horrors battled at his gate, Adams heads to a space as yet untouched by the world: his son's innocent gaze.

From the uncertainty infiltrating the homestead, Dr. Adams flees to the outside, where the old hemlock's comfort and his little boy greet him. Hemingway significantly ends his story here with this final exchange between father and son. If Mrs. Adams symbolizes a dying value system, and that, along with the boy, Dr. Adams is an initiate into a new world order, then Mrs. Adams's parting words to her husband work to push him out the door: "If you see Nick, dear, will you tell him his mother wants to see him?" (75). Even the sanctum shared by father and son is not sacred. The doctor's response is understated: he simply slams the door. More than a bristling reaction to emasculation, though, his anger and frustration are an answer to dead rhetoric. As the voice of reason in the darkness, Mrs. Adams becomes a living ghost for the doctor and the reader. Adams's abrupt flight is a response to the rhetorical trap he sees being set for the next generation. Fittingly, young Nicky sits alone, reading, in the woods.

The tension between the couple is apparent even in the son's declaration that he wishes to follow his father instead: "'I want to go with you,' Nick said" (76). Longing for companionship on his lonely quest for understanding, Dr. Adams grants his son's request. When young Nick declares that he knows "where there's black squirrels," Dr. Adams responds with "All right. . . . Let's go there" (76). This sequence is emblematic of the story's entirety as Dr. Adams, with psychic wounds still fresh from the tangle with Boulton and then his own wife, longs for the simple polarities of days passed. Nick's green eyes still see the world in definite shades (of black and white). This is important in the context of a vastly changing societal landscape. Both outside the gated yard and within the bedroom walls, others challenge Dr. Adams's divine right (as white male), and thus lines of clear delineation blur. This is the initiate's greater lesson, and the doctor is the true initiate here. Calming the discord, Adams seems to suggest, becomes a matter of simply knowing where to find those black squirrels.

CHAPTER TWO

Beyond the Camp, Behind the Myth

Native American Dissolution and Reconstituted Whiteness in "Ten Indians," "Fathers and Sons," and "The Indians Went Away"

> We are what we imagine. Our very existence consists in our imagination of ourselves. . . . The greatest tragedy that can befall us is to go unimagined.
>
> —N. Scott Momaday

> Since the original inhabitants of the Western Hemisphere neither called themselves by a single term nor understood themselves as a collectivity, the idea and the image of the Indian must be a White conception.
>
> —Robert F. Berkhofer Jr., *The White Man's Indian*

So far, we have seen Hemingway explore and dispel the myth of racial primacy by delving into the depths of the gray spaces between red and white. Woods, water, and gate worked well as spatial separators between civilized and savage. If the camp stories exploit difference along general primitive lines, then several of Hemingway's remaining Native tales complicate the formula considerably. In them, the author explores and exploits interstitial race spaces through the lens of degeneracy and moral corruption. In each instance, per our established paradigm, that degeneracy, that corruption, begins as a seemingly Native phenomenon and end as a shared experience with whiteness a bit worse for the wear.

Hemingway's predominant devolutionary tropes of choice in these particular Indian stories are drink and sex. Critic Bonnie Duran suggests in her "Indigenous versus Colonial Discourse: Alcohol and American Indian Identity" that "the imagery of the stereotypical Drunken Indian—violent, lawless, impetuous—emerges clearly in this analysis as one of the instruments that attuned

Western collective consciousness to the notion of a North America awaiting the civilizing and rationalizing mission of European settlement." (113). Clearly, Hemingway did not invent the type, but he did recognize early on its inherent power, and he exploited it accordingly. The inebriated Native, whom I will examine later, litters Hemingway's literary landscape. However, in "Ten Indians," he explores a singularly different aspect of man's "otherly" nature—sexuality—in an attempt to draw clear lines of racial division between red and white. Once again, though, our emphasis should be not so much on the end result as on the means to that end—that is, Hemingway's initial narrative strategies employed to both forge this degenerative picture and wrest agency from alien clutches, only to subvert the totem again and question white inheritance in the end.

"Ten Indians," like "Indian Camp" before it, is very much an initiation tale. In it, a young Nick Adams learns about love, heartache, and rejection. Nick, still a preadolescent at this stage, is teased by neighborhood children about the wandering eyes (and other parts) of his crush-of-the-moment: a Native American girl named Prudence Mitchell.[1] Importantly, his father confirms the rumor after stumbling upon young Prudence mid-dalliance with another neighborhood child, Frank Washburn. While he never expressly tells Nickie what the young couple was doing when he came upon them, Dr. Adams's circumlocution leads us to believe she and the boy were engaged in some kind of sexual play. Most scholarship emphasizes the beginnings of a sexual awakening for a boy being initiated into the world or else sees it as a young boy's first dealings with the harsh realities of love and matters of the heart.[2] But I would venture to say that something more than heartache deserves our attention here—focus should also be on what precipitates that disappointment.

"Ten Indians" is very much a story about corrupted virginity. Further, Hemingway racializes sex as he examines that sullied space; he explores and ultimately aligns sexuality—more specifically, promiscuity—with stereotypical savagery. "Ten Indians" becomes a formal testament to the marginalized figure's moral decadence (with Nick Adams and the reader as principal witnesses to his decline). And with an added emphasis on miscegenation's threat (miscegenation here being actual, real), on the surface, this story serves as Hemingway's reminder of its perceived dangers. Hemingway seems to venture that such a reading of the Indian's apparent degradation begs some questions: Is depravity essential? Is decadence corruptive? And is the white immune to such corruption? To be sure, the sexual act is a union, a merging of disparate bodies; momentarily, two become one, each potentially indistinguishable from the other. Thus, to the fearful and squeamish, the physical divide here between the races becomes Hemingway's tenuous Gothic separator, and the threat of actual miscegenation is the most feared entity. In the failed sexual connection between Nick and Prudence at story's end, then, Hemingway silently underscores and assuages contemporary (read: *white*) fears about race transgression and its prospects, prospects that necessarily begin and end with white America's lost authority.

In a bold move, Hemingway opens "Ten Indians" with a cogent confluence of Indian life and white Americana: "After one Fourth of July, Nick, driving home late from town in the big wagon . . . , passed nine drunken Indians along the road" (253). Again, Hemingway begins with Independence Day as a reference point.[3] To be sure, he reminds us of the date as the story closes with Nick recounting the day's events to his father over dinner. Hemingway's deliberateness smacks of irony as the author juxtaposes two conceptions of America, one for the Native American, and one for his white counterpart. Marking the anniversary of the nation's own break with bondage, Independence Day is paramount to our reading of this tale through the lens of race.[4] The immediacy of the reference gives us an instantaneous portrait of two Americas at odds with each other.

Hemingway, in spare form, gives us a vibrant and wholesome America, one rooted in tradition. This America is the middle America of families breaking bread at suppertime; of neighborhood children converging for games; of baseball, barefoot walks through the woods, and apple pie. Joseph Flora reminds us in fact that this is—especially at the turn of the century—a holiday of family, community, and goodwill. However, juxtaposed with this picture of nurturing comfort are images of another America. Let us call this the "other" America or, more appropriately, the America of "otherness." This America is an America of taboos, both racial and sexual. It is an America of clandestine affairs, of deviant behavior, of decadence. More importantly, it is an America of marginalization, polarity, and strife, all rooted in this holiday. Within the white imagination, and battling for its very survival, is an America at war with itself. And Hemingway complicates matters by giving us an American conscience, on this fine Fourth of July, haunted by its ultimate betrayal of the Native and, in turn, itself.

Hemingway's narrative opens with this clear juxtaposition of these two Americas at odds with each other. And in the end, he uses as his barometer an understood American value system. He engaged that model early on with Dick Boulton, and here he reconnects to the tried-and-true formula and an audience he knows well:

> After one Fourth of July, Nick, driving home late from town in the big wagon with Joe Garner and his family, passed nine drunken Indians along the road. He remembered there were nine because Joe Garner, driving along the road in the dusk, pulled up the horses, jumped down into the road and dragged an Indian out of the wheel rut. The Indian had been asleep, face down in the sand. Joe dragged him into the bushes and got back up on the wagon-box.
>
> "That makes nine of them," Joe said, "just between here and the edge of town."
>
> "Them Indians," said Mrs. Garner. (253)

Mrs. Garner's "Them Indians" solidifies the separatist sentiment and Hemingway's initial intent in the opening sequence: from the beginning, it is "us" against "them." Further, Mrs. Garner's diction assures us of a blanketing of identity: in "them," one becomes all, and Hemingway gives us a mass indictment of a people. When the question arises concerning who exactly that last individual was whom Joe dragged from the road, one son tersely remarks to another, "All Indians wear the same kind of pants" (253).[5] Put another way, all Indians look alike. In just a few lines, Hemingway toys with stereotype and summarily links Native American to drink, to vice and degradation, to otherness. And with this, he begins to forge the divide between white man and red.

In *White Man's Wicked Water*, William Unrau traces the origins of the drunken Indian as a common trope in American lore, concluding that the formulation of this image owes as much to fiction as it does to actual fact.[6] Substance abuse among Native Americans during the nineteenth century, in particular, was as much a result of socio-historical factors—high-pressure government-sanctioned liquor sales, for example—as it was symptomatic of actual community dysfunction. However, the typology conveniently survives for a subject bent on defining himself in terms of what he is not. Irrespective of the fact that alcohol consumption was rampant in many instances among poor whites living in outpost towns who were just as starved for escapism during the same period, the image of the drunken Indian endured well into the twentieth century as a matter of course. Shrewd man that he is, Hemingway knows and exploits this reality in "Ten Indians."

As Unrau posits, "Immoderate, antisocial consumption was then viewed more as evidence of savage deficiency than as an individual malady or community pathology afflicting humans irrespective of social, ethnic, or racial boundaries" (118). Depicting the Native American in constant prostrate inebriation (Hemingway splays many an oblivious Indian across his literary landscape) elevates the "better man"; *razing* the red man in effect *raises* the white. In speaking of contemporary governmental propaganda, Unrau asserts that "uncontrollable passion and moral deficiency were recurrent themes regarding the abandon with which the Indians consumed alcohol" (52). Reminders of this "truth" abound already in the opening paragraph of "Ten Indians"; during the Garner family exchange, we learn that several of the neighboring camp's Indians litter the town's roadsides, drunk and immobile, and Hemingway's iceberg principle is in full form as whiteness becomes the amalgam of all things outside Indian debauchery.[7]

Hemingway immerses us in this debauchery—much of it coming in the form of young Prudence—as Nick and the two Garner boys discuss their father's recent encounter with a skunk. He ran over one while driving just days before this outing. The two brothers relate the story to Nick and disagree about the exact location of the unfortunate event. Their father's answer hardly settles things; in fact, it serves to complicate matters, as it begins a short exchange between Nick and the Garner family about sex and race. More importantly, the exchange becomes key in reading "Ten Indians" as a work invested in racial stereotype: "One place is just as good as another to run over a skunk" (254). This statement takes on metaphoric meaning as racial pejoratives and the person of Prudence Mitchell conflate and become the object of Carl Garner's inquiry. Just what was it that Nick saw the night before in the darkness? The back-and-forth exchange between the boys and their parents suggests much about the way these folk see the world and the way in which young Nick is initiated into it:

> "They were coons probably," Carl said.
> "They were skunks. I guess I know skunks."
> "You ought to," Carl said. "You got an Indian girl."
> "Stop talking that way, Carl," said Mrs. Garner.
> "Well, they smell about the same."
> Joe Garner laughed.
> "You stop laughing, Joe," Mrs. Garner said. "I won't have Carl talk that way." (254)

Carl's reply encapsulates the Garner clan's global conception, and white America's (re)vision. His statement is more than pejorative teasing; it is an active dehumanization.[8] Not only do ethnicity and species conflate, but so do individuals as Prudence becomes a stand-in for the skunk, and then implicitly *all* Indian girls ("they smell about the same").

And while Hemingway implicates Carl in this racial diminution, the elder Garner family members must share equally in his indictment for what they do *not* say. Joe and his wife, in their indulgence, share in Carl's guilt. Joe's immediate reaction to Carl's words is not righteous indignation but unabashed laughter, for which he too is reprimanded. Further, while Mrs. Garner does reprimand her son for his cavalier remarks, her chastisement is indirect and without bite. However, Hemingway would have us examine Mrs. Garner's tough talk. Her scolding is less for a family's blatantly racist attitudes than *for their exhibition.* Through her choice words, Hemingway underscores the *communication* of attitudes, *not* the views themselves ("I won't have Carl talk that way"). In this woman's tough talk, we can almost hear echoes of Dr. Adams's admonishment to Dick Boulton in "The Doctor and the Doctor's Wife" ("Don't talk that way"). We get it again as Mrs. Garner whispers something in her husband's ear after their son proudly assures us of his father's personal standards—his father declares that he would never pursue a "squaw" romantically: "Don't you say it, Garner," she warns. Most importantly, Mrs. Garner's admonishment belies the "truth" in her eyes. Mrs. Garner teases, "Carl can't get a girl . . . not even a squaw" (254). Thus, in this light, even Mrs. Garner's apparent righteousness is diminished.

Meanwhile, Hemingway cements our judgment of Prudence Mitchell with Nick's own father, who verifies the rumors surrounding the young Indian girl.[9] While engaged in intimate dinnertime talk with Nick, Dr. Adams fills in the rather conspicuous blanks for his inquisitive son.[10] As the story's tenth and last Indian, Prudence Mitchell becomes a dubious racial representative; when paired with the sexually naive Nick, she is licentious, aggressive, and potentially monstrous. Thus, not only does the chat between father and son introduce the young boy to love's perils, but it also underscores valuable lessons regarding matters of race and white privilege. Indeed, the Garner exchange proves quite fruitful.

Hence, Joe Garner's admonishment to young Nick that he "better watch out to keep Prudence" gains particular importance in this context. Suddenly, with emphasis on the right word—"keep"—friendly fatherly advice foreshadows the boy's impending crisis of the heart and indicts the Native American girl; Nick should be on his guard. Add to that Joe Garner's final declaration to Nick at the end of the verbal sparring session, and the profile is solidified: "'Nickie can have Prudence,' Joe Garner said. 'I got a good girl'" (254). If we place the emphasis on the word "good," Joe Garner's joking declaration and his affectionate reassurance to his wife (and nod and wink at the "goodness" of Nick's own girl) become an unabashed contrast of essentialities. Mrs. Garner's goodness implicitly runs counter to the Indian girl's "good" nature and that of her inebriated community members. Hemingway shows us that Prudence's sheer volition (and by implication, the hapless naïf's relinquished control and impotence) is that thing haunting white imagination. Her alleged deviance, her will (wanderlust in its broadest sense), is monstrous.

The truth about Prudence's dubious nature comes to pass later, naturally, with the doctor's allusion to Prudence's indiscretions with Frank Washburn. Nick, vexed at this point by all the teasing he's endured on the way home, prods his father for something, anything, to allay his worst fears: that the Garners are right about Prudence. The doctor's hesitation makes it apparent that the two young people were indeed engaged in some kind of sexual play when he happened upon them. When first asked for the particulars, Dr. Adams responds that "the Indians were all in town getting drunk," once again reminding us of the line separating civilized from savage. And when pushed for specifics, the doctor, quite aware of his son's concerns, suggestively tells him that he did in fact see something (or someone) of note: Prudence Mitchell. She and Frank Washburn, he adds, were having quite a time as they were "thrashing around" in the woods together. Averted eyes and circumlocution do much to paint the rest of the picture for both Nick and the reader. The conventional reading stops there.

But Hemingway pushes further, giving us yet another life lesson on this day of days: this experience and its recounting work both to affirm the racialized figure's decadence and decline and to reify whiteness, as evinced in the stable nuclear Garner and Adams families. Prudence—clearly not living up to her name—is that racial deviance and decay incarnate. Maintaining the myth of Anglo purity and progress means displacing perceived foible and fault and racializing it; doing so becomes a matter of underscoring certain "facts," namely, that the hyper-sexualized other is *not* the self. Hemingway kindly obliges with his character sketches. For Joe Garner and even Dr. Adams, clearly delineating difference becomes paramount; doing so gives permanence to otherwise fluctuating conceptions of self and society. And Hemingway gives us a narrative seemingly bent on preventing actual miscegenation and maintaining such an order, all within recounted memory. But for a nation grappling with its own restless demons, this story is less a prescriptive than a mirror.

Perhaps nowhere is the internalized angst and struggle against racial mixing more urgently expressed than in the later Nick Adams story "Fathers and Sons," in which Hemingway demonstrates Nick's further understanding of the world through the familial prism as he figuratively confronts and effectively exorcises that haunting demon called miscegenation. Nowhere are the latent fears of racial transgression and white erasure more evident than in this heavily autobiographical story. Mining his own memories, Hemingway presents us with an older, more mature Nick Adams ("Nicholas" now) who travels the roads with his own son. All of the story's observations are framed within the confines of this trip's conversation and spurred memory; the triggers are familiar settings and questions from his boyhood. Nick's remembrances are never expressly enunciated for his son; instead, he summons them for us through quiet recollection.

Very quickly the sights passing by Nick's moving car windows trigger memories of long-ago conversations between father and son and remembrances of sexual lessons learned (and not learned). And, significantly, sexual lessons become racial lessons. This is key because, in this story especially, sexual matters are representative of things unspoken, things unknown, and things feared. His own father, after all, Nick tells himself, "was not sound about matters of sex" (370), and therefore moments of miscommunication and misinformation abound in memories of his early education. Hemingway's narrative necessarily binds this same education to matters of race.

Our own education begins with Nick's earliest childhood recollections. Nick shares with his son and with us boyhood memories of hunting with his own father and, in one instance, of being bitten by a red squirrel after shooting it. The bite elicits a profanity from Nick ("The dirty little bugger"). Dr. Adams responds with a key question that not only underscores young Nick's oft-mentioned sexual (mis)education but, more importantly, acts as catalyst for the story's greater social lesson. In response to young Nickie's exclamation, his father asks, "Do you know what a bugger is?" (371). The doctor's definition is rooted in sin and perversion (more specifically, bestiality). Using this question as a trigger of sorts, Hemingway then deftly forges connections to Native demise, that same moral regression we get in "Ten Indians" and "The Indians Went Away." (While in these texts the sins assume other names—drunkenness most especially—racial decadence, deviance, and demise are still all pervasive.)

Indeed, Nick's initiation in "Fathers and Sons" fits our paradigm of relative othering quite well. Immediately, Hemingway's strategies of placement and association conflate as he again emphasizes physical location and polarity: "Nick's own education in those earlier matters had been acquired in the hemlock woods behind the Indian camp. This was reached by a trail which ran from the cottage through the woods to the farm and then by a road which wound through the slashings to the camp" (371–72). Like "Indian Camp" and "The Doctor and the Doctor's Wife," "Fathers and Sons" unabashedly exploits racial and spatial polarity.[11] Even with the mingling of red and white, the two remain markedly separate. And Nick's informal education, an education of the clandestine and unspoken variety, begins in the woods surrounding the camp, separated from the cottage and civilization. Received amid the trees and swamp, his education is almost primordial.

Hemingway uses setting once more as his metaphorical moral indicator in constructing his disparate model. The Indian woods, stripped and gutted as they are, become an outward manifestation of Native moral decline:

> The hemlock bark was piled in long rows of stacks, roofed over with more bark, like houses, and the peeled logs lay huge and yellow where the trees had been felled. They left the logs in the woods to rot, they did not even clear away or burn the tops. It was only the bark they wanted for the tannery at Boyne City; hauling it across the lake on the ice in winter, and each year there was less forest and more open, hot, shadeless, weed-grown slashing. (373)

With barkless trees and treeless thickets, with hemlocks felled and robbed of their outer covering, this is a scene of utter desolation. Hemingway gives us a structural (and social) fabric in decay ("rot," "burn," "weed-grown"). And for the white—as he pushes the shadow figure toward the margins—that decadence is a reminder of his own culpability in crimes against the red man; in turn, the "rot," the "burn," and the overgrown weeds are reminders of his own fallibility. All this—materialized misery—proves too close for comfort.[12]

Hemingway translates the metaphor for us, turning memories of the woods' decline into memories of Nick's first sexual dalliances in that formerly fecund, wooded space. Nick's recollections begin with narrative attempts to underscore racial difference. Getting to the camp, Hemingway tells us, is a matter of walking a trail through the hemlock forest. We can almost sense reverberations of Dr. Adams's camp sojourn to deliver the baby and of Dick Boulton's trek (apparently from the forest's far reaches) to help clear the white man's land of driftwood. In each instance, Hemingway's narrative creates a spatial divide, a divide that is eventually transgressed by the story's principal players.

From the spatial differential, Hemingway shifts gears a bit but never loses sight of his objective; he maintains those lines of racial delineation with linguistic markers, something he used to great effect in "The Doctor and the Doctor's Wife." While certainly well beyond the reductive primordial screams, grunts, and marked silences encountered in "Indian Camp," the Native American voice of "Fathers and Sons" is far from being that threatening force of Dick Boulton. In "Fathers and Sons," English is the domain of Nick and Nick alone. With her broken descriptors ("I no mind Billy," "He my brother," "That all I want do," "Make plenty baby what the hell"), Trudy hardly commands the language. Nick underscores this point, recollecting how "it was a long speech for her" as she tries to link multiple simple declaratives (373). Meanwhile, Billy, the story's only other featured Native American figure, is all but mute. In suggestively linking such concrete examples of lost voice with their relative associations, Hemingway reminds us that these are, after all, ethnic others "with funny names" living outside the established power structure; linguistic mastery—or failed mastery—underscores the difference already marked by blood.

However, at precisely the same moment, Hemingway also reminds us with hyper-racialized conceits—in a meta-moment of sorts—that the power structure is first and foremost just that: a construct. While armed with the powerful memories he mined for these vignettes, Hemingway, we can see, recognized, on some level, the pure absurdity inherent in the essentialist argument and its attendant tropes. We hear echoes of Trudy's verbal struggles in the grunts and broken English of Yogi Johnson's Indians in Hemingway's 1926 Chicago school send-up *The Torrents of Spring*. That knowledge only solidified with time. Here, too, he packages subversion and crossed racial lines in the very concept of name. Trudy, Billy, and Eddie, all Native Americans, have names of the dominant culture. Nick's own young son, upon hearing of his father's childhood friends, underscores this notion of constructed difference, declaring, "Those are funny names for Indians." Such "funny names" flout expectations. Clearly, even young Nickie sees that the color line has been crossed with the Native American's taking of "standard" Anglo names. In fact, the entire sequence bolsters this insistence on difference and divisional markers in spaces where they clearly no longer apply, and Hemingway invites us to discover this anachronism for ourselves.

Deliberate transgression assumes an even more aggressive form as the three young children of Nick's long-ago memories shift the topic of conversation to the eldest of the Indian siblings. Nick learns that Eddie, the oldest (and absent) brother, has been longing for the Adams sister, Dorothy. The children's exchange is extensive and important. That being said, it is especially useful to examine the sequence in its entirety, especially Nick's reaction, to appreciate its full implications:

> "If Eddie Gilby ever comes at night and even speaks to Dorothy you know what I'd do to him? I'd kill him like this." Nick cocked the gun and hardly taking aim pulled the trigger, blowing a hole as big as your hand in the head or belly of that half-breed bastard Eddie Gilby. "Like that. I'd kill him like that."
>
> "He better not come then," Trudy said. She put her hand in Nick's pocket.
>
> "He better watch out plenty," said Billy.
>
> "He's a big bluff," Trudy was exploring with her hand in Nick's pocket. "But you don't kill him. You get plenty trouble."
>
> "I'd kill him like that," Nick said. Eddie Gilby lay on the ground with all his chest shot away. Nick put his foot on him proudly.
>
> "I'd scalp him," he said happily.
>
> "No," said Trudy. "That's dirty."
>
> "I'd scalp him and send it to his mother."
>
> "His mother dead," Trudy said. "Don't you kill him, Nickie. Don't you kill him for me."
>
> "After I scalped him I'd throw him to the dogs."
>
> Billy was very depressed. "He better watch out," he said gloomily.
>
> "They'd tear him to pieces," Nick said, pleased with the picture. Then, having scalped that half-breed renegade and standing, watching the dogs tear him, his face unchanging, he fell backward against the tree, held tight around his neck, Trudy holding, choking him, and crying, "No kill him! No kill him! No kill him! No. No. No. Nickie. Nickie. Nickie!"
>
> "What's the matter with you?"
>
> "No kill him."
>
> "I got to kill him."
>
> "He just a big bluff."
>
> "All right," Nickie said. "I won't kill him unless he comes around the house. Let go of me."
>
> "That's good," Trudy said. "You want to do anything now? I feel good now."
>
> "If Billy goes away." Nick had killed Eddie Gilby, then pardoned him his life, and he was a man now. (377)

The sexual implications loom large for these preadolescents. And the convergence of sex and violence is visceral and powerful. Hemingway deliberately crafts a dialogue that is rife with innuendo. Immediately, the narrative presents us with two possible readings of Nick's reaction. First, there is the knee-jerk reaction of an overprotective brother armed with his own brand of sexual knowledge and coming to the aid of his vulnerable sibling. However, Hemingway gives us something much more ominous as well. Nick's reaction is arguably more than proffered brotherly love and protection, and it is extreme to say the least; his strong and very select language bespeaks a young white male vowing to protect the honor of not only his sister but, by extension, all white women. In young Nickie's sworn and open declarations (of war), Hemingway makes use of a very particular tradition, one with southern mythological origins: the so-called Cult of True Womanhood, which called for nothing less than the unqualified preservation of white maidenhood.

Ironically, the transgressive act itself is what first spawns Nick's rage at Trudy's mention of her brother's bolstered prowess and boastful talk. I say *ironically,* because Nick rages against the very thing responsible for his own sexual awakening and initial lessons in all things amorous. His most vivid memories are attributable in part to "the things done" by Trudy, things "no one has ever done better" (376). And Nick's remembrances of these encounters are nothing more than a catalog of body parts and sensations: "Plump brown legs, flat belly, hard little breasts, well-holding arms, quick searching tongue, the flat eyes, the good taste of mouth, then uncomfortably, tightly, sweetly, moistly, lovely, tightly, achingly, fully, finally, unendingly, never-endingly, never-to-endingly, suddenly ended, the great bird flown like an owl in the twilight" (377). In this sequence, Hemingway demonstrates Nick's deliberate taking and what I will term a relative knowing of the Indian. His chain of remembered sensations evokes a sense of passionate conquest and self-satiation as the catalog builds from robust and functional parts ("plump brown legs," "well-holding arms," "quick searching tongue") to the "flat eyes," whose only purpose, it seems, is to reflect the will of he who stands before them.

Bolstering this idea of relative knowledge gained from this "taking" are the words immediately following the "suddenly ended" experience:

> So that when you go in a place where Indians lived you smell them gone and all the empty pain killer bottles and the flies that buzz do not kill the sweetgrass smell, the smoke smell and that other like a fresh cased marten skin. Nor any jokes about them nor old squaws take that away. Nor the sick

> sweet smell they get to have. Nor what they did finally. It wasn't how they ended. They all ended the same. Long time ago good. Now no good. (376)

Hemingway seems to suggest that discovery and conquest have engendered a new kind of knowledge. Suddenly, an entire people's complexity is distilled into a primal understanding and a sensory chain of knowing; suddenly, a sexual encounter gives way to a profound essential knowledge of a race and a culture. Interestingly enough, it also portends a culture's apparent demise. Implicit in this is a marked state of fallen-ness, and it is a fallen-ness precipitated by moral weakness. Nobility gives way to ignobility, simplistic perfection corrodes, and the romantic lapsarian conception is complete (see Berkhofer 88).[13]

Hemingway also, quite importantly, shows us that this kind of knowledge, this means of reading the world via the branded body, is not meant to be a reciprocal act. Or, more accurately, this kind of epistemological probing becomes an aggressive act of racial exclusivity. And, completing Hemingway's Gothic homage, the things Nick most cherishes in those backwoods memories are the very things that haunt him as a young (white) man decades later.

Conversely, Eddie's suggested interest in Dorothy as a sexual object represents the marginal figure's greatest encroachment, and, as with Dick Boulton before him, his "half-breed" indeterminacy only fans those fearful flames ("half-breed bastard").[14] In the new century's early years, such an encroachment was, for many, the most heinous of crimes. Well into the twentieth century (some would argue well into the twenty-first century), the mere charge of rape (of a white woman) levied against a man of color was often enough to warrant conviction both in and outside a court of law; mob rule and the noose were behind scores of lynchings at the turn of the century. Suddenly young Nickie, heeding the call of Thomas Dixon, slips into the realm of Arthurian legend and the Cult of True Womanhood and dons the garb of white knight. Eddie then becomes the dark dragon that must be slain. There is more at stake, then, than protecting the sanctity of feminine sexuality; it becomes a matter of staving off a threatening minority presence. The evidence lies in Nick's choice words; his reaction is one of marked terror. And in the young boy's voice, Hemingway channels the greater fear of converging generations: the fear of miscegenation and anticipated social upheaval.

Young Nick's fears stem from the same space as Dr. Adams's frustration in "The Doctor and the Doctor's Wife," frustration born from the challenges inherent in the racially nebulous Dick Boulton. But complicating Nick's fears is the perceived threat of reciprocal transgression—something easily initiated from *either* side of the color line—and sullied purity challenging whiteness as great inviolate space. Hemingway's translated fears are certainly nothing new; such fears have deep roots in this nation's history, with laws concerning miscegenation, particularly "violations" of white women, dating back to the seventeenth century.[15] So when rumors of Eddie Gilby's interest in Dorothy reach Nick's ears, his (white) imagination and national history allow him to murder the Indian with impunity ("After I scalped him I'd throw him to the dogs"). Thus, Nick's psyche is, as Philip Young rightly suggests, a psyche that is vulnerable and scarred by life experience. But, Hemingway demonstrates, it is a psyche scarred by the unsettling fact that racial definitions (and ideas of superiority) and notions of assured racial dominance are fast becoming unraveled and, in some instances, altogether irrelevant.

As a response to "Fathers and Sons," if these stories are looked at critically as a thematic unit, "The Indians Moved Away" works as a coda of sorts to a people's history and the greater body of the author's Indian stories. In the last of the Indian tales, the story of the Indian formally comes to a close as the narrative relates not an individual's fate but that of an entire people. In it, Hemingway once more momentarily indulges in the romance of the fading historicized race consumed by drink and debauchery. And if we trace the Native's (d)evolution from the early stories ("Indian Camp") to the later tales such as "Ten Indians" and "The Indians Moved Away," we see definite lineal connections between them. The points of commonality are several, and no matter what their particular dynamic, each story points to the same inevitability, which is enunciated perhaps most clearly in "The Indians Moved Away."

Like the other stories in this examination, "The Indians Moved Away" begins in that clearly delineated comfort zone. It begins with a marked bifurcation, with Hemingway once more painting a portrait of polarity. The opening paragraph is both a simple homage to the bucolic and the beginnings of an overt sociological cleavage with which Hemingway invests most of the text: "The Petoskey road ran straight uphill from Grandpa Bacon's farm. His farm was at the end of the road. It always seemed, though, that the road started at his farm and ran to Petoskey, going along the edge of the trees up the long hill, steep and sandy, to disappear into the woods where the long slope of fields stopped short against the hardwood timber" (34). On the one hand, even with Nick's picture-postcard remembrance of Grandpa Bacon's farm, the narrative focus at all times is the road to Petoskey. With small-town America coursing through his veins, young Nick sees all things emanating from the farm. In terms of a more universal importance invested in the road, it stands as a prominent signifier of progress and all its relative associations; the road is a civilizing agent linking the farm with the town of Petoskey, fittingly, a white space bearing an Indian name. (Hemingway's deliberate choice itself playfully anticipates the complexity and conflation of identities toward which he works.) This is Nick's initial memory and the narrative's very first utterance. Completing the spatial divide, and juxtaposed with the farm and the connected road, are the woods that pervade the story and Nick's imagination.

The woods are a site of mystery and relative uncertainty. As such, Hemingway remains true to both the geography and the trope. He would revisit these images again and again, relegating the Indians in *The Torrents of Spring,* for example, to a great "beyond, where you could not see it" (52). Always, they are the stuff of imagination. Nick's imagination roams with the same freedom that his hands enjoy on the family farm as they rummage, spade, and till the soil for worms; the surrounding woods and its inhabitants do not seem to enjoy the same sense of reassurance. Images of Grandpa Bacon's farm open the tale, and there is nothing to suggest it does not outlive the storyteller; Hemingway attaches a sense of permanence and intractability to the land in general. It is to this essence that Nick—and, for that matter, whiteness—attaches himself in his grasping for authoritative reigns.

Actively and sharply contrasting this sense of permanence are Hemingway's associations with all things "other," associations inherent in the figures haunting the literary landscape. From its inception, the narrative aligns the Indian with impermanence, perpetually dressing him in the garb of variability. Implicitly consumed by his own foibles, destroyed by his own decadence and moral corrigibility, he is a dying figure.[16] He is a living ghost, and, as such, he becomes a mute expression of racial uncertainty.[17] From the story's beginning, the Native American figure takes on the vestiges of a Gothic spook. Just as the farm and whiteness become visible signs of the essential and the enduring, Hemingway's Indian becomes a sign of the unknowable (recall Dick Boulton) and the mutable as evinced in the woods. This contingent includes both the slightly desperate, nameless horde and the singularly respectable Simon Greene, a Native figure from the neighborhood.

Hemingway introduces us to the dying Indian early on, as memories of farm and road and woods become quick flash memories of a people:

> In the summer the Indians picked the berries along the road and brought them down the cottage to sell them, packed in the barrels, wild red raspberries crushing with their own weight, covered with basswood

> leaves to keep them cool; later blackberries, firm and fresh shining, pails of them. The Indians brought them, coming through the woods to the cottage by the lake. You never heard them come but there they were, standing by the kitchen door with the tin buckets full of berries. (34)

These Indians are the Ojibwa. Once proud hunters, fur traders, and fishermen of the Great Lakes region, the Ojibwa of Michigan are reduced to a landless people; when we meet them, they are Gypsy-like, picking berries by the side of the road to support themselves in a new and adversarial economy. The reality of this diminution is accurately depicted by the artist here; this is the sobering reality undergirding Hemingway's hyper-divisive narrative. As a student of history, Hemingway would have known this reality well.

A multiplicity of treaties crafted in the late nineteenth and early twentieth centuries by both the Canadian and American governments promulgated a policy of dependency as thousands of Ojibwa were "relocated." The Ojibwa slowly signed their lives away by treaty, more than any other Native tribe (involving the peoples and lands of St. Louis, Saginaw, and Chicago, for example).[18] Once the most powerful and largest Great Lakes tribe, at the twentieth century's dawning, the Ojibwa found itself confined to reservations. Furthermore, commercial mandates and regulations pushed many a Native farmer to the brink of economic insolvency and into other forms of subsistence (see, for example, Waisberg and Holzkamm). Hemingway depicts this socioeconomic mutability in a people without history, without voice, and without footsteps. Like ghosts, Hemingway tells us, the Indians seemingly appear from nowhere, haunting the landscape and memory alike.

Racial knowledge now comes through sensory perception. Nick, the narrative tells us, often "smelt the Indians coming through the gate past the woodpile and around the house" (34). This description works perfectly within Hemingway's Gothic framework; for the white, the Indian's dehumanization is the first step in exorcising latent feelings of guilt and responsibility. In this segment, the native is a mass phantom presence. The narrative more fully engages this active exercise in homogeneity in its insistence that Indians all "smell about the same." We can almost hear echoes of Frank Garner's declarations in "Ten Indians" that "all Indians wear the same kind of pants," and his brother Carl's unabashedly racist remark (in an attempt to hurt young Nickie's feelings) that skunks and Indians "smell about the same."

As the narrative works to dehumanize the Indian, it pushes him increasingly toward the fringes of reality and affixes to him the Gothic sensibilities of spook and specter; in so doing, he becomes less real and more romantic. Meanwhile, the Anglo acquires a supernatural kind of knowledge (therein lies the paradox) of the objectified Indian as he works to quantify even as he mystifies. The "smell" then becomes a means of both orientalizing and making palpable the projected unknown. As a romantic sublimation, this newly conceived Indian works to simultaneously maintain a distance between subject and object, all the while drawing that feared specter closer. At the very least, then, in "The Indians Moved Away," Hemingway paints for us a composite of conflicted white consciousness.

Beneath the sublimation lies a profound guilt; more importantly, it is a guilt that implicates the inviolate white, and a guilt that, Hemingway shows us, makes white man and red not all that different. A ghostlike Native American presence is a metaphysical reminder to whites of the debts owed to a broken people; more than a cheap conceit, Hemingway's Indian is a flesh-and-bone manifestation of the guilty collective white conscience, a conscience clearly still at odds with its past sins. The dying Native is that reminder incarnate.

Further, Hemingway's Native figure is also a reminder to the white man of his own very precarious position within this model; by virtue of his close alignment with these purportedly foible-laden people, the white subject finds himself dangerously close to that very decadence. Robbed of his land, his individuality, and his dignity, and reduced to noble and ignoble stereotype, the Native American stands before us a diminished figure. Yet, Hemingway demonstrates, his diminution does not guarantee continued racial disparity and white primacy. With blood on his hands, both figuratively and literally, the white man is greatly responsible for the state of Indian decadence and decline. As a result, he too necessarily finds himself a reduced figure.[19] Time and again, our author holds up for scrutiny Anglo claims of purported greatness. Hemingway paints this problematic picture with relish, showing us a twentieth-century white America with its own questionable character and moral rectitude hardly distinguishable from that of the degraded other. And as the Indians move away, color lines blur, identities conflate, and all racial claims to authority and privilege disappear.

CHAPTER THREE

The Truth's in the Shadows

Race in "The Light of the World" and "The Battler"

> As master and man stood before him, the black upholding the white, Captain Delano could not but bethink him of the beauty of that relationship which could present such a spectacle of fidelity on the one hand and confidence on the other.
>
> —Herman Melville, *Benito Cereno*

> The story of the life I have led may . . . not only contain some interest if told for its own sake, but may also shed some light on the life of our times.
>
> —Jack Johnson, *Jack Johnson: In the Ring and Out*

In the summer of 1908, up became down, black became white, and the world as many knew it changed forever. In that year, Jack Johnson became the first African American heavyweight boxing world champion. Some seven years later, Johnson would lose that title to the last of several so-called great white hopes looking to knock the defiant smile from the black man's face. In the spring of 1915, Jess Willard became that man, seizing the crown for himself, and reclaiming it for all of white America.

It was a moment etched into the national consciousness, and a reality that Ernest Hemingway subtly infuses as backstory into the narrative threads of "The Light of the World" and "The Battler," stories I refer to as his black-and-white stories.[1] These tales take us away from the wilds of the Indian camp and transplant us to the outskirts of town and anticipated civilization. Hemingway replaces red man with black as he negotiates yet another racial space. Like the Indian stories, the black-and-white tales anticipate (white) reader assumptions just to subvert them altogether in the end, and Hemingway's means to that end—as it was in the Indian stories—is a nod to the Gothic as he employs the grotesque in both tales to draw truth from the mouths of each story's soothsayer. Truth-telling once more means exposing the myths of both racial essentiality and the totem.

Like Flannery O'Connor's deformed characters, Hemingway's grotesques shock the system, awe, and teach. In each of his pugilistic stories, the marginalized figure—Johnson in "Light" and Bugs in "The Battler"—steps out from the shadows to wrest power from white hands. In each instance, dark figures transgress the all-important color line and the story becomes the black man's as much as it is that of the young naïf, Nick Adams. With each transgression, Hemingway shows us how the color line is the stuff of imagination and how white supremacy is the material of myth, and Hemingway's imagination would push the limits of this truth for years. The boxing ring becomes the perfect forum in which to explore the concept of the so-called great white hope, a racialized messiah destined to reclaim white primacy both in and, symbolically, outside the ring; in each of these spaces, tempered violence dictated by prescriptive rules within the ring and social protocol without maintained at least the semblance of order. Both stories anticipate and seemingly validate contemporary (white) reader assumptions. Then, through moments of violence, they altogether subvert and question expected racial definition and whiteness's seemingly inherent greatness.

While many critics note Nick Adams's piecemeal initiation into manhood in these stories and others in the Hemingway canon, few go beyond standard readings of innocence lost amid sex and violence. Even fewer recognize the importance of race within this same paradigm.[2] The majority of the few Hemingway race readings only go so far as to offer critiques of his Indian stories. This raises several questions: If we can concede that literature is a way of reading the world, why have scholars not applied a racial lens to more of the Hemingway oeuvre?[3] Further, what does the overall trajectory suggested by Hemingway's writings and his sustained interest in race throughout his career really mean? The import of Hemingway's racial tales extends beyond what I will call "racial cognizance" on the part of a resistant white figure; the true significance lies in the traditionally marginalized figure and *his* awareness of the tenuous, even illusory, nature of the color line. So, how does "The Light of the World," with Jack Johnson at its center, largely escape such a critical reading? Related criticism has been relatively sparse, debate relatively quiet. Race has been the pink elephant in the room that, by and large, Hemingway critics have refused to see, and like Ralph Ellison's invisible man, Hemingway's Johnson is the black man who simply refuses to be ignored.

During the first two decades of the twentieth century, racial tensions in America were palpable. World war, increased foreign immigration, and a sizable African American migration from the South to the North all marked the American landscape during the new century's first decades. So did increased xenophobia and related immigration laws, a resurgence of the Ku Klux Klan, and lynching and race riots. And, as any good social realist would, Hemingway imbibed what he saw. What many scholars and general readers alike seem to overlook in assessing the author's modern vision is that Hemingway, the voice of Anglo American masculinity, saw the world in more than shades of white. And in "The Battler" and "The Light of the World," he explores blackness and the gray spaces where black and white collide. For Hemingway, the allusive boxing ring in each tale becomes an appropriate metaphor for the violent energy both holding together and threatening to tear apart the present social order, an order predicated on understood rules of racial construction.

Hemingway's "The Battler" is a fine entrée into the realm of his black-and-white tales. Each story is in fact an Anglo-centered text, with a young white male protagonist being initiated into a world of violent racial negotiation. However, here the minority presence works to both indirectly illuminate the Anglo character and properly educate the reader.[4] I choose to examine this story first for two reasons. First, published in 1924 as part of the early Nick Adams collection and included in *In Our Time,* it is an early reflection of Hemingway's awareness of the African American presence. Hemingway's prospective descriptions of the tale before its publication casually suggest the proper racial lens through which the story's principal players should be viewed.[5] Second, "The Battler" forecasts and anticipates nicely this and other ancillary motifs visited repeatedly in the author's later works, including "The Light of the World." Here Hemingway consciously underscores then deconstructs the fault(y) lines separating the races.

"The Battler" opens in line with reader expectation as Hemingway introduces us to a harsh landscape and a young, impressionable naïf, Nick Adams. The story unfolds amid violent environs with Nick battered and bruised, much worse for the wear after a scuffle with a train's brakeman. His pants, Hemingway tells us, are torn and "the skin was barked." His hands prove to be in no better shape, as "there were sand and cinders driven up under his nails"

(97). Nick has been tossed from a train for playing (rather poorly) the part of a stowaway intent on riding the rails for free. The brakeman has other ideas and passes along the lesson to Nick.

The greater lesson for Nick, though, is not necessarily one of economy or ethics; it is one of racial negotiation, and the story, which transpires at the foot of the embankment below the rails, follows Nick's brief encounter with the brakeman. Nick suddenly comes across a wandering duo: a white ex-prizefighter and his African American ex–jail mate and traveling companion. Hemingway's story begins ostensibly with Nick's meeting of this roving twosome, and the narrative's true racial implications are not readily apparent until well into the text. Hemingway does not disclose the tale's narrative import until the last sequence unfolds and Nick Adams wanders onward: "He must get to somewhere" (97). The physical site then becomes secondary to the encounter itself as a site of newfound racial knowledge.

Hemingway chooses a darkened clearing underneath the rails as his site of conveyance, carefully crafting a new Gothic space within which to divide then conquer old myths. Nick happens upon a fire burning for one Ad Francis, former boxing champion, and his black compatriot and former cell mate, Bugs. Bugs, we quickly learn, acts as caretaker and confidant to the former fighter; further pertinent details are revealed later. However, the narrative's initial sequences involving the two strangers serve to underscore white reader expectation as we quickly get typology at its strongest. Nick meets Ad first: "The fire was bright now, just at the edge of the trees. There was a man sitting by it. Nick waited behind the tree and watched. The man looked to be alone. He was sitting there with his head in his hands looking at the fire. Nick stepped out and walked into the firelight" (98). The man in deep thought is Ad Francis. Immediately, the narrative forges an associative linkage of sorts among Nick, the former boxer, and the thriving fire. The connection is bolstered by the seemingly automatic bond between young Nick and the fighter, contrary to Joseph Flora's perceived disjuncture between the two figures.[6]

The point of convergence for the two is the evidence Nick sports as proof of his encounter with the train's brakeman—his black eye—as Nick's "Hello!" is followed by "Where did you get the shiner?" (98). The connection between the nameless man and the fire, and soon enough Nick himself, is significant in that fire stands as the first sign of civilization for Nick as he walks through the darkness with "three or four miles of swamp" between himself and the next town, Mancelona (98). In this sequence, Hemingway elicits unspoken racial typology as shared images of whiteness and civilization conflate in the form of the fire.

And as Ad and Nick rail against the brakeman ("The bastard!"), man and boy forge an alliance against a system seemingly intent on constricting them both. They implicitly share an understanding of violence's place in this world:

> "You're a tough one, aren't you?"
> "No," Nick answered.
> "All you kids are tough."
> "You got to be tough," Nick said.
> "That's what I said." The man looked at Nick and smiled. (98)

They both know that this brand of violence is best left relegated to the realm of tough talk and hard-boiled machismo. This violence is born of a mythical kind of bravado celebrated in the ring and the back alleys of crime fiction lore. Confined to tough talk, theirs is a violence of story. It stands in stark contrast to the actual violence we get with our introduction to Bugs, Ad's African American sidekick, whose brand of violence promises to be both unexpected and terrifying.

A bit later, the ex-fighter touts his toughness and insists that the strange boy call him by his first name, Ad. Conversely, his friend of several years, Bugs, never moves beyond the formalities of surname. The bond between white men appears to be instantaneous, and the black man immediately moves outside the circle. In fact, he shows deference to both white figures with a last name address for each. In keeping with the racial constrictions separating the men, at work even in this space, even young Nick is afforded the title of "Mister." When asked by Bugs who he is, Nick offers his last name first to convey the lineage and history denied the black man; it is important to note that Hemingway's narrative never grants Bugs those entitlements. All demonstrations of respect are reserved for Ad.

On the surface, Ad is the epitome of the great white hero and the Hemingway code hero. Anticipating white reader expectation, Hemingway initially casts the boxer as the embodiment of white masculinity (Early).[7] Fittingly, his original working title for the story was "The Great Man." The former champion has apparently weathered a life's storm, and he has endured; his battered body and psyche (he admits to being "not quite right") stand as testament to this. Even in his worn state, though, he assumes quasi-mythic proportions as a man with a storied past. And this story is not lost on Nick, who instantly recognizes the name. He was once a fighter of some renown and comes to us as a conqueror of men. Nick's reaction is one of earnest awe as he credulously verifies the former boxer's identity ("Honest to God?"), just knowing that "it must be true." Ad names no opponent, cites no particular fight, as he recounts his past glory; instead, Hemingway gives us mythical allusion to a boundless nameless corpus of slain warriors. His success, he says, is due in part to an unnaturally slow-beating heart, the marker of fine physicality.

> "You know how I beat them?"
>
> "No," Nick said.
>
> "My heart's slow. It only beats forty a minute. Feel it."
>
> Nick hesitated.
>
> "Come on," the man took hold of his hand. "Take hold of my wrist. Put your fingers there."
>
> The little man's wrist was thick and the muscles bulged above the bone. Nick felt the slow pumping under his fingers. (99)

Nick counts his pulse to quantify that prowess. Joe Flora asserts that "the touch leads to no epiphany or communal fellowship" (88). To the contrary, the sequence demonstrates a young white boy's hero worship and evinces his connection to this white superman as something that is both race-based and immediate.

White reader expectation is met yet again as the focus shifts to the boxer's black traveling companion and confidant, Bugs. Juxtaposed, at least initially, with a pronounced Anglo masculine model is the African American type. Again, Nick's initial encounter with this apparent secondary figure is one of blatant typology and fulfilled narrative expectation. Nick's first impressions of the black man exemplify this point best: "A man dropped down the railroad embankment and came across the clearing to the fire" (100). Immediately, the black man's presence is phantom-like and Gothic, bearing all the markings of "otherness." He comes to the fire from the void of brush, darkness, and night. But even under the shroud of darkness, Bugs reveals enough of himself to Nick for the boy to make a race-based identification, to know him as an African American man: "It was a negro's voice." Nick listens, watches, then knows: "Nick knew from the way he walked that he was a negro." Later as he cooks for the group, Bugs "crouch[es] on long nigger legs over the fire" (100). In each instance, Hemingway paints a picture of crafted racial difference.

Further, Hemingway tells us that Nick immediately recognizes the voice coming from the fire at the story's outset as that of a Negro. Race bears sensory marks, and Hemingway knows it, and he appropriately plays on this association. Type suggests that the Negro is meekness incarnate. In fact, the narrative subtly interchanges name with racial manner and racial manner with racial epithet as Bugs becomes the "polite negro," and the polite "negro" becomes "nigger." Bugs speaks with a Negro's voice, walks with a Negro's gait, and often is simply "the negro." As he warns Nick against handing the former boxer his knife, he is "the negro"; as he tends to the cooking requests, he is "the negro"; as he and Nick speak of the former champion's bouts with the press, the public, and the law, he is "the negro"; and he is "the negro" again as Nick finally takes leave of the duo at story's end. Hemingway cunningly refuses to allow the reader to forget that this is a story of racial exchange and difference.

The relationship between the two vagabonds initially fails to escape this polar paradigm. At first, the dynamic appears to be anything but complex. Anticipating reader expectation, Hemingway simplifies the complexities with an exaggerated color line. Bugs is deference and servility embodied, and outside his sense of allegiance to the former fighter, we know little about the man as the story begins. Bugs has no discernable past of his own. What we glean is through association and manner only. Whereas Ad is brash and purposeful in his exchange with Nick, Bugs is all quiet deference. The black man clearly knows his place. Financial support is apparently Ad's domain, while Bugs's is primarily domestic. Appropriately, once the proper introductions have been made, Bugs immediately launches into meal preparation for both friend and guest: "When are we going to eat, Bugs?" With a quick "Right away," the black man's response is automatic (100).

The narrative's racial divide further reveals itself in the short history the two vagabonds share. Their paths crossed, Nick learns from Bugs, in prison. Both men were prosecuted for violent crimes, and both paid their debts to society with time served. However, Hemingway makes clear a very important distinction between the two men, a distinction demonstrated through connotation. The former jail mates are men with similar fates, but altogether different guiding principles. Hemingway's narrative goads ever so slightly, coaxing both Nick and the (white) reader to judge the two men differently. Bugs's terse recount of Ad's collapse after his wife's desertion is telling: "'I met him in jail,' the negro said. 'He was busting people all the time after she went away and they put him in jail. I was in for cuttin' a man'" (103). Immediately, nuanced division overshadows any solidarity between the two mates. And that difference is notably one of racial association. Hemingway paints Ad as a man of brawn and bodily might (he "bust[s]" people with his fists), Bugs as seemingly less than a man, requiring a blade to even the score. The narrative links white with might and fair play, and blackness with inadequacy and cheating. Bugs's storytelling anticipates the black underhandedness that we see in Nick's encounter with the prostitutes of "The Light of the World." In each instance, Hemingway intentionally drives a wedge between characters with racial discourse.

However, as we saw in the Indian stories, division is only one part of the Hemingway racial equation; revelation is the other. Bugs's purpose here is more complicated than a typological reading suggests. In "The Battler," the racially charged narrative—especially its descriptions of the black man—both demonstrates Nick's race consciousness or hyper-cognizance and reveals the very new and often terrific realities of a color line in constant flux. These are realities Hemingway exposes with relish.

The first racial myth dispelled by Hemingway is perhaps the greatest of them all, and one that toppled quickly with the fall of Tommy Burns and the rise of Jack Johnson: that of the indomitable white hero. We have a hero in this tale who is in fact unheroic. When we meet him, the fighter's best days are behind him. From the story's inception, Ad Francis is very much a diminished figure: "In the firelight Nick saw that his face was misshapen. His nose was sunken, his eyes were slits, he had queer-shaped lips. Nick did not perceive all this at once, he only saw the man's face was queerly formed and mutilated. It was like putty in color. Dead-looking in the firelight." Later in the same exchange, Nick sees that Ad "only had one ear. It was thickened and tight" (99). Note that the emphasis is on exteriority, on the physical marker. Hemingway all but dehumanizes Ad with his beaten, almost monstrous countenance; the prizefighter becomes a grotesque, offering the wayward kid wisdom and a new racial truth. At its core, Hemingway's story is about a fluctuating color line and shifting racial authority, seen first in markers of physicality and then, more importantly, in characterization and action. Hemingway's corporeal focus furthers his experiment with the grotesque, anticipating an interest revisited in "The Light of the World."

Hemingway's narrative explores the grotesque in its exaggerated characterization: characters are super-masculine ("the muscles bulged above the bone") and overtly racialized as black or white ("his face was white," "crouching on long nigger legs"). In each instance, the distortion approaches the absurd. With a form and figure severely misshapen, the ex-champion is the grotesque incarnate: of the downtrodden boxer the narrative tells us that his skin is "like putty in color," and his face is "queerly formed and mutilated." However, Hemingway goes beyond the initial physical distortion to expose and exploit the incongruities of race. And the true incongruity, the true distortion, Hemingway shows us, is the one between racial mythos and racial reality. When viewed through the racial lens, the encounter between Nick and the two vagabonds shifts from one of pure typology and a clearly marked racial divide to one of floating definitions and an unraveling construct. Hemingway's original title, "The Great Man" (*Selected Letters* 155), thus becomes one of marked irony, not nostalgia, and one that challenges, rather than satisfies, white reader expectations.[8]

Ad Francis is a former ring warrior, a pugilist of some repute whose muscular wrists, scarred face, and seemingly perpetual income are proof of a man with history and legacy. However, the case of Ad Francis is also one of loss and degeneration, not of greatness (regained). Hemingway repeatedly employs the word "little" in his descriptions of the former fighter, suggesting a narrative deliberateness. Twelve times the former slayer of men and great white hope is cast as "the little man." Hemingway's cognizance of racial construction becomes clear as he (de)constructs the character.

When he first meets Ad, Nick confirms the great man's claims to "superhuman" conditioning: "Feeling the slow hard throb under his fingers Nick started to count. He heard the little man counting, slowly, one, two, three, four, five, and on—aloud" (100). Ad's physical prowess is undeniable. However, at a key point in the narrative, Ad asks to hold Bugs's knife and is summarily denied his request. Appropriately, the former champion asserts himself, and at the moment of his supposed resurgence, the narrative tells us that "the little man" glared at Nick, and then "came toward him slowly, stepping flat-footed forward, his left foot stepping forward, his right dragging up to it" (101). Even in this moment of apparent self-affirmation, Hemingway marks Ad's attempted rise with diminution. The former champion is ultimately met with a knockout blow from Bugs. As Nick departs, with Ad prostrate on the ground and Bugs nursing him after having struck him down, he listens to the private conversation between the two men and notes Bugs's low soft voice and "the little man" complaining of a terrible headache. Thus, from beginning to end, whiteness is made small time and again.

While attention to exteriority (and its disintegration) allows for the beginnings of a subversive reading, there is another more profound truth hidden in the grotesque face and form of Ad Francis. The image of the powerful white champion whose money sustains him years after he has left the ring is supplanted by the reality of an *ex*-champion with one foot squarely planted in the soil of a past that is anything but glorious. This former great white hope is also a convict and a degenerate. If he is a master of men when in the ring, outside it, Ad Francis is conversely an irrational law breaker and an unbridled slave to his emotions. Outside the ring, he is effectively feminized: unable to control himself, he goes to jail for "busting people all the time [after his wife] went away and they put him in jail." Bugs refuses to expound upon the known, simply suggesting that Ad's wife deserted him. The desertion poses, for us, a greater question of dubious (white) manhood.

With his wife's departure and his release from prison, Ad becomes an "other" of the Anglo imagination—bereft of his livelihood and his glory, he is a vagabond dependent on the personal kindness of his former cell mate and the monetary support of a former spouse who sends him money. Further, he is a man whose sanity ("I'm not quite right," he posits) becomes increasingly questionable as the narrative progresses. Most importantly, he is a man who, in spite of his white skin, is clearly *not in control of himself,* let alone those around him. Thus Ad Francis is a man robbed of any and all authority. Gone with the glory, Hemingway seems to suggest, are the clear markers of racial primacy.

Hard on his luck, very much at the mercy of a black man, and only a shell of his former (supposedly greater) self, Ad Francis is the great white hope dashed. As such, he is living testament to the illusionary nature of racial configuration. If boxing is a crafted manhood, then dark dominance in the ring by Jack Johnson—whose capture of the heavyweight championship galvanized the race issue in America decades after Reconstruction—becomes a metaphor for a palpable black volition and an encroachment of white authority outside the ring. For Hemingway, the advent of Johnson's world championship marked the opening of a new epoch in American social history. The perpetuation of clearly debunked myths—the white reign over the square jungle—is the greater absurdity to which Hemingway seems to point.

Ad's traveling companion, Bugs—not Ad himself—becomes the true agent of action and control here and Hemingway's ultimate site of subversion. The black man effectively commandeers white authority while the white male subject becomes pliable and putty-like, at the mercy of those around him. Once more, focus on exteriority, the white man's "dead-looking" color, underscores this malleability. We get the ultimate moment of white diminution at story's end with Ad's complete physical submission to Bugs, who stands over him as he lies prostrate and small on the ground. Hemingway gives us a racial inversion as he morphs and even transposes black and white bodies. To that end, Ad's realization of his own marked impotence, of the fact that he, Ad Francis, former world champion and white agent, is in reality no better than the seemingly simple dark figure frying his eggs, is enough to drive him to lunacy. Black has become white, up has become down. Truth be told, the only thing separating white master and black servant here are illusory racial truths, a consciously imposed color line, and a contained violent will.[9]

From the outset, Bugs is deceptively cast as the essence of dark typology: he is servile, he is genial, and he is gentle. He invites Nick to sup with him, he cooks for the group, he even serves the gathering. And he does all this with a gentle smile, a smile that belies a latent knowledge and power. George Monteiro, drawing a correlation to Benito Cerino, says of Bugs's smile, "That smile, I would venture, is Melvillean. It is the smile of a black who, too, would be seen as 'less a servant than a devoted companion'" (128). I would amend Monteiro's statement and suggest that this smile is less hopeful than knowing. While inexplicable rage incapacitates Ad, a tempered violence empowers Bugs. Bugs becomes the new danger. He relates to Nick how he served time for cutting a man, recounting his crimes in clinical fashion. Thus, in the "cowardly" razor lies actual empowerment. Ad's amusement at Nick's enthusiasm ("Hear that, Bugs?") elicits from his dark companion a telling response: "I hear most of what goes on" (100). Here Hemingway paints Bugs as shrewd and adept at reading the racial landscape. Even as he dons the garb of servility, Bugs directs the exchange, propels the narrative, and becomes the oracle of personal history for the crew.

Hemingway bestows upon Bugs the story's true agency and power. The blow Bugs delivers to his friend at story's end instantly orders the rage and squelches any resurgence of white might: "I have to do it to change him when he gets that way" (102). Black dictates predominate. After relaying to Nick some personal history regarding the ex-champion and himself, Bugs again becomes the forceful agent as he ushers Nick out, suggesting that it would be best if he were not around when the little man awakes: "I don't like to not be hospitable, but it might disturb him back again to see you. I hate to have to thump him and it's the only thing to do when he gets started. I have to sort of keep him away from people" (103). There is a method to the apparent madness, as he suggests most tellingly, "I know how to do it" (102). In the tense exchange just prior to the knockout blow, Ad's refusal to respond to Bugs's request draws a suggestive rebuke from the black man: "I spoke to you, Mister Francis" (101). Again, the minority voice boldly asserts itself. All this, Hemingway shows us—the dialogic authority, the self-assertion, the minority's physical dominion—is in each instance carried out willfully and skillfully *within* the parameters of the established order itself.

To this effect, civility and gentility color Bugs's words and actions. Bugs's insistence on an answer from his ignorant and violently preoccupied crony is tempered with deference ("Mister Francis"). After striking the white man, Bugs almost immediately resumes the servile posture, caring for his now-ailing friend, "pick[ing] him up, his head hanging, and carry[ing] him to the fire . . . and la[ying] him down gently" (102). And as he tends to his friend, Bugs addresses Nick in subservient phrases littered with "Misters," "all this in a low, smooth, polite nigger voice" (103). Just as quickly as the violence commences, it ceases, and suddenly Bugs is nurse and companion again. Master of his rage, he sips coffee and smiles.

Unlike his compatriot, Bugs proves himself to be a master of tempered violence. Joseph Flora also notes the temperamental divide between the two figures and suggests that "the difference between Bugs and Ad is seen in the cool efficiency of Bugs" (89). The key to Bugs's "cool efficiency" is control. Here Hemingway inverts the tried-and-true model wherein—as critic Gerald Early posits in a marked criticism of Norman Mailer's overdependence on such tropes—"the black male is metaphorically the white male's unconsciousness personified" (138). In "The Battler," Hemingway toys with the natural order and Ad is the id-driven primordial figure, Bugs the rational being constrained by ego/superego. The unexpected literal blow to whiteness is a metaphor for the greater anticipated racial violence of Hemingway's day.

These social prescriptions were being tested during the last years of the nineteenth century and early part of the twentieth century. Lynchings were rampant as the ruling order desperately tried to reassert itself and to erase meager minority gains following Reconstruction. The second decade of the new century, especially after the First World War's conclusion, was marred by racial unrest and a black community in active revolt. It was revolution on a national level, sparked in part by the rise of an American icon. And within the pages of his boxing stories, Hemingway gives voice to a national conscience troubled by the rise of Jack Johnson.

Johnson's successful title defense against Jim Jeffries on July 4, 1910, set off racial strife all over the country. There were riots in cities nationwide following the fight, leaving no doubt as to the correlation between racial strife and violence.[10] Many cities around the country, fearing more violence, enacted a moratorium prohibiting the official fight reel from being shown in theaters. Local and state administrators feared a reignition of racial passion (not so much on the part of whites, but blacks), passion stoked by ideas of racial equality and personal value—ideas internalized, lived, and symbolized by Jack Johnson.

Johnson played on Hemingway's psyche as well: the author once again revisits the Gothic as he infuses a national angst in the subtext of "The Battler."

Bugs comes to symbolize the reprehensible Jack Johnson: the willful minority. Ad conversely comes to symbolize white degeneration and self-deception. Both men—especially Ad, in his freakish ghoulishness—are monstrous Gothic operators within Hemingway's benighted world. We see this in Bugs's forays across the color line, in his apparent Jekyll-and-Hyde racial negotiation, and in his eerily proffered truths; we see this, too, in Ad's ravaged body and exaggerated diminution, his lost dominion and lost sanity, his helplessness before the knife-wielding black man. Bugs's proffered truths and racial realities are written all over the white man's ghastly countenance.

Further, the Bugs-Ad commingling and conflation is representative and expressive of racial mixing's nightmarish potential. Bugs, after all, says he "like[s] living like a gentleman" (103) and tellingly, more than his white cohort, he has *mastered* the art of the civilized. Hemingway crafts a black character who skillfully negotiates that color line and shows us several key things: that the clearly defined separator between primitive and civilized is illusory, that the color line's transgression is *not* a unilateral exercise, that checked violence is often the only thing maintaining such an order, and that white primacy is a myth. A physically deformed Ad bears the markings, as a grotesque, of this new truth, and we encounter this truth again eight years later in "The Light of the World."

In "The Light of the World," the nameless narrator and naïf generally thought by most scholars to be a teenage Nick Adams, travels the road with a friend.[11] He and Tom make short work of a nameless midwestern town, arriving and departing in the same evening, but not before being initiated into the violent world of racial negotiation. The narrative's brief description proves quite telling as the tale unfolds: "We'd come in that town at one end and we were going out the other" (293). During the course of what cannot be more than hours, though, Nick confronts yet again the violent realities of racial strife.

Hemingway, in what was to have been an introductory segment to a student edition of his stories (the introduction did not see the light of day for another twenty-two years), suggests that there is more to "The Light of the World," a story that reads deceptively easily, than meets the eye.[12] He goes on to suggest that it is, more than anything, a "love letter to a whore" (Trogdon 314) and an homage to memory seen through rose-colored glasses. In giving us a surface reading himself, Hemingway is deliberately only telling us part of the story, and giving us only part of his aesthetic strategy; while the gendered story can be granted credence, so too can the racial one, and Hemingway goes to great lengths to show us the complexities of racial construction. However, "The Light of the World" stands as perhaps the best example of a Hemingway text whose racial implications have generally been ignored by critics.[13] Like "The Battler," with its paradigm of "unnatural" racial divisiveness and a crafted subtext pushing for a subversion of that constructed order, "The Light of the World" also begins with the polarized racial paradigm. Significantly, the world we see, hear, and smell as we enter the nameless town, encounter the hostile barkeep, and experience the exchange with disputing prostitutes is Nick's world. With Nick's first-person narrative, conjecture regarding what is internalized is unnecessary as the world unfolds in stark black and white.

Hemingway deliberately has Nick survey his surroundings as he and Tom leave the diner in the opening scene and enter the local stationhouse, and his description is most suggestive: "Down at the station there were five whores waiting for the train to come in, and six white men and four Indians. It was crowded and hot from the stove and full of stale smoke. As we came in nobody was talking and the ticket window was down" (293). The description reads like a catalog as individuals are instantly counted, typed, and labeled. Distinction is not the aim here; generality is, as those populating the train station become "whores," "white men," and "Indians." Hemingway grants just six amid the crowd relative respect and humanity: the white *men*. To the others he affixes just sexual pejorative or racial label. As the boys enter the station, one of the white men waiting in the crowd breaks the collective silence. As if to underscore this key point, Nick notes the whiteness of faces that greet him (293). From this point on, a white voice predominates and becomes the story's sole voice. First, Nick becomes the narrative voice, the ultimate arbiter of what is seen, heard, and experienced by the reader. Then Hemingway passes the narrative baton to whites engaged in verbal skirmishes unfolding before the boy's eyes. Hemingway paints a world with a doe-eyed Nick at its center, and Nick's descriptions become our window into this world in all its various shades of white.

Conversely, Hemingway deliberately mutes the Native American voice from beginning to end. While the white voice colors the exchange between the cook and the group and that of the prostitutes who debate a shared memory, the Native remains forcibly silent. His purpose, it seems, is only to bolster the forged racial divide: "Two Indians were sitting down at the end of the bench and one standing up against the wall" (294), "The ticket window went up and the three Indians went over to it" (295), and "The Indians had gone outside on the platform" (296). In each instance, Hemingway gives us a virtual narrative pantomime. In each instance, the Native's voice is nonexistent, his stark silence deafening, even as his body crowds the landscape.

However, the most pronounced silence emanates from the most conspicuously absent body in this painted scene: the black. Nowhere to be seen, the black man is the most expressly referenced figure in the work. Toni Morrison's assertion that the minority presence becomes a necessary referent for the self-fulfilling prophesy of the white literary imagination rings most true here (see Morrison, *Playing in the Dark*). While in "The Battler" the minority presence is an actual corporeal presence—Bugs—here the black body is altogether physically absent; in its stead, Hemingway crafts a phantom presence. While in "The Battler" the black body assumes a feared corporeal reality, here Hemingway relegates it to the realm of imagination; our only encounter with blackness comes via recalled images and disputed memory. And to his credit, Hemingway shows us just how this phantom presence produces a greater fear in the white collective imagination than any reified body ever could.

We see this played out most expressly in Hemingway's warring whores. In a heated dispute that becomes the story's central focus, two of the original five prostitutes tussle over a distant memory involving a former boxing champion who may or may not have once been the lover of either or both women. He is Steve, according to the two prostitutes, Stanley according to formal history.[14] The women both lay claim to the heart and soul of one Steve Ketchel, one-time middleweight boxing phenomenon. Hemingway clearly has Stanley Ketchel in mind as he mines actual history. Most importantly, the man against whom Ketchel measured himself was the nation's first African American heavyweight champion, Jack Johnson (see Lardner).[15]

For many whites during the twentieth century's first decades, Johnson represented a new racial reality of unbridled black will. The black champion brazenly flouted his in-ring prowess and the many acquisitions that came with his newfound celebrity, including money, cars, and white women. In bold fashion, Johnson repeatedly crossed the color line, baiting fears of miscegenation by openly cavorting with several white women. He even married a white prostitute, and he did all this even as the burgeoning film industry exhausted the monstrous black male–helpless white damsel trope and expressly exploited latent racial anxieties.[16]

Jack Johnson dressed the part of the dandy and, like Hemingway's Bugs, spoke the language of a "gentleman." In short, Johnson did what few minorities could, all the while daring the establishment to stop him. As Andrew Lindsay suggests in *Boxing in Black and White,* Jack Johnson's impact on a nation ripped by racial anxiety cannot be overstated:

> During the six full years of Johnson's reign, 359 black Americans were lynched, an average of five every month, while this black champion rubbed his physical superiority, sexual conquests, and wealth in white faces. The vast majority of these mob murders were for crimes either petty or imaginary, many carried out under the pretext that a white woman's virtue or safety had been violated. These lynchings spelled out to the black population where it stood, and must remain. (14)[17]

If we see the lynching bee as white America's method of checking black advancement, then we can readily see the significance of a Jack Johnson in the era of Jim Crow. Of the catalog of violations, the brazen sexual conquest, black of white, carried the greatest weight and smarted the most in the white collective conscience.[18] America's visceral reaction to Johnson's transgression was the lynching bee; America's legal answer was, out of the ring, new legislation (state and local acts to halt the showing of his fight films, a call from Teddy Roosevelt for an outright ban on the sport, and the Mann Act, which eventually put Johnson behind bars). Within the ring, Americans engaged in a national search for a great white hope to dethrone the presumptuous black man.

Jim Jeffries, as one of those white hopes, was coaxed out of retirement not by riches, not by the promise of celebrity alone, but by an American populace hungry for a champion who looked like them. Gerald Early's reminders regarding the pastime so many loved to hate at the turn of the century are particularly salient, and they underscore the profound investment in racial claims made upon the sport: "Boxing is an American pastime. Moreover, one must not lose sight of the fact that modern professional boxing in its traceable history was a product of Britain; boxing in its course to its present identity is not just Western, not simply American, but particularly Anglo-Saxon" (134). In this sense, Johnson was a usurper of sorts to many, having stolen the title two years before in his knockout of Tommy Burns in Australia.

Before the Jeffries fight, a series of "white hopes," including Jack O'Brien, Al Kaufman, and Stanley Ketchel, had tried to reclaim the title. It was an effort with national investment.[19] Johnson's title defense against Jeffries—held, significantly, on July 4, on American soil, and billed officially as "the fight of the century"—was about, most of all, reaffirmation of white supremacy, both inside and outside that square jungle.[20] To white Americans, a defiant Jack Johnson represented a perversion of sorts, a de-formation of normative concepts. And Hemingway thoroughly explores and exploits this (de)formation in "The Light of the World."

To do so, Hemingway once again employs the grotesque and revisits the Gothic in telling his tale and exposing national fears. We see this investment both in the ghostly presence of the curiously absent black champion and in the figures relating his story. Like Ad Francis, whose smashed facial features approach the absurd, prostitutes Alice and Peroxide, and even the cook, are the bizarre lenses through which Nick and the reader see truth. The cook in particular becomes the story's true conduit of quantitative fact. As the story's whitest character, literally, the cook plays *the* fundamental function of inquiry, questioning the narrative and subverting expectation along the way. This very sense of absurdity itself, glowing white, shakes the racial truth free from the narrative. With his allusion to Jack Johnson, the cook forcibly reminds us that this is more than some "love letter to a whore"; it is very much a story about race in America.

Nick too participates in this ludicrous narrative exercise in polarity, as his initial impressions of the train station personalities attest: "I looked to see who said it. It was one of the white men. . . . His face was white and his hands were white and thin" (293). Just as he fosters difference with the emphatic silence of the red man shuffling in the background, Hemingway drives a wedge between the races with an exaggerated whiteness. Nick fittingly describes the prostitutes as "ordinary looking," and "peroxide blondes" (293). In the absence of specified color, whiteness shines brightly. Such linked images also establish white as something both normative and exceptional. The skin color and therefore the Caucasian ethnicity of the cook, the story's featured pariah, are greatly exaggerated and ultimately called into question, so that this also becomes for Hemingway an interrogation of whiteness as well.

Nick finds the cook's coloring especially remarkable; other white men in the diner openly mock it, directing Nick to "look at his hands" (293). This begs the question: if white masculinity is the standard against which all else is measured, why then do other whites mock it? The cook falls well short of the prescription and is made to suffer for it for the same reason Ketchel's composite fails to sit well with the modern reader: his whiteness is an absurdity. The cook's whiteness is metaphysical; he is *beyond* white in complexion and becomes another Hemingway grotesque. With his tightly puckered lips and hands all aglow, he is further pushed to the margins as a figure of effeminacy, yet another figure of otherness. However, his perverted mouth gives us verifiable truth. The cook follows the lead established by Dick Boulton, Bugs, and others in the litany of Hemingway characters who step from the shadows to convey wisdom. The cook utters Johnson's name and also quickly corrects

Peroxide in her remembrance of Ketchel, insisting that Stanley Ketchel is in fact the Steve Ketchel over whom the women squabble. This fact alone is worth noting, as Stanley Ketchel's name was synonymous in early twentieth-century boxing circles with cheating (see Plimpton).

Thus, the mere mention of Ketchel's name undermines the reader's confidence that this is truly his name and in any claims that he makes. As for the prostitute's recollection, boxing lore suggests that Johnson and Ketchel agreed to what was supposed to be a simple exhibition match. But with the sheer vitriol surrounding Johnson, and racial tensions being what they were, an exhibition quickly became a test of racial prowess; the match between two of boxing's best—Ketchel as middleweight champion, Johnson as heavyweight powerhouse—ended with a knockout. True to form, Ketchel abrogated the deal, taking cheap shots that floored a surprised champ, and the bout ended with Ketchel on the mat for the count. Ketchel's loss sits at the core of the prostitutes' debate, with Peroxide reviling Johnson for foul play and, of course, for derailing Anglo plans. This is the truth hidden in the cook's inquiry and allusions, a truth lost on Peroxide (and many contemporary readers), whose vision has been clouded by her own fearful racial myopia.

Again, Hemingway's narrative approach initially is one of polarity, as he actively pits white against black. And polarity is what we get in the whores' praise of the white boxer. Peroxide, Ketchel's biggest champion, marvels over Ketchel's essential beauty and physical prowess: "He was like a god, he was. So white and clean and beautiful and smooth and fast and like a tiger or like lightning" (296). Later, to support her claim that Ketchel loved her, Peroxide offers, "We were married in the eyes of God and I belong to him right now and always will and all of me is his. I don't care about my body. They can take my body. My soul belongs to Steve Ketchel. By God, he was a man" (296). Yet Peroxide's catalog of virtues is meant to make Steve Ketchel into something more than human. Fervently extolling his skin color, Peroxide deifies Ketchel. What makes him "like a god" are the carefully strung-together descriptions: "clean," "beautiful," "smooth," and "white." In *Blacks in Eden*, J. Lee Greene explores totemic construction in relation to a nineteenth-century southern white hegemony and a legacy of black literature engaging it. As one of the more "significant motifs" employed in such texts, Greene points to "a focal character's adherence to (or rejection of) a value system that privileges whiteness to the point of deification" (213). The prostitute's absurd elevation of Ketchel testifies to the universality of such systems.

In contrast to the godlike white man, Johnson is the villainous "big dinge," the "big black bastard," and "the nigger" (295).[21] Implicitly, though standing brazenly atop the world as champion for the better part of seven years, Johnson is everything Ketchel is not: he is unclean, he is ugly, he is unskilled, he is black. Speaking of Negrophobia in the Antilles, Frantz Fanon posits in *Black Skin, White Masks* that "everything that is the opposite of these Negro modes of behavior is white. . . . In the collective unconscious, black = ugliness, sin, darkness, immorality. In other words, he is Negro who is immoral. If I order my life like that of a moral man, I simply am not a Negro" (192).[22] We can easily apply Fanon's fifty-year-old commentary to Hemingway's racialized narrative. Ketchel is deified; Johnson is demonized. Peroxide's claim that the world just doesn't produce fighters like her man Ketchel anymore underscores the notion of—if not a paradise lost—a world transformed.

Fittingly, Alice, who, like the cook, disputes particulars of Peroxide's story, wears a silk dress that "change[s] color" as she moves, emblematic of her acceptance of a morphed world reality (293). And inherent in Alice's challenge is a questioning of racial essentiality; Hemingway builds up white reader expectation only to raze it in the end. Alice proposes an alternative to the story being told, challenging Peroxide's narrative authority. Both she and the cook are grotesques, he with his glowing white hands, she with a girth the likes of which no one has seen. Nick tells us, "You couldn't believe she was real when you looked at her" (293). The truth, like the bodies that convey and contest it, is also a grotesque distortion of a still-greater truth.

The cook's periodic interjections do more than demonstrate the dubious nature of one woman's memories; for Hemingway, his comments also underscore the inherent absurdity of the value system undergirding those perceptions and crafting those memories. Peroxide's memories represent a warped congregate memory. The whiter the skin, the greater the man, it seems, with racial superlatives forging the all-important necessary linkage. If we create heroes as amalgams of all things we deem important, then Peroxide's statement that Ketchel was the "greatest, finest, whitest, most beautiful man that ever lived" (295) is a collective memory built upon a shared perception of glory and greatness steeped in the trappings of racial discourse.

If the cook's simple but consistent questioning of Peroxide's memory proves it false, then that greater collective perception must also be questionable. Stanley Ketchel was in fact just a man. As for his bout with Johnson, Ketchel was a man out-classed by his larger, stronger, and darker opponent. He was also a man just desperate enough at times, legend has it, to enlist the help of others in "winning" his matches, and this part of the legend clearly played on Hemingway's mind.[23] While Peroxide's reminiscences paint a picture of a hyper-adaptable fighter with the requisite transferable skills, the historical records indicate otherwise. Reflecting on the Ketchel-Johnson fight footage, noted essayist and sports historian George Plimpton suggests in *Shadow Box* that "at one stage of the bout, Johnson bulled him to the canvas, and then, almost apologetically, picked him up and set him on his feet as one would a child, so that watching the film, I half expected Jack Johnson to dust him off" (154). Suddenly, when viewed through the prism of historical truth, Peroxide's words appear false and a greater accepted white mythos crumbles.

The cook continues with his inquiry, insisting, "Didn't Jack Johnson knock him out though?" Ever the good woman, Peroxide stands by her man; ever the good demagogue, she stands by her fallen idol and shaken rhetoric: "It was a trick. . . . That big dinge took him by surprise. He'd just knocked Jack Johnson down, the big black bastard. That nigger beat him by a fluke" (295). Peroxide gives us no concessions, just excuses, racially charged vitriol, and an affirmation of whiteness. She actively twists fact as the bigger (and blacker) Johnson becomes the trickster and social miscreant, Ketchel the victim. Hemingway thus demonstrates the slippery nature of racial definition and the increasing difficulty of building upon racial polarity. Peroxide's recollections are an emphatic whitewashing of historical fact. Just as she romanticizes her often lurid sexual liaisons and cleanses her body with rhetoric, the prostitute consciously sanitizes a painful memory. In fact, the entire exchange between the prostitutes, specifically Peroxide's fairytale treatment of her life, is an active employment of "white face," as re-creation of the self necessarily becomes a performative act, a hiding of the unclean. In the end, Hemingway shows us that theirs is a false whiteness. As Alice challenges Peroxide's story and her (re)constructed mythological model, Peroxide meets the barrage with desperation, "This is true, true, true, and you know it. Not just made up" (296), and later, "Leave me with my memories. . . . With my true, wonderful memories" (297). The real truth, Hemingway shows us, is buried beneath the absurdity: white primacy is myth, and that myth, like memory, is fast fading.

Hemingway even imbues the story's title itself with this marked irony. "The Light of the World" proves to be a false beacon not to be followed. Thus, Nick's lesson is a simple one: racial truths, like so many others he has encountered on his sojourn, are not necessarily truthful at all. Hemingway's narrative inversion is complete as good becomes evil, hero becomes demon, and white becomes black within the retooled race paradigm. In the end, Hemingway boldly questions racial essentiality's veracity, and this new paradigm is perhaps too much for young Nick to fathom. His horrified response to the cook's inquiry at story's end ("Which way are you boys going?") suggests as much: "The other way from you" (295). In this sequence, we can almost hear the echoes of Uncle George's verbal barbs and his fleeting footsteps at the end of "Indian Camp."

Both within and without the perimeters of the ring, lines between civil and savage blur with each transgression, each casting off of the typological garb. White authority and associated truths, Hemingway suggests, fade with the challenge. But they do so reluctantly. Even in the face of new truth, certain quantifiable realities can be re-created, but only momentarily, Hemingway says. As Nick engages a past glory, Ad Francis is "the battler" again. In "The Light of the World," through skewed memory, whiteness is made great again. Peroxide's revisionist reaction is America's wish to cope, its will to power. But the din of America's Jack Johnsons insistently clamoring for recognition, for reification, could no longer be ignored, and Hemingway took his cue from that black man. Both tales become, then, deliberate explorations of black humanity. "The Battler" is as much Bugs's story as it is Ad's or Nick's, and "The Light of the World" is more the story of Jack Johnson, and all of America's Jack Johnsons, than the story of Stanley Ketchel. Moreover, these stories show us an author whose very investment in white masculinity necessitates the subversion at the core of each. In both instances, we see a very modern artist slyly exploring blackness, interrogating whiteness, and mapping the nebulous space between them. Yet with these two tales, the first of his black-and-white stories, Hemingway was just getting started in his racial inquiry; he would save his most explosive racial statement for a work that would never see the light of day in his lifetime.

CHAPTER FOUR

Killin' 'Em with Kindness

Hemingway's Racial Recognition in "The Porter"

> Be not deceived, for every deed you do I could match—out-match.
>
> —Claude McKay, "To the White Fiends"

> I want you to overcome 'em with "yeses," undermine 'em with grins, agree 'em to death and destruction, let 'em swoller you till they vomit or bust wide open.
>
> —Ralph Ellison, *Invisible Man*

Ernest Hemingway had seen the world in shades of black and white long before his first African adventures of 1933–34. As a boy, he'd dreamed of following in the footsteps of Theodore Roosevelt on a trek to the African continent. A few years later, he had watched with great interest as a young African American boxer named Jack Johnson captured America's heavyweight crown and forever rewrote the rules of the (race) game. Not long afterward, and perhaps with great anxiety, he watched as his beloved city, in the still-new century, experienced one of the nation's worst race riots to date. As a social realist of sorts, and as a young white man, Hemingway imbibed and, in some sense, wrote what he saw. What he saw was a changing American sociological landscape and the unsettling of a nation; what he wrote were stories brimming with that tension. His black-and-white stories demonstrate this beautifully, and "The Battler" and "The Light of the World" work as wonderful precursors to what we find in one of Hemingway's least-known works.

"The Porter" brings us one step closer to the nightmarish maelstrom plaguing white America's collective imagination during those first formative years of the twentieth century, when whiteness and blackness collided and racial definitions conflated. Hemingway's piece about a young white boy, his father, and the African American porter who serves them on an overnight train trip is an exploration of twentieth-century American race relations. Hemingway gives us few character details, very little plot, and a narrative that is deceptively simple: a father and son ride the rails together, unaccompanied by wife, mother, or siblings, without a specified destination, and without, it seems, much of a bond between them. We learn little about any of the primary characters. However, that fact only works to underscore the author's overall intentions in this segment: to illuminate the world in which they live.

Hemingway pushes the reader, initially, to see the world through the young boy's eyes, through the bifurcated lens of racial stereotype; but then, through the skillful handiwork of the black porter, the reader soon recognizes that that lens is imperfect—faulty even—and that notions of white supremacy and the line separating the races are illusions. Befriending the young boy—whose name is the only one the author does not withhold—and temporarily acting as his custodian while the father sleeps is the train's primary porter. In the father's absence, he has the boy join him on his rounds as he visits with the train's staff; he then proceeds to give the boy a mini-lesson in razor fighting between his assigned duties. So ends the fragmentary tale.

This apparent absence of plot point forces the reader into an existential posture, to make something from (apparently) nothing. But, with his iceberg principle squarely in mind, Hemingway gives us so much more than what this bare-bones plot suggests. In "The Porter," Ernest Hemingway pushes us to the razor's edge—of race war—before skillfully pulling back from the color line and demonstrating its illusory nature (see Strong, *Race and Identity*).[1] Through the exchange between a young white boy and a black Pullman porter, Hemingway dissects the complexities of identity, demonstrates his belief in the socially constructed nature of race, and explores the seething violence that both works to maintain and threatens to erase America's color line.

Surprisingly, over the past two decades, the fragment has garnered very little critical attention. While Hemingway scholarship is rife with critical analysis of Uncle George from the Nick Adams stories, virtually nothing exists on Hemingway's other George character, his other "uncle" figure. Initially conceived as part of a novel that Hemingway never finished, "The Porter" was finally published in 1987, some twenty years after the author's death, as part of *The Complete Short Stories of Ernest Hemingway*.[2] Like *The Garden of Eden* and a handful of other unfinished pieces, this one does not come with the author's final blessing. In fact, Hemingway walked away from the project frustrated, after less than a year, some twenty chapters into it, and with no apparent end in sight.

Begun in earnest in late September 1927, on the heels of the very successful *The Sun Also Rises* (1926) and the wildly popular, though critically dismissed, story collection *Men without Women* (1927), the much-anticipated (by Hemingway, especially) new manuscript quickly lost its luster. What was to have been Hemingway's second novel—a plot-driven story about crime, revolution, and a young boy's instructional road trip with his father—quickly devolved into a dialogue demonstration with an ever-inconsistent point of view. Michael Reynolds notes in *Hemingway: The American Homecoming* that Hemingway himself watched a stellar idea become something stale with "too much talk and not enough action" (152).[3]

Just as quickly as the idea was born, it died, and in the late winter of 1928, plagued by a series of interruptions (repeated illness and an injury sustained from a falling window pane) and a stagnant story, Hemingway willfully abandoned the idea altogether. Conveniently, at the behest of friends who urged him to revisit his wartime experiences in his fiction, and inspired by popular dictates of the day, Hemingway put down one would-be road story and began looking ahead to the next. That story, which Hemingway called a "sure thing," would become *A Farewell to Arms.* What Hemingway's final version of that abandoned crime novel would have looked like is anyone's guess. But what he left us is the kernel of something grand, and a text that can stand on its own; further, this fragment of Hemingway's writing demonstrates beautifully his keen insights into racial construction and early twentieth-century America's attendant fears.

That said, "The Porter" is rife with social observations, and perhaps more than Hemingway's other finished pieces, the fragment underscores the author's keen awareness of America's color line, its illusory nature, and the critical part tempered violence plays in its maintenance. To be sure, we have seen Hemingway's flirtation with race and tempered violence in other works. We saw it prominently featured in Dr. Adams's dealings with Dick Boulton in "The Doctor and the Doctor's Wife," and then again in Nick's confrontation with the threat of miscegenation in "Fathers and Sons." We saw it most especially in the author's boxing stories. However, in "The Light of the World" and even the "The Battler," for example, the two strains—race and violence—never quite fully intertwine and remain squarely in the background. In "The Porter," though, the narrative takes us entirely outside the bounds of the boxing ring and out into the wild, where rules and measure ultimately lie exposed as arbitrary and irrelevant. Here lines between civilization and established decorum and savagery, like those separating black and white, prove altogether illusory.

As he explores these nebulous spaces—as he has done all along—Hemingway paints in shades of black and white and, at least initially, with exaggerated strokes, fervently pointing to difference and the line separating the races. But all the while, he seems to mock the color line, ultimately questioning racial essentiality. In this work especially, Hemingway explores head-on the clash of white and black bodies completely *outside* the contextualized ring; in "The Porter," he transports the black-white conflict and the potential for unbridled violence from the square jungle to the streets of America. Clearly, Hemingway mined from localized memory as he fictionalized his "what ifs" for this piece; less than a decade before, Chicago, as well as several other cities across the nation, had endured a hellish week of unprecedented racial violence.

For the longest time, Chicago seemed immune to the racial ills infecting the country after Reconstruction. Stalwart optimist and favorite son Carl Sandburg pointed to the city's perpetually welcoming posture and seemingly unmatched liberal attitudes regarding matters of race and ethnicity. Just weeks before rioting erupted in 1919, the writer took to the streets of his beloved city, on assignment for the *Chicago Daily News*, to document a metropolis's growing pains. Even as he noted the stark increase in immigrants and a doubling of the city's black population, even as he observed the resulting competition for jobs and increased crime, he proudly proclaimed Chicago to be a model city, perhaps *the* model city, and provocatively suggested that if that model failed, there was no hope.

However, even Chicago proved vulnerable during the so-called Red Summer of 1919. That summer, the city bled openly as it bore witness to one of the most brutal race riots in the nation's history. What seemed to begin as an isolated incident—a young black boy's death at the hands of a white man—ended with almost forty dead, hundreds more wounded, countless numbers displaced by looting and fire, and a painfully exposed color line running down the center of this model town after days of retaliatory violence (see Tuttle).[4] The reported images and recorded stories of the red summer would lie dormant for years before a young Hemingway would mine them for the raw emotion and anxiety inherent in the porter's story. The true horror, Hemingway suggests in "The Porter," is that the only thing stemming the tide of violence between the races—and, ironically, the very thing stimulating it—is that imaginary color line.

Hemingway fixates on the color line as he crafts his narrative in "The Porter," a story predicated on difference. The story's setting is a train, its time frame a day, its featured characters a white man; his young son, who describes the scene; and the train's hired help, all black. In its original form, the tale was one of a father and son living a transient life, visiting America's greater cities, and—because of the father's underworld associations as a professional revolutionist—eluding authorities along the way. Of equal importance to the proposed criminal arc was the educational one that had the boy learning valuable lessons from his exposure to the harsh realities of American urban life. The fragment Hemingway left gives us no gritty city underworld, and really no substantive father-son exchange; instead, we get a young white boy acting the part of hanger-on, learning valuable lessons concerning race relations in America and notions of difference along the way as the black porter makes his rounds aboard the train. Significantly, these lessons are doled out not by the father but by the black porter who shines his shoes.

Our introduction to young Jimmy Breen, the tale's protagonist and narrator, and his father establishes the racial dichotomy early on as Hemingway quickly links whiteness with literacy and civilization.[5] Jimmy's father winds down his day with a book and instructs his son to lay out his shoes that night:

> "Get a good sleep," he said and closed the suitcase and put it back under the berth.
>
> "Did you put your shoes out?"
>
> "No," I said. They were in the hammock and I got up to get them but he found them and put them out in the aisle. He shut the curtain.
>
> "Aren't you going to bed, sir?" the porter asked him.
>
> "No," my father said. "I'm going to read a while up in the washroom." (571)

With this casual exchange, Hemingway draws the imaginary color line. Historically, Pullman travelers would leave out shoes for the train's staff to shine during the night. Rather significantly, the train's staff at this time would have been almost exclusively black, and Hemingway subtly exploits this reality and a nation's racial history.

After Reconstruction, few professional organizations embraced blacks in so inviting a manner as the railroad industry did. In fact, the Pullman Sleeping Car Company was, at the height of its success, the nation's single largest employer of African Americans, boasting numbers during these years of nearly

10,000, all porters. The industry made the transition for the newly freed slaves a seemingly natural one; as David Perata notes in his *Those Pullman Blues,* "There were no special job requirements beyond the domestic skills to which so many African Americans had been confined" (xvii). The difference, at least in theory, was that these domestics were now being compensated for their work, but compensation was comparatively minimal. Early twentieth-century Pullman porters supplemented their rather meager incomes by buffing shoes and completing other menial tasks for the train's predominantly white patrons.[6] Jimmy and the porter serving him represent that fixed social system predicated on an unspoken code.

During the new century's formative years, Jim Crow and the impact of *Plessy v. Ferguson* left a mark on the national consciousness, and, artist that he is, Hemingway masterfully exploits the unspoken.[7] As with the rioting of 1919's Red Summer, personal connection again marks the author's own consciousness as he once more subtly mines local memory in painting the scene. The riots of 1919 were not the first of their kind in Chicago. Less than two generations before, Chicago had witnessed a class war of sorts when, in 1894, the Pullman Company's porters went on strike for increased wages and decreased hours. Although the stakes were apparently financial, with its predominantly black labor base, the Pullman Sleeping Car Company, the great strike itself, and the ensuing violence were all inextricably tied to race.[8] Exemplifying Hemingway's minimalist technique, and standing as proof that less is indeed more, our story's porter embodies all this and serves as grand symbol; much history courses through his veins. So, for Hemingway, mining hometown history proves fruitful, and connotation alone draws the racial binary.

With Jimmy's interaction with the train's porter, Hemingway builds on this divisive foundation. In the morning, Jimmy automatically reaches for the shoes left out the night before; the protocol is unquestioned and natural. As if by magic, the young boy's shoes have been polished and buffed: "I got dressed in all but my shoes and reached under the curtain for them. They were shined and I put them on and unbuttoned the curtain and went out in the aisle" (572). Jimmy awakens early only to find virtually everyone else asleep, including the porter.

The boy's initial encounter with the porter tells us much about his own place within this paradigm: "I was hungry and I looked out of the window at the fall country and watched the porter asleep. It looked like good shooting country" (572). Diction proves all-important here as the narrative opts to move beyond merely *seeing* the porter asleep. Jimmy intuitively engages in the privileged rites of his father and his father before him as he actively *watches* the older black man. From the outset, a color line separates the subjective "seer" and objective "seen." The gaze quickly shifts from the oblivious manservant to the alternating scene of the countryside flitting by the train's window, forging a definite linguistic association between the two. Inherent in the gaze are authority, privilege, and conquest, and Hemingway deliberately makes it difficult to separate gaze from land from man.

Jimmy tells us that he "went down to the washroom and looked in. The nigger porter was asleep in one corner of the leather cushioned seat. His cap was down over his eyes and his feet were up on one of the chairs. His mouth was open, his head was tipped back and his hands were together in his lap" (572). Immediately, the narrative reduces the still-nameless porter to racial epithet and function ("nigger porter"). A black man asleep, feet in the air, mouth wide open, becomes an amalgam of the lazy, foolhardy caricature popularized by the day's minstrelsy and the carefree servile "Tom," images Hemingway wagers that his audience will recognize. In *Miles of Smiles, Years of Struggle: Stories of Black Pullman Porters,* Jack Santino notes that even the Pullman Company's own advertising contributed to the crafting of the kindly servant type:

> In its publicity photos, the Pullman Company showed the public a kindly, avuncular porter. These images were directed at travelers who may have wondered at some time or other if these men ever resented their menial status. The figures in the publicity shots reassured passengers. They created misleading images of happy, simple men who got no greater pleasure in life than waiting on rich white people, and who wanted only a pat on the head and perhaps a shiny quarter for their efforts. (116)

This crafted buffoonery works to maintain a totem both within and outside the company, exorcising blackness of any threatening mystery. Hemingway is well aware of the artful image and uses it to great effect in his own work.[9]

The Torrents of Spring, an exercise in wit written early on in his career, serves as a great reference point in underscoring the author's cognizance in crafting character and the conceit. In that work, a nameless African American cook is an absurdly "happy darky" (Hemingway labels him a "merry fellow"), whose sole purpose, it seems, is to serve and echo those around him, and whose (haunting) laughter (what Anderson called his "dark laughter") echoes throughout the tale: "From above floated the dark, haunting sound of black

Negro laughter" (67). This same laughter resonates in the voices of the train's black staff in "The Porter." A bit further into the text, Hemingway gives us more blanket typology relying similarly on connotation as he tells us about "four other niggers sitting at a table playing cards" (573). Again, the description is terse, but the linkage, in Jimmy's eyes, between racial "other" and leisure and vice is clear.

Hemingway even exploits the most blatant of stereotypes in the naming of the porter himself. As the two become acquainted, Jimmy addresses the perpetually smiling porter as "Uncle George," a wink to this nation's love affair with the plantation tradition and its evocative images of the kindly (and seemingly vacuous) black "uncle" figure of yesteryear. Elder black figures on plantations were often granted familial labels ("Aunt" or "Uncle") and a false sense of authority that was undermined by childlike tendencies. Stowe's Uncle Tom stands as a prominent example of this. To the young white boy, the porter is and forever will be "George." Much of Hemingway's contemporary (white) audience would have intuitively accepted this narrative conceit as unvarnished truth. Appropriately, we never learn his real name.

As Santino asserts, the George label is a blatant white assumption of ownership of blackness, becoming yet another labeling or branding of human chattel. While the exact genealogy of the label is debatable, most scholars agree, as does Santino, that the one-size-fits-all George label probably emanated from the founder and owner himself; in this way, George Pullman, "father" of the railroad company itself, became father to his predominantly black employee base. His model town, yet another variation of the company town, fostered a sense of dependency among its employees and tenants, who looked to Pullman for work, for housing, and for sustenance. The company town was, in effect, a rebirth of the Southern plantation.

Years earlier, Hemingway had drawn from both memory and long-standing (southern) tradition in "Fathers and Sons" as he configured Nick Adams as brother, protector, and defender of his sister's honor when he suspects amorous advances by one Eddie Gilby, a Native American child from the neighborhood. Hemingway looks to the South again in "The Porter" as he reconfigures within the confines of the sleeper car the plantation tradition with its benevolent master and its "happy darky," George. With such a broad-stamped labeling, any attempts by the many Georges to establish individual identities separate from that of the "father" were an exercise in futility. The childlike black porters were seen to be in the charge of their employer—George Pullman—and nothing more.

In fact, Santino suggests, many Pullman porters saw their employment with the Pullman organization as a double-edged sword. The company both gave them status among blacks because of its relative high pay scale and travel opportunities (compared to the few opportunities afforded the African American community at large) and entrapped them in a cycle of hours upon hours working for that increased pay. Often, on the basis of well-crafted technicalities favoring the company, they worked hours on end without any pay at all. Indeed, for many of Pullman's "children," the company's promised high life turned out to be a modern iteration of indentured servitude, with Pullman as a new kind of master.

Within Hemingway's initial configuration, the train's chef also never becomes more than a person who is known by his job title. He too never rises above the status of type. Hemingway's characterization ensures this reality. Like his brethren playing cards through the night, the chef is a beastly black driven by impulse and vice. His weakness, it seems, like that of his red brethren peopling the landscape of the Indian stories, is alcohol. In Pavlovian fashion, the chef salivates at every turn in anticipation of his next drink. Constantly, lustfully, Hemingway tells us, "he wipe[s] his lips" (573). In this sense, he is expressly the "bad nigger." And George, his proclaimed kindred spirit—one who shares his "same point of view"—is the Tom figure, happy to do his master's bidding; however, his own lust for drink lies buried through the story's opening sequence.

Accordingly, as he interacts with whites, the porter's words are at first all business, servile, and understandably deferential. All inquiries to Jimmy's father are addressed to "sir." Clearly, Hemingway initially takes great strides in erecting the color line. In a conversation between the two black workmates, the chef appropriately echoes this sentiment as he jokes about the pecking order aboard the train:

> "How did you eat last night?"
> "With that collection of yellow boys."
> "They all together still?"
> "Between Chicago and Detroit. We call 'em the White Eskimos now."
> "Well," said the chef. "Everything's got its place." (573)

During the exchange between these two black men, Hemingway underscores the importance of color to the order.

Bolstering our model of crafted difference is the black man's apparent aggrandizement of Jimmy's (white) father, whose physical presence is limited to the tale's opening lines, but whose influence extends much further. The incomplete nature of the story and the father's limited appearance should not disqualify Mr. Breen from scrutiny. At the beginning of their time together, George heaps praise upon the boy's father for his phenomenal drinking ability, often a universal measure of manhood both within and outside the Hemingway literary universe. Then, in an interesting juxtaposition, George further demonstrates his reverence for the father in his emphatic insistence that Jimmy's father is a "type of noble Christian gentleman" (575). From our limited engagement with the elder Breen, we are apparently meant to connect him with goodness, with the civilized, and with Western-ness.

Hemingway plays this binary game to the end of the narrative as George momentarily initiates the young boy into the world of savagery. In it, the porter demonstrates for Jimmy his proficiency with a razor. Hemingway slyly juxtaposes images of apparent civilization ("noble Christian") with the racially loaded image of savagery (the razor). Clearly this conceit is the product of some deliberation. He overtly mocks it in *The Torrents of Spring,* in which one of the novella's protagonists, pump factory worker Scripps O'Neil, learns a very sad truth regarding his Indian co-workers at the plant: they notoriously lust for metal parts from which they fashion razors to sell (or use?) on the outside. George's own words here are racially charged as he labels the razor a "nigger weapon" and confides to the boy that "bending a razor back over the hand is the only progress the nigger ever made" (576). This proves to be a key admission, given the era's economic, socio-historical, and political associations with progress. Hemingway's own interests in progress were bound up with those of his childhood idol, Theodore Roosevelt, a crusader for the ideal early in the century.[10] Conveniently, as George *razes* his race, seemingly disassociating himself from his own people in this candid moment, he *raises* the white.

The razor's edge, it seems, holds many secrets, as does Hemingway's narrative: "'Returning to the razor,' George said. He reached in the inside pocket and brought out a razor. He laid it close to the palm of his hand. The palm was pink" (575). Like Bugs in "The Battler," who crouches on "long nigger legs" (100) and "wipe[s] his lips with the pink palm of his hand" (103), George is a physical marker of difference. Hemingway further connects the two seemingly ancillary black figures in the conceit of the razor; in "The Battler," Bugs admits rather matter-of-factly that he was jailed for cutting a man. More importantly,

George, who also wields a black-handled weapon, is by profession a caretaker whose wisdom extends beyond his deferential smile. Hemingway shows us that George, in fact, provides us with more than an opportunity to read difference; like Dick Boulton, Bugs, and the cook in "The Light of the World," the character of George allows us to question racial dividers and white primacy. And running counter to this simply painted picture, that judgment, like the binaries themselves, is already there in the beginning.

Hemingway's juxtaposition of the white gentleman traveler with the servile and apparently docile black figure at the opening of the story is an instantaneous but quickly dissolved model. In "The Porter," Hemingway intentionally makes whiteness a phantom presence. Its relative absence forces the reader to reconsider its implications and contextualize its value. Whiteness's purpose here is singular: to haunt the reader, phantom-like in its limited presence. We saw this same narrative strategy used to great effect with blackness in "The Light of the World." Power resides in association. And here Hemingway inverts his Gothic paradigm to make whiteness the haunting specter. Why is the father figure, a figure featured so prominently in Hemingway's Indian stories, markedly missing from this text? Would we have seen much more of him had the author completed the novel? The fact that Hemingway abruptly aborted the project altogether does not help us answer such questions. Still, what he does give us lends itself quite nicely to my investigation. The opening scene marks the last time the narrative gives us any direct contact with the father. And what we do get is a filtered presence and a very questionable glory.

Mr. Breen is more ideal than real. But patriarchal mythmaking is nothing new for the author; Hemingway establishes the precedent early on in the Nick Adams canon. In "Fathers and Sons," Nick's father is a master hunter, a wicked marksman whose keen eyesight is, according to many, unmatched. And in "Indian Camp," Dr. Adams casts himself as a master healer, a doctor so skilled in his art that he is able to perform a cesarean section without much more than what's found in a tackle box.[11] In "The Porter," Jimmy's father is also labeled a "great drinker." However, as in "Indian Camp," as suggested by Uncle George's quip at the end of the story ("Oh, you're a great man, all right"), *this* George's compliments are meant to be dubious.

We actually know very little about *this* great man. Again, we are working dangerously here, without a net, in assessing a work Hemingway abandoned. However, with the author's iceberg principle in mind, we look for what the author *does* give us and make necessary adjustments and imaginative leaps. When we meet him, Jimmy's father is a man bereft of both occupation and name; at this stage of the composition, Hemingway gives us neither. Importantly, both are often defining barometers of manhood and both become glaring barriers to our ability to determine this man's identity.

Again, though, if we focus on what we do have, we see that Hemingway's offerings are sufficient. The father's initial associations are with book and bottle: "My father took a suitcase out from under my berth, opened it on the bed, took out his pajamas and tossed them up to the upper berth, then he took a book out and the bottle and filled his flask" (571). Embracing his artistic license, Hemingway expressly highlights the bottle.

The all-but-absent father's capacity for drink becomes the material of mock epic, and George gently shapes our perspective:

> "That your father that stayed up here reading?"
> "Yes."
> "He certainly can drink liquor."
> "He's a great drinker."
> "He certainly is a great drinker. That's it, a great drinker."
> I did not say anything.
> "I had a couple with him," the porter said. "And I got plenty of effect but he sat there half the night and never showed a thing."
> "He never shows anything," I said.
> "No sir. But if he keeps up that way he's going to kill his whole insides."
> I did not say anything. (573)

The black man deftly commandeers the exchange. He initiates the apparently praise-laden conversation, and he sets his dialogic sights on the father in the process.

The tone is ironic, the civility proves specious, and the implications are great. Jimmy's father, as "great drinker," "the world's champ" (573), is arguably an alcoholic. He spends his night hours immersed in drink. The fact that he "never shows anything" suggests, at the very least, a very high level of tolerance and a proficiency reserved for the experienced.

Like the father, George loves his libation. Unlike the father, he openly lusts for it. Also unlike the father, George *does* show his "weak" constitution and is unable to handle his liquor; he complains at story's end that he needs a remedy for a body sick from drink. Indulging in the spirits with both Jimmy's father and the chef, he suffers great effect and pays for it dearly. However, Hemingway rather keenly juxtaposes George's weakness with the father's strength, and the porter's commiseration with the chef (they are kindred spirits, says George) with the father's solitary binges, and in the end, the white man appears worse for the wear. Jimmy's father simply drinks, and he drinks alone. In this particular sequence, Hemingway boldly tears away the trappings of type and emphatically blurs set racial boundaries as he pairs whiteness with intemperance and self-serving euphemism, and blackness with a frank and reasonable truth. Fittingly, George, as purveyor of this new truth, comes to embody that new, (con)fused, and feared racial nexus. As such, he is this text's Dick Boulton.

And as he does with Boulton in "The Doctor and the Doctor's Wife," Hemingway further muddies the waters here with his treatment of name. In several of his racial texts, we see Hemingway's nonwhite characters taking ownership of the naming act. Dick Boulton's confrontational perversion of Dr. Adams's professional title ("Doc") in "The Doctor and the Doctor's Wife" marked the first of several reversals in the Nick Adams canon. The sequence is also reminiscent of Bugs's, not Ad's, insistence on knowing Nick's name as he joins the vagabond party of "The Battler." And we see that same high degree of marked cognizance again here. The disparity between white and black treatments of the naming issue speaks volumes, suggesting a white reliance on assumption, typology, and specious knowledge, and a black level of inquisitiveness heretofore unseen and certainly unexpected. Jimmy's surprised response to George's bold familiarity and informality ("How do you like the railroad business, Jimmy?") suggests as much: "How did you know my name?" (574).

George's response conveys astuteness meant to serve notice to whites. The seemingly happy servile "darky" in "The Porter" knows more than his vacuous smile suggests. As discussed in chapter 3, in speaking of Bugs in "The Battler," George Monteiro suggests that "his smile, I would venture, is Melvillean. It is the smile of a black who, too, would be seen as 'less a servant than a devoted companion'" (128). Monteiro's "Melvillean" label is appropriate both in that story and in this one.

In each instance, in the vein of Herman Melville's *Benito Cereno*, Hemingway's black manservant tempers his shrewdness with a smile. In Melville's novella, a ship captain's seemingly devoted black manservant is in reality a slave engaged in active, though silent, revolt. However, a placid demeanor and smile work to preserve the appearance of order to all who look on from the outside. Hemingway clearly mined Melville in sketching his own black servant.[12] In "The Porter," George's nominal awareness subverts expectation; the black man gains intimate knowledge of the white, and through acts of subterfuge, at least momentarily, he holds some authority.

In the fragment's final and most important sequence, Hemingway fully realizes the subversion. As the porter and chef commiserate, we see the black man foray farther across the color line, encroaching on the "gentleman's" space.[13] As the porter and the young boy in his charge get better acquainted, Jimmy witnesses black life seldom seen by whites, a life outside his imagination. Through some nifty histrionics and affected gentility in an exchange between the two servants ("Does the young gentleman drink too?" "It's a pleasure, sir," "Good-bye to a noble soul" [574]), we see the depth of black consciousness and cognizance: so much of racial definition depends on observation of a code of expected behavior. Hemingway shows us the black man's awareness of performance and its role in constructing racial identity. The black man dons a smile to mask his pain, his rage, his true self.

A scene of apparent black mirth drawn from caricature and type (they laugh and engage in seemingly meaningless banter) takes on the vestiges of the blues. Their mockery is the blues reconfigured, in that like a blues composition, their dialogue is multilayered and tells a sad story. Ralph Ellison speaks of a blues aesthetic in his "Blues People," asserting that:

> The blues speak to us simultaneously of the tragic and comic aspects of the human condition, and they express a profound sense of life shared by many Negro Americans precisely because their lives have combined these modes. This has been the heritage of a people who for hundreds of years could not celebrate birth or dignify death and whose need to live despite the dehumanizing pressures of slavery developed an endless capacity for laughing at their painful experiences. (*Shadow and Act* 256)[14]

And Hemingway's George is no exception to the prescriptive life for blacks in early twentieth-century America. His smile masks much.

The verbal exchange between porter and chef, brief and playful as it is, marks the text as an authentically bluesy moment:

> "We got to get back to the car. How is the railroad business?"
> "Rails are firm," said the chef. "How's Wall Street?"
> "The bears are bulling again," said George. "A lady bear ain't safe today."
> "Bet on the Cubs," said the chef.

"The Giants are too big for the league." George laughed and the chef laughed.

"You're a very courteous fellow," George said. "Fancy meeting you here."

"Run along," said the chef. "Lackawannius is calling you."

"I love that girl," said George. "Who touches a hair—"

"Run along," said the chef. "Or those yellow boys will get you."

"It's a pleasure, sir," said George. "It's a very real pleasure." (574)

Far from frivolous, this segment is a pain-laced mockery of two American institutions; the railroad, America's lifeblood for so long, and baseball, the national pastime, become easy targets for two men looking in from the outside.[15]

George, as a representative of all Pullman porters, may actually know "the railroad business"; he most certainly knows the trains themselves, through and through. He may even find himself wearing multiple hats while riding the rails over the years, including, at times, that of the conductor. However, aboard that train, any train, he will never *be* the conductor; limited by his very skin, he can only imagine and play the role. Thus Hemingway's simple story of a white father and son abruptly becomes the black man's story of struggle in America.

Once we strip away the whimsical veneer, we see a raw truth exposed: a porter's life is a hard life, something we miss altogether as we, along with young Jimmy, first encounter George as stereotype, asleep at the story's inception.[16] Through the porter's interaction with the chef, Hemingway reveals the black world as something painful, real, and meaningful. The two black men commune in this experience of shared marginality, singing their sad song in tandem, one conversationally riffing off the other. They are, after all, "kindred spirits," says George, "gentlemen with the same outlook on life" (575). But it takes two to carry off the revelry effectively. Alone, George cannot bear the weight of his smile; so it disappears as the chef takes his leave.

With his friend's departure, George becomes serious again and assumes the teacher's role, engaging the boy in lessons of razor war. This scene demonstrates Hemingway's deliberateness in delving deeper into marginality's pitfalls. Now the porter speaks candidly about the razor's art. As if to grab young Jimmy (and the reader) by the jugular, George initiates the conversation with, "Did you ever see a man cut with a razor?" (575).

The question and image evoke type, but the entire sequence acts as part of a greater metaphor for the African American predicament. Like Bugs in "The Battler," the porter reveals himself here to be a wise man, shockingly aware of himself as a black man in a white world. In "The Battler," Bugs, exhibiting full gentility as he speaks, candidly admits he served jail time for blade play of his own. The racial lines blur with each line of his politely whispered, bloody confession. In that story, too, stereotype quickly gives way to complete *mis*-type as Bugs, not Ad, asserts himself as oracle and purveyor of wisdom.

Also like Bugs, the porter demonstrates in his interaction with young Jimmy his own hyper-awareness of racial construction. And he distills this truth with his razor demonstration. Prompted by the boy's apparent curiosity regarding the use of the razor, George asks Jimmy, "Would you like to have it explained?" Thus the lesson commences:

> "The use of the razor," he said, "is an art not alone known to the barbering profession." He looked at me. "Don't you make them big eyes," he said. "I'm only lecturing."
>
> "I'm not scared."
>
> "I should say you're not," said George. "You're here with your greatest friend." (575)

This exchange suggests three things of importance. First, things are not always what they seem. The wielding of the razor is not exclusively the purview of the barber, posits George. With this assertion, the narrative pushes both Jimmy and the reader outside normative parameters. Suddenly, the shift from gentleman to would-be brute is seamless. Jimmy's horrified reaction ("Don't you make them big eyes") underscores this lost moment where definition fails. Second, the black-white "relationship," specious and steeped in performance, is a tenuous one at best. Only the performance of expected roles keeps this totem intact. Having rattled the boy with the mere allusion to a breakdown of social order (through violence), George quickly steps into the familiar role: the nonthreatening caretaker, nurse, uncle figure ("I'm your greatest friend," he says reassuringly). Finally, the sequence suggests that, as things stand, fear dictates the order. Here the fear is one of racial violence and of the upheaval inherent in such violent revolution.[17]

George's metaphorical razor talk is a reminder to the hegemony that the established social order teeters on the razor's edge, and that the balance is fragile. The only thing maintaining that balance and keeping that blade sheathed is a tempering of the violent will. Hemingway suggests that what is even more potentially terrifying for many (whites) is the prospect of this violence being *controllable* by the servile underling; fittingly, George's lesson proceeds in an eerily calm and methodical fashion.

Our porter's didactic moment continues with what he sees as the three functional essentials of razor mastery. The first two qualities he links to the tool itself: "'You have observed,' he said, 'keenness of edge and simplicity of action. Now a greater than these two. Security of manipulation.'" Sharpness and ease of use are necessary attributes of the blade. The porter's primary focus, though, is on the third factor, and this deserves our greater attention: "'You observe it?' George said. 'Now for that great requisite skill in the use of'" (576). True mastery is found in the *manipulation* of the instrument, not in the instrument itself. The magician, he assures us, not the wand, holds the power.

George demonstrates with great alacrity the nuances of razor fighting before his mesmerized young pupil. The older man takes apart his imaginary foe with great skill and a marked methodology. Then, just as quickly as the lesson begins, it ends. As if to assuage a growing fear in his audience of one, George ends his performance with a curt reminder that "the razor's a delusion, Jimmy. It's a nigger weapon. A regular nigger weapon" (576).

First glance suggests racial division and underscores the associative power of image: blackness, razor fighting, savagery. However, a closer reading also reveals the crafted quality of these narrative associations. Hemingway infuses a great deal of pathos in George's words to the young boy:

> Only nigger ever knew how to defend himself was Jack Johnson and they put him in Leavenworth. . . . It none of it makes any difference, Jimmy. All you get in this life is a point of view. Fellow like me and the chef got a point of view. Even if he's got a wrong point of view he's better off. A nigger gets delusions like old Jack or Marcus Garvey and they put him in the pen. Look where my delusion about the razor would take me. Nothing's got any value, Jimmy. Liquor makes you feel like I'll feel in an hour. You and me aren't even friends. (576)

The razor becomes a metaphor for the black man's plight and his lack of progress in the shadows of whiteness. Jack Johnson's dominance—as a black man—in the ring and his capture of the heavyweight championship served as an answer, albeit exceptional, to claims of arrested development among blacks and galvanized the race issue in America all over again decades after Reconstruction. He, more than anyone else during those years, became a symbol for a palpable black volition and an encroachment of white authority outside the ring. Conjuring bloody images and engaging a Gothic moment, Hemingway gives voice to a national conscience troubled by the rise of Jack Johnson and those he inspired.[18]

The first two decades of the twentieth century were christened the era of progress. But for the black man, progress was slow in coming as philosophical and political ideals strategically intertwined themselves with accepted theories of social Darwinism; the woes of the black community conveniently provided a basis for the supposedly scholarly promotion of racist ideology.[19] Black subservience (and suffering) was simply part of the "natural" order of things.

George astutely reminds us that Jack Johnson was king, but only for a day, and only within the confines of the ring. The rules of the ring could not and did not protect him on the streets of America. Death threats dogged him for years before, during, and after his capture of the coveted crown, and the Mann Act eventually put him behind bars, like the animal so many convinced themselves he was.[20] Hemingway followed boxing and, as a young man, could not have helped but follow Johnson's career. The boxer is a phantom presence in Hemingway's short fiction, and this latent history quietly informs our reading of the black porter.[21] As does that of Tiger Flowers, America's first black middleweight champion, also mentioned in our porter's social indictment. Crowned in 1926, he too had big ideas. All a (black) man has in the end, George reminds us, is "a point of view," a mind and will of his own. But that, in and of itself, is a defiant stance for a black man. So, even as his voice quiets, seemingly deflated in apparent defeat, George stands before us with a razor in hand and ideas in his head, and the implications are quite clear.

The narrative suggests that (black) awareness of America's racial illusions is the key to beating the system. "Skill in the use of" becomes the prescriptive template for African Americans constricted by that system, and George sees this quite clearly. So while the narrative relies heavily on typecasting and racial dogma—as does every other text in this examination—it also quickly subverts expectation by pushing those recognized boundaries aside and asking, What if? George's lesson demonstrates Hemingway's keen awareness of America's racial dynamics and the illusory dividing lines separating its citizens. George's candid commentary about black stagnation in America is thus a passive warning to the powers that be.

The porter's critique suggests that discretion and true understanding are necessary for survival. The bold and seemingly strong—the Jack Johnsons and the Marcus Garveys—are eventually broken by their boldness, cut down by their own razors. It is the man skilled in its use who walks away victorious. Those who engage the enemy knowing full well the dynamics of the relationship, those knowing the established boundaries well, and those knowing the nuances of the power structure stand empowered. Simply put, knowing how the game is played is the key to surviving and, quite possibly, eventually winning it.

The nightmarish point of convergence for many, says Hemingway, is where black and white identity markers conflate and black supplants white. Hemingway knew this truth, and George conveys it. He and the chef are "kindred spirits" who share this "point of view," this secret knowledge. In the end the question Hemingway seems to posit is, What does one do with this newfound knowledge? Our porter chooses to hold onto this secret knowledge, at least for the day.

With this life lesson over, George reverts to the familiar. Jimmy admits: "I wish I could have gone back with George to the kitchen. But during the regular daytime George talked like anyone else, except even less, and very polite" (577). With that regularity, that marked return to normalcy, all hints of the latent violence revealed in the faux fight are gone. Dividing lines are reerected with the return of protocol, and he again becomes the minstrel.

Santino rightly employs language of the stage in assessing the porter's self-perception and self-awareness: "Being a servant was a role the porters played. They put it on and took it off along with that white jacket they once admired from afar. . . . To give service was a job, a skill, even an art. They vigorously resisted the tendency to internalize the role, with its attendant stereotypes, and confuse it with their personal identities, their self-worth" (111–12). Minstrelsy is acting, and acting is artifice. At lesson's end, the costumes return and on go the masks.

This duality, this racial binary of white and black, provided comfort to a nation seeking to preserve a quickly fading social order. Hemingway demonstrates that blackness and whiteness and redness as race markers are conceptual and subject to inquiry and (re)negotiation. Like Uncle George and Dick Boulton in the Indian stories, and like Bugs of "The Battler" and the cook in "The Light of the World," George the porter prompts a questioning of a racially defined ruling order. Through George, we see the arbitrary and rather tenuous nature of the color line. A work like "The Porter," then, even in its apparently incomplete state, provided Hemingway with an aesthetic space within which to stretch and test the parameters of identity, particularly those steeped in race, showing race for what it is: part social animal, part performance, and aesthetic fodder for one poised to engage in social experimentation. Hemingway's text becomes the nexus where past and present America engage in a tug of war. Accordingly, the author must make concessions and face down this new reality. Ultimately, Hemingway shows us, (racial) identity is something quite fashionable. Therein lies the wonder and terror of the specter.

Ultimately, this same attempt at self-fashioning and, to some degree, self-preservation drove Hemingway to Africa on two extensive safaris, one in the mid-1930s and another some twenty years later. Hemingway's trips to the African continent, particularly his first, became in one sense quests for that which he could no longer see in America: the promise of racial stability. What formerly drove men west in what I will call the invention of America is part of what drove Hemingway east in his attempt to preserve that same ideal: "to construct geographical racial boundaries."[22] In Africa, he could re-create that totemic stability; in the African bush, the white man's shadow is always dark. Simultaneously, Hemingway recognized in that reconstructive push the opportunity for aesthetic experimentation and growth. Thus, the safari becomes both a metaphorical crusade to maintain boundaries and salvage all-important ideas of whiteness and an opportunity to challenge those same notions of racial essentiality. In both instances, Hemingway ultimately shows identity for what it is: something to be fashioned. Harry's constructed whiteness in "The Snows of Kilimanjaro" is at its core—like George's minstrel mask in "The Porter"—artifice, and it is an art that Hemingway deftly exposes and exploits with relish.

CHAPTER FIVE

"The Snows of Kilimanjaro," "The Short Happy Life of Francis Macomber," and *Green Hills of Africa*

(Re)drawing the Color Line, or Reimagining the Continent in Shades of Black and White

> Should . . . the conjecture . . . that the immense and rich interior of the country is pierced by a fine navigable water be realized, we may expect such an advance in the civilization and commerce of Africa as will give to it a real place in the society of nations, and a sense of completeness to our own ideas of the globe.
>
> —J. C. Frémont, *Four Years in the Wilds of Africa*

Africa: a single word with a multiplicity of associations. The continent's image is a virtual Rorschach test, a polarizing form of black and white. Since childhood, Africa had always been a place of high adventure and imaginative wandering for Hemingway. Theodore Roosevelt—president, paragon of self-reliance, and fellow adventurer—would cast his spell on the impressionable young boy at a very early age. In *The Young Hemingway,* Michael Reynolds tells of young Ernest's first viewings of Roosevelt's famous safari movies in 1910 and of his pledge not long before his high school graduation to follow in the footsteps of his childhood idol and explore the wilds of Africa.[1] In those interim years, Hemingway maintained an especially close connection to the continent; he made special trips with his father to the Field Museum's Hall of African Mammals to see Tsavo's infamous man-eating lions, and clad in authentic safari gear like his hero Roosevelt, he heard lectures at home in Oak Park, Illinois, as a slew of special speakers addressed a sleepy community celebrating the efforts of explorers and missionaries alike.

The author at last realized the most fantastic of his juvenile dreams in late 1933 as he and a small but merry band—including his second wife, Pauline; friend Charles Thompson; and revered British hunting guide and mentor

Philip Percival—trolled the East African hills for kudu, rhino, and adventure. These adventures would spur the author's imagination in the months and years following his excursion. If we can say that the Indian stories and the black-and-white tales of the 1920s are largely a progressive aesthetic exercise for Hemingway, one that ultimately questions and all but levels America's racial totem, then the stories spawned by that initial African trip are, at least on the surface, a regression of sorts. While Hemingway's first African stories continue his interrogation of white primacy, and while they affirm his ideas regarding identity construction, they ultimately stand as a firmer re-entrenchment in the old and familiar. We can see them, by and large, as a slight lapse in the artist's forward-thinking racial experiment.

Surely, *Green Hills of Africa* was both a narrative experiment and a response to the author's critics in that Hemingway worked to do something new and rare, sought to overcome time and space constrictions in bringing home the African experience to the reader. Still, those two variables—time and space—worked to mute, if not quell temporarily, the raging race questions that seem to drive so much of his earlier American material. Physical and metaphorical distance from the racial rumblings of home—Hemingway was some 8,000 miles from his native Illinois and over three years removed from his proposed crime novel and George's lamentable blues in "The Porter"—would do much to refocus the writer a bit, and to free him of the attendant racial angst that informs his American short fiction, at least for the moment. His writings from this period bear out this truth.

Missing from the African narratives are the truly Gothic moments, the deep forays into stark darkness, both metaphoric and real (recall Nick's trek into the deep woods with his father or his lonely meeting with a broken-down boxer and his black handler); missing too, for the most part, are the outward signs of an individual psyche wrestling with piercing totemic questions or a collective conscience grappling with guilt (recall a suicidal Indian husband incapable of aiding his ailing wife, unable to "stand things," and a town littered with inebriated Indians). Further, there are no literal spooks to be found inhabiting Hemingway's African space. (*Green Hills*'s Kandisky is, as we shall see in this chapter, less haunting Western presence than annoying reminder of ideological failings.) To be sure, grotesques remain a standard fixture of the landscape, reminders of race's instability, but in Africa alongside each grotesque moment is always the promise of white renewal, the possibility of being made whole again. What remains are the spectacle of race, the marked divide, and ultimately a resplendent whiteness.[2] While the essentially "great" white man invariably falls short time and again at home, in Africa, Hemingway shows us, he can redeem himself. In Africa, it seems, anything is possible.

To be sure, "The Short Happy Life of Francis Macomber" and "The Snows of Kilimanjaro" give voice to a young man's racial angst. Hemingway at thirty was, after all, a man reflective of his own celebrity and of his time, and these stories, at least in part, articulate an era's longing to reinscribe the color line. In *Green Hills of Africa,* his longer fictional memoir of his 1933 trip, he indulges this angst, almost gleefully. The African narratives—as a collective—serve a dual purpose for the author: the earlier African texts, including *Green Hills,* work as an antidote to fearful dis-ease, stabilizing and reaffirming, in part, the perceived crumbling social order at home. In his later years, Hemingway would come full circle in his racial attitudes; in fact, the last African writings reaffirm what a young Hemingway had already thought at sixteen years old: race and racial primacy are indeed purely constructed, a truth he would exploit with relish while on his second safari in 1953.

But this was 1933, and Hemingway, as a young man mirroring his environs, was still evolving socially, politically, aesthetically. With racial strife as the norm and the color line as the law of much of the land at home, and with a burgeoning super-state in Nazi Germany waving the eugenics flag for all of Europe and the rest of the world to see, the ideas of social Darwinism were bound to shape the artist's consciousness. Not purely the cerebral stuff of academic circles, eugenics was popular fodder for discussion in the tiniest of towns in small-town America during the days of Hemingway's youth, and Oak Park was no exception. Further, the social argument raged on well into the 1930s, both in America and abroad. Perhaps, for some, the concept of the Aryan superman, employed and exploited by Hitler's Nazi party, seemed but an extreme (per) version of Hemingway's "code hero": strong, exceptional, and white.

So, in late 1933, Hemingway embarked on his African sojourn, like Harry in "Snows," with the intention of "work[ing] the fat off his soul" (44), of challenging himself as an artist, and, it seems, of reconstituting shattered (racial) identity. Yet even with his polarizing racial conceptions, he toys with the boundaries, and the very act of reconstitution, of reclaiming that whiteness, ultimately affirms Hemingway's aesthetic promise. Even those first African writings then become yet another testament to the young artist's aesthetic cognizance and promise, to his awareness of race as social construction. He would use this cognizance to rebuild a social bedrock many saw crumbling before them. The road to realized promise is sometimes fraught with many a trap, and the trappings of colonialism lay before Hemingway on that first visit to the African continent.

The Indian stories and the African American–centered works all demonstrate an intention to forge racial difference and establish Anglo primacy where, the author eventually shows us, there is in actuality none. Hemingway pays homage to the myths only to subvert them in the end. However, the early African writings show us something slightly different. In *Green Hills of Africa,* for example, the narrative heavily extols notions of sameness and egalitarianism, *not difference,* only to prove them false in the end. Colonialism's differential dictates become *the* order of the day. The short works spawned from that first safari follow suit. Both the African short stories and the fictionalized memoirs, especially his first, ultimately employ what Toni Morrison, in *Playing in the Dark,* insists drives much of the American literary canon—the "Africanist presence" and the black-white binary. In the end, polarity becomes a means of white self-discovery, and the late-1933 safari proved to be an illuminating moment for one such literary sojourner.

Hemingway's African fictional memoir is, more than anything else, a memoir honoring its creator and political ideology. In it, the hunter (particularly Hemingway) becomes the great man figured so prominently (and ultimately dismissed) in his earlier American stories. His first African book is both an answer to his critics—those who balked at Hemingway's brand of celebrity and his seemingly arrested style—and a Whitmanesque celebration of himself. In *Green Hills of Africa,* Ernest Hemingway consciously casts himself as aesthetic deity, creating for himself a world in which he is ultimate seer, doer, arbiter; in it, he is both (great white) hunter and craftsman. He is pursuer as well, as the titles of his book's sections indicate: "Pursuit and Conversation," "Pursuit Remembered," "Pursuit and Failure," and "Pursuit as Happiness." If this is a work concerned with competition and winning, with taming the wilds and subduing beasts, the thread linking each of these realizations is *conquest,* and conquest is the business of empire.

In his first African book, Hemingway attempts to negotiate between two seemingly distinct worlds: a sublime aesthetic and the authentic, or the real. In 1933, that African reality was necessarily entrenched in colonial dictates. In answering his critics and in reaching for artistic perfection, Hemingway expressly strives to move beyond the reality of a collective colonial consciousness. He struggles with an ideal (artistry with both rifle and pen) and its base, real counterpart (mastery with rifle and pen). Channeling Whitman, he suggests in *Green Hills* that the ideal lies in the fourth and fifth dimensions, where time matters not and perfection is perpetual. Unfortunately, though, he taints his work of veritable art with a baser imposed reality. At every turn, empire's indelible brand threatens to tarnish his sublime creations. *Green Hills* is less a work challenging conventional thinking than it is a work set on perpetuating those conventions; it is less a work about an artist's attempts to tame time and subdue space than one white hunter's documented struggle with a savage world. Truth be told, Hemingway's grand experiment, with its mighty, self-indulgent (white) hunter, its tamed frontier and catalog of kills, and its muted Native masses, follows the narrative form established by Richard Burton, Lord Stanley, and, appropriately enough, his childhood hero, Theodore Roosevelt.[3]

Hemingway's choice for co-hunter and guide on this trip was none other than Philip Percival, a man whose reputation as a master huntsman was beyond question and whose expert counsel alongside Roosevelt years before was legendary. His addition to the small party made the experience all the more special for the author, who as a child voraciously consumed tales spun by the "rough rider." Hemingway transposes the safari experience to fiction in *Green Hills of Africa,* and Pauline, Thompson, and Percival become "Poor Old Mama" (P.O.M.), Karl, and Pop, respectively. Hemingway assumes the name Papa. But while names change for the fictional translation, the colonial sensibility itself does not. If anything, Hemingway's transposition seems to heighten that part of the experience. While a self-proclaimed narrative experiment, *Green Hills*—and, to some extent, each of the shorter works coming out of that 1933 safari—remains faithful to ideals inherent in country (nationhood) and color.

Hemingway's aesthetic effort begins earnestly enough. Almost immediately, our author gives us the Kandisky character, an Austrian transplant managing an Indian-owned plantation whose absurd colonial allegiance becomes the narrative's biggest joke. Note that East Africa, including Kenya and what was then Tanganyika, the site of Hemingway's first safari, was largely under British rule at this time. Tanganyika, originally a German colony, came into British hands—officially as an international protectorate, unofficially as yet another colony—after the First World War. Hemingway's Austrian, in all his comic glory, is actually typical of the hangers-on in both government and industry after the fall of the former Central powers.[4] Hemingway opens his work by telling us that Kandisky's rattling automobile disrupts and ultimately ruins his kudu hunt for that day. Not long after he makes Hemingway's acquaintance, Kandisky makes the connection between the Ernest Hemingway of recent international fame, featured poet of Germany's literary magazine *Der Dichter,* and the writer standing before him. Hemingway is clear to emphasize the difference between the two men even as the Austrian tries to engage our writer.

At this point, the Austrian and American conveniently lapse into literary discussion.[5] Kandisky initiates this illuminating segment with talk of books, brilliant minds, and literary greatness: "And tell me, who is the greatest writer in America?" With P.O.M.'s obligatory nod to her husband, Kandisky persists, asking, "I mean who really? Certainly not Upton Sinclair. Certainly not Sinclair Lewis. Who is your Thomas Mann? Who is your Valéry?" (19). After P.O.M.'s ego-stroking affirmation, Hemingway gives us his artistic vision's most pronounced pieces.

Hemingway's aesthetic mission to convey the real begins with a Whitmanesque charge to re-member the body. Terry Eagleton notes in *The Ideology of the Aesthetic* aesthetic philosophy's persistent and long-held denial of the sensate. Tradition sanctioned a divorce of material and immaterial, often placing greater credence in the latter. For the materialist Eagleton, one needs the other to thrive, to exist. He expressly calls for a return to the body, and Hemingway, in his *Green Hills,* heartily complies. Hemingway insists to Kandisky that *true* artists strive to realize a fourth and a fifth dimension. The fourth and fifth dimensions are time and space. Few, if any at all, he says, ever attain it. A writer's aim is to transcend chronological and spatial boundaries, bringing the subject matter to the reader as it occurs, "as it is," unaffected.[6] The artist's job is to conflate time and space through the sensory experience. Realizing this is Hemingway's aesthetic objective. Thus, while his journey is cerebral, his vehicle is corporeal.

Through a catalog of examples, Hemingway draws and perfects his own aesthetic definition and schematic—with all its whats, wheres, and hows. We see expressly externalized examples of this very internal struggle in the Hemingway-Kandisky literary discussion itself. Kandisky's anticipation of the discourse of his new acquaintance suggests as much: "This is what I enjoy. This is the best part of life. The life of the mind. This is not killing kudu" (19). Hemingway would beg to differ; in his kill talk, he invests himself in the corporeal. In this sequence, with Kandisky's help, Hemingway both anticipates his aesthetic engagement and foreshadows the struggle that will engulf him long before his tale ends.

Jilted in the wake of the Great War, left to fend for himself after sacrificing so much for the German cause, Kandisky, self-professed man of ideas, stands wide eyed and slack jawed before a morally bankrupt establishment. Hemingway would have us see him as divesting himself of all imperial attachments; he suggests that like Immanuel Kant and so many others before him, Kandisky naively clings to foreign intangibles that offer no return for his investment. The Germans, we learn, have met his material and spiritual sacrifices for the war effort with a flat denial of responsibility. Even in the face of this, though, Kandisky remains foolishly steadfast in his opinions and duty-laden discourse.

Confined to the mind's recesses, the Austrian arises from his scuffle with abstraction psychically bruised, but no wiser than before his abrupt abandonment by his country.

Hemingway seizes upon this same compulsion in his criticism of America's early men of letters. Of Hawthorne, Emerson, and Whittier, Hemingway says: "They were all very respectable. They did not use the words that people always have used in speech, the words that survive in language. Nor would you gather that they had bodies. They had minds, yes. Nice, dry, clean minds" (20). Hemingway speaks less than flatteringly here, ever critical of the sanitized artificiality of mind in exile. He suggests their writing is respectable but ultimately simply unnatural. And he implicates Kandisky in this fondness for "blue sparks" (22) over substance (the actual dynamo) in his catalog of artistic criteria: "Writers should work alone. They should see each other only after their work is done, and not too often then. Otherwise they become like writers in New York. All angleworms in a bottle, trying to derive knowledge and nourishment from their own contact and from the bottle. Sometimes the bottle is shaped art, sometimes economics, sometimes economic-religion. But once they are in the bottle they stay there" (22). The bottle imagery here is important. Whether it is art, religion, or economics, the bottle signifies conformity, constraint, confinement. This conceit anticipates and underscores Hemingway's fixation on containment, an obsession that drives empire and one that we quickly see colors the work's entirety.

Hemingway juxtaposes this analogue with Kandisky's literary discussion. In it, the Austrian describes a life bereft of new books but steeped in interesting intellectual exchanges: "We have a very interesting mental life. Formerly, with the shamba, we had the *Querschnitt*. That gave you a feeling of belonging, of being made a part of, to a very brilliant group of people" (19). This nicely formulated world is Hemingway's sanitized bottle. Rather than forge something wholly his own and risk being "lonesome," Kandisky strives to be a part of something greater than himself. Eagleton would suggest that such an absorption in mental activity is an abandonment of the body; for Hemingway, this is self-abandonment for life in a bottle.

Hemingway's definition of good writing again goes to the body, drawing on the sensate to bring home the point for both the Austrian and the reader: "We have had writers of rhetoric who had the good fortune to find a little, in a chronicle of another man and from voyaging, of how things, actual things, can be, whales for instance, and this knowledge is wrapped in the rhetoric like plums in a pudding. Occasionally it is there, alone, unwrapped in pudding, and it is good. This is Melville. But the people who praise it, praise it for the rhetoric which is not important. They put a mystery in which is not there" (20). Most important is Hemingway's emphasis on the real. The greatest gift a writer can give to a reader is a sense of "how things, actual things, can be." This explains Hemingway's affinity with Mark Twain.

The quasi-empathetic power of Twain's *The Adventures of Huckleberry Finn* is found not so much in the river tale's particulars as in the storytelling itself. As Carlos Baker notes of Hemingway's connection to Twain, "the shared quality—and one comes on it dozens of times in the course of Huck's journey downstream—is one of direct and 'simple' transcription of things as they are" (*Hemingway: The Writer as Artist* 181). Baker labels this verisimilitude. Along with architectonics (a creation of drama through structural manipulation of fact), it is the pillar upon which Hemingway builds his African narrative. However, in *Green Hills,* Hemingway crafts a self-serving narrative that, in the process of truth-telling, turns a blind eye to much of Africa itself. This is where Hemingway's sublime aesthetic comes crashing down. In fact, his entire text runs contrary to Baker's assertion that in *Green Hills of Africa* "there is no neglect of humankind" (172). Toying with description and crafting association, Hemingway reconfigures Africa and the African as only a white man can; the "as is" he gives us is a carefully crafted reality with the West and whiteness at its center.

If containment is Hemingway's ultimate end in Africa, veiled rhetoric is his means to that end. He gives us not Africa proper but a representation of it reshaped by white hands and saturated in stereotype. Edward Said speaks to Hemingway when he points to the "so-called truthful text" as a primary perpetrator of "unnatural" presentation. "These representations," notes Said, "rely upon institutions, traditions, conventions, agreed-upon codes of understanding for their effects, not upon a distant and amorphous Orient" (22). Colonial discourse becomes a virtual catalog of perceptual instructions and a formulaic guide for seeing the world. "Sometimes," says Hemingway, "Sometimes the bottle is shaped art, sometimes economics, sometimes economic-religion." Sometimes too the bottle is shaped like social politics.

From the work's inception, Hemingway gives the reader colonial Africa. Littered throughout the literal and the actual African landscape are empire's remnants. The work's opening sequence sets the tone as the reader is invited to follow this white man's trek into the visible darkness of Africa: "We were sitting in the blind that Wanderobo hunters had built of twigs and branches at the edge of the salt-lick when we heard the truck coming" (2). At once, we see a portrait painted in colonial hues as the beast of the West, the machine, abruptly breaks an implicit natural tranquility. The opening sentence yields an irony of sorts as well; while the lorry is resented by all, the most pronounced grievances come from Hemingway the hunter. The machine serves as an important reminder to both the author and the reader of the hunter's inextricable link to this intrusiveness. While he voices his disgust at the lorry's arrival, and while he makes Kandisky the butt of an extended joke, Hemingway's symbolic ties to this man and his machine are unbreakable.

Kandisky's sole function early on is to elevate our narrator, and in doing so, he becomes a type himself, a Western "other," a spectacle of sorts, against which Hemingway the accepted, Hemingway the near-Native, who dons a mask of sameness (what linguist Norman Fairclough calls "false egalitarianism" [18]), may gauge himself. As such, from the narrative's inception, Kandisky assists in rebuilding the great man. The first chapter of *Green Hills* serves as a grand stage for the interplay of sameness and difference between Hemingway and Kandisky. For the wary reader, though, Kandisky becomes more of a mirror than a transparent glass through which we are to view and judge the Austrian's absurdity. To the discriminating eye, Kandisky becomes not a foil to Hemingway but the reflection of a shared ideology, the exaggerated whiteness shown to be his own.

Through Hemingway, we see Kandisky hovering over his lorry, hood raised, in the dark. Hemingway's description, though brief, is thick with implication: "I told Kamau to stop and go back and as we backed into the firelight there was a short, bandy-legged man with a Tyroler hat, leather shorts, and an open shirt standing before an unhooded engine in a crowd of natives" (6). In the midst of the African bush, Kandisky is a walking representation of his European homeland. Hemingway wastes little time with physical description, instead paying special attention to posture and dress. Kandisky sports leather shorts and a Tyroler hat, pants and headdress with a specific history; he wears the clothes of Austria. With an ever-discriminating eye, Hemingway simultaneously turns his attention to space and location as well. Kandisky stands before the stalled lorry—Westerner inextricably linked to machine—surrounded by Natives. The picture is markedly Eurocentric, and deliberately so. But again Hemingway relishes anticipated reader uncertainty.

The stalled vehicle has the effect of skewing our impressions and cultivating a peculiar ambiguity. Kandisky, the most blatantly Western of the bunch, is surprisingly dumbfounded by the vehicle's sudden arrested state. He quickly shrouds the incomprehensible in mystery. In uncharacteristically un-Western fashion, Kandisky reduces the complexities of auto mechanics to superstition;

this engine, like all engines, simply dislikes him, and it dies merely to torment him. Hemingway, until now suppressing his Western-ness, comes forward as shrewd observer, asking, "Do you think it could be the timer? It sounded as though it might be a timing knock when you went past us" (6). In contrast to his emotional Austrian counterpart, he assesses the situation with cool detachment and reason. The relationship between the two men is in a constant state of flux, each positing then severing ties to empire.

However, when the artist seems to diverge from his banal associate most, Hemingway steps through the looking glass and we get a point of convergence:

> "And you know what you want?"
> "Absolutely, and I get it all the time."
> "But it takes money."
> "I would always make money and besides I have been very lucky."

Hemingway links the two figures instantaneously with ideology and language: both are familiar with the notions of wanting, getting, and having. The two become one, and through the dollar's transcendence, they reach an understanding, but only for an instant.

In the conversation between Kandisky and our narrator, the writer constantly strives to distance the two men. Questioning Hemingway's patient yet utterly exhaustive and singular tracking of the kudu, Kandisky opines, "But you should hunt for a year. At the end of that time you have shot everything and you are sorry for it. To hunt for one special animal is nonsense" (8). Kandisky does two things here: in the most obvious sense, he promotes a more practical approach to the hunt and, in a more suggestive fashion, he posits for the reader another of the many myths of empire: the Edenic plenum. Implicit in Kandisky's advice is an undeniable presumptuousness: the colonialist's new-world perception of abundance, availability, and assured acquisition. This too is something of which the contemporary reading audience is, Hemingway wagers, fully cognizant.

Later on in the same conversation, the Austrian remains unchanged in his opinion of this obsessive hunt, remarking, "You should not take it so seriously. It is nothing. In a year you kill twenty" (14). Hemingway as Papa immediately seizes upon this remark with reminders of license and legal allowances, and Kandisky backpedals abruptly. After this apparent slip of the tongue, Kandisky dons the garb of superiority, also attempting to distance himself from empire with a quick qualification: "I kill nothing, you understand" (14). The Austrian constantly razes and rebuilds himself before our very eyes; his self-righteous impulse and longing for approval are almost laughable. Hemingway's pen draws on this vacillation in wicked fashion.

"I represent European organization," announces the Austrian proudly (17). The significance (and irony) of this statement is amplified in light of the other details concerning his African enterprise. His place atop the racial totem is unclear at best; the Austrian has lost everything associated with his shamba, the plantation he once possessed. Once the proud owner of a landed estate with laborers of his own, Kandisky is now painfully alone, with just the single sputtering lorry in his possession, and now that too, he freely points out, is gone. Kandisky retains a managerial position on a plantation owned by an Indian tycoon; the colonized now render *him* servile. However, while his own commodity status is apparent to everyone (most especially the reader), he arrogantly shrugs off this reversion and, like Kant, holds fast to old ideals. Emphasizing the color line himself, the Austrian stresses his importance to the new owner and to the entire operation, asserting, "He values me. I represent European organization" (17).

Seemingly insistent on distancing himself from all things imperial, Hemingway extends the joke heartily and shows us in the Austrian's personal history and attendant arrogance yet another white man fallen. Like his counterparts in the American tales, this white man can only stand idly by and watch as his world slowly inverts itself, but this casualty our writer is willing to acknowledge, because redemption here is still very much in the offing, just not for the Austrian; Papa reserves this privilege for himself, and that leaves room for a little levity. The truth in Kandisky's sad story makes him this text's requisite absurdity, this text's grotesque; his is a cautionary tale. It is painfully funny and becomes the narrative's grand joke. The humor lies partly in the fact that, unlike his American counterparts, this fallen man continues to delude himself.

While his personal empire has crumbled, the Austrian naively clings to his ideal's founding principles. Even as he stands before us all but divorced from his glorious past, Kandisky openly declares himself a monarch in this land of plenty: "I am king here. It is very pleasant. Waking in the morning I extend the one foot and the boy places the sock on it. When I am ready I extend the other foot and he adjusts the other sock. I step from under the mosquito bar into my drawers which are held for me. Don't you think that is very marvellous?" (31). Here the irony and the distance between the two men could not be any greater. And the humor reigns supreme as Hemingway, through Kandisky, boldly reinscribes a faded color line, a line Papa seems to shrewdly cross as he (and we) laughs at the Austrian's absurdity. In a sense, Kandisky becomes this text's grotesque, the book's incongruous marker of truth. Unlike his American counterparts, though—Uncle George, the cook, the porter—he is somewhat oblivious to the depths of this truth. However, Hemingway's seemingly obligatory affirmative response is rife with more than simple irony. "I am king here," declares Kandisky. The Austrian's ridiculously arrogant moment arguably becomes Hemingway's as well. With Kandisky's departure, the American resumes his reading and then naps in the coolness of the African breeze as Molo (his Native traveling companion) arranges the tent flaps for the comfort of the Colonel (Hemingway's name for himself).

With Kandisky staring at him from within the glass, Hemingway at times engages in a game of imitative pantomime, mocking the Austrian's absurdities and hypocrisy while simultaneously committing the very same sins himself. "Why are you not more interested in the natives?" asks Kandisky (14). Time and again he posits the same question; time and again the author blatantly, conspicuously, and altogether dismisses it. Bernard DeVoto suggests in a 1935 review that the black characters of "Droopy, Garrick, and The Wanderobo are splendid creations; one sees and feels them, accepts them, experiences them" (see Trogdon 179). But does one know them? The short answer to this question is simple: hardly. DeVoto answers this question himself in his praise's conspicuous omission. *Green Hills* is, more than anything else, the white hunter's tale. Chapters into the memoir, miles into the bush, and seemingly years after our introduction to Kandisky, the Austrian's words still ring lucid: "Why are you not more interested in the natives?"

Kandisky tells us, unabashedly, that he studies the Natives, literally observing them with pen in hand, and Hemingway seems to mock him for it. Yet what the Austrian does literally our author does figuratively, and through an act of displacement, his mockery thinly disguises his own lack of interest. Throughout the narrative, he manages to keep both friend and associate alike—black of course—at a marked observational distance. In each instance, they remain background silhouettes, undefined shadows in the presence of the resplendent Hemingway. M'Cola, the most intimate of Hemingway's Native companions, is described in nothing short of servile terms. Of M'Cola, Hemingway says early on, "He was Mr. Jackson Phillips' gunbearer and he had been loaned to me" (40). Hemingway simply defines M'Cola by the services he provides and, gauged by his utility, this "old man" becomes yet another exploited body.

At the height of the shooting competition between Papa and friend Karl—the two chase the elusive kudu and, hypercompetitive as they are, they separate themselves with imaginary boundaries cutting through the Great Rift Valley—Hemingway tersely describes M'Cola's role as simply "to carry shells and birds" (128). Toni Morrison suggests of Hemingway's black characters in general that "the black man is not only nameless" but nothing more than "a kind of trained response, not an agent possessing a job" (*Playing in the Dark* 70). From beginning to end, Hemingway's black countrymen in *Green Hills,* even those closest to him, *are* their jobs, and little more. The competition between Karl and Papa only heightens the secondary position of those at their service.

As anticipation builds, and time dwindles, the hunting party enters "Droopy's country" with guarded optimism. By now, with frustration unquestionably setting in, Papa bears the burden of insatiable desire and ego; M'Cola and Droopy bear all else: "The five of us in single file, Droop and M'Cola with a big gun apiece, hung with mussettes and water bottles and the cameras, we all sweating in the sun, Pop and I with guns and the Memsahib trying to walk like Droopy, her Stetson tilted on one side, happy to be on a trip, pleased about how comfortable her boots were" (68–69). This scene and others like it stand in utter opposition to those in which Papa and his band share victuals and hunting stories (manifest instances of Fairclough's false egalitarianism). Droopy and M'Cola are workhorses and little more. The Native as beast of burden is one of many recurring images littering the narrative landscape that work to reinscribe the color line separating Papa from those darkened by his shadow. Anonymity, label, and epithet become wondrously powerful tools in the process.

As we trek with Hemingway on this first African excursion, we encounter countless nameless and faceless dark bodies along the way; most engender little more than the label of savage. For example, early on, in the midst of preparations for a rhino hunt, Hemingway notes the complexion of Karl's Native entourage, which he describes as "forty M'Bulus, good looking savages with a pompous headman who wore the only pair of shorts among them" (61). Placing immediate emphasis on exteriority, Hemingway subtly reads the nakedness of those standing before him. According to David Spurr, within the imperial vision, "the body, rather than speech, law, or history, is the essential defining characteristic of primitive peoples" (22). Thus, the body is at once aestheticized, utilized, and economized, depending on imperial needs and desires. And Hemingway's evaluation of others in his hunting group consistently fails to move beyond this marked superficiality.

During his initial encounter with Garrick and Abdullah before the actual kudu tracking begins, Hemingway sizes up his prospective guides. Garrick and Abdullah are but two of four potential guides available to the party, and our writer lumps all the agents together and simultaneously categorizes them: two are clothed, two are naked, all are "savages." Of the clothed guides, Abdullah, Hemingway tells us, is "the short, thick-nosed educated one" (163). Unlike his Native companions, apparently, he can read. However, Hemingway expressly notes how thoroughly unimpressed he is with Abdullah's literacy skills as he watches the African scratch his name on his leg with a twig. The tension pervading Hemingway's narrative voice emanates from the fact that Abdullah, the "educated one," is also Garrick's personal tracker. This fact only adds to the already pungent distaste the American has for Garrick. It seems the theatrical one has his own entourage. And, according to Hemingway, he is all histrionics. For this, Hemingway quickly christens him "the bloody tragedian," "Theatre Business," and "Garrick" (163–64). While the humor is at once apparent and undeniable, Hemingway's labels and the Natives' dramatic sensibility assume a life of their own and we never learn his real name. In this sense, Hemingway's narrative engages in a kind of ontological thievery as it erases personal story, as fiction supplants fact, as white supplants black.

As for M'Cola, whose close connection to Papa seems to stem from his utility and his ready embrace of all things Western (Hemingway emphasizes the shorts and khaki army tunic he sports), he too loses his story, his essence, to narrative expedience. By narrative's end, the old man is the same empty cipher (bereft of personal story) he is at the beginning of the narrative. While Hemingway repeatedly describes him as an old man, and rightfully so—he is at least fifty years old and significantly older than Hemingway—M'Cola does not garner the same sort of reverence that Philip Percival does; Percival is a sage, he is a father figure, he is "Pop." Conversely, this old man, time and again, is referred to as "boy." Further skewing reader perception is a narrative that insists the black man's children are "no good, worthless" (41). And a sequence in which Hemingway compares the various sleeping states of his companions only underscores the divide between black and white. Of Pop, Hemingway notes that "you could see his soul was close in his body." M'Cola, on the other hand, is simply "an old man asleep, without history and without mystery" (73). The narrative actively and completely divorces M'Cola of history, an act whose import cannot be overstated. A denial of African history by empire, notes Spurr, is in fact a stratagem initiated by the imperialist "in order to construct [his] own vision of an African future" (100). We can amend this assertion by suggesting that the imperialist necessarily (de)constructs an African present as well, and Hemingway's narrative sleight is just that: a (de)construction. In this divorce proceeding, Papa, as part of a long tradition, performs a literary exorcism of sorts as well as he effectively denies M'Cola his soul (see Hegel 93, 99).

Just as Hemingway reconfigures this "new" land's people, so too does he impose a Western vision upon the land itself. In fact, at times the two (Native and landscape) are seemingly inextricable—both simultaneously refashioned and assimilated into the great Western vision. In one instance, Hemingway actively traverses continents and transforms a Masai villager and his son into Romans. Of these people, Hemingway notes: "They looked like no negroes I had ever seen. Their faces were a gray brown, the oldest looked to be about fifty, had thin lips, an almost Grecian nose, high cheekbones, and large, intelligent eyes. He had great poise and dignity and seemed to be very intelligent" (224). In an uncanny moment, Hemingway makes blackness both unfamiliar and instantly recognizable as he reads the African duo from the outside; in forging an outside-inside correlative, Hemingway ascribes an inherent dignity to the Masai men, insists on some non-tangential European connection, and in the process engages a phrenological tradition of which his reading audience would have been quite aware.[7]

The narrative implications here are clear as Hemingway effectively appropriates identity and history and manipulates them to his liking. The Masai engagement furthers Hemingway's reconstruction of whiteness. Dressed in togas like Romans, the Masai assume a spiritual sensibility, seemingly unconfined, unbound, unfettered by time. With this painted vision, Barbara Lounsberry posits, "Hemingway clearly wants the reader to recognize the difference between the 'true' and the 'better than true'" (23). I would amend this statement, substituting the words "real" and "romantic" for "true" and "better than true." While M'Cola evokes no sense of history for Hemingway, these black men, the Masai, do—but the associations are shamelessly Western. Even Hemingway's description of the Natives, which gives them classically Anglo features—"thin lips, an almost Grecian nose, high cheekbones" (and skin that is a tempered brown)—reveres whiteness in the end.

Borrowing Lounsberry's notions of the "true" and "better than true," I would say that Hemingway gives us two Africas in the book, each a creation of the white imagination: the East Africa true to stereotype and cursed expectation, and the Westernized Africa formulated in mythology, imbued with mystery and reverence. One is something to be conquered, the other something to be discovered. Each serves its purpose in placating the white psyche. Most importantly, Africa, even an Africa shrouded in mystery, is a knowable or potentially knowable quantity.

Toni Morrison reiterates this point in her double-storied vision of Hemingway's *The Garden of Eden,* stating that "*Africa, imagined* as innocent and under white control, is the inner *story*; Africanism, *imagined as evil, chaotic, impenetrable, is the outer story*" (*Playing in the Dark* 89). With its "impenetrable" bush, its "solid, scrubby-looking undergrowth," its "typical desert country" (*Green Hills* 115), the East African landscape is the Africa often ignored, cursed, or, like M'Cola's progeny, deemed worthless. Even the Natives, Hemingway tells us, trek westward, fleeing famine. These deserted lands are Pop's "million miles of bloody Africa" (159). Droopy's country, then, the country to the west, represents a more forgiving Africa, a fabled Africa, a mythic Africa. Appropriately, Hemingway's excitement in his encounter with a country imbued with both history and novelty translates well: "It was a new country to us but it had the marks of the oldest countries. The road was a track over shelves of solid rock, worn by the feet of the caravans and the cattle, and it rose in the boulder-strewn un-roadliness through a double line of trees and into the hills. The country was so much like Aragon that I could not believe we were not in Spain" (146). Like the Romanesque Masai villagers, the country itself is steeped in history, but not just *any* history; old Europe resonates throughout the hills and valleys of this "new" country. Hemingway's love for it is thus justified. Yet there is mixed with that historic sensibility an undeniable newness associated with the land as well, and for that, Hemingway's excitement as explorer is warranted.

From its inception, *Green Hills* perpetuates an Edenic mythology; this new Eden is a land teeming with wildlife and brimming with possibility for one willing to seize it. We see this almost immediately in Hemingway's provocative admission to Kandisky early on that he would indeed kill an elephant if it were large enough, contrary to legal restrictions and the Austrian's expressed philosophical convictions (8). Later, this same sentiment echoes throughout the marsh as Hemingway and M'Cola hunt for ducks, Hemingway "brown[ing] a bunch to get cripples for decoys and then tak[ing] only fancy shots because you know now you can get all that we can use or carry" (133). With M'Cola's shooting coat filled to capacity, the shooting continues and our American's appetite is only temporarily satiated. The entire foray into the forest is thus in many ways nothing more than an active, often cavalier, stripping of the land. All told, Hemingway's kills during that 1933–34 safari consisted of "three lions, a buffalo and twenty-seven other beasts" (Meyers, *Hemingway: A Biography* 263). Such an extensive hunting catalog suggests that Papa too falls prey to empire's peculiar brand of wanderlust.

From its creation of a new Africa to its perpetuation of colonial mythologies, *Green Hills of Africa* is a celebration of the imperial ideal and an underscoring of the color line. Within its scope, the land, the animals, the people that are Africa—all fall prey to the white man's gaze. Thus, Hemingway's first

African book is an homage to the adventures played out in his youth and the hunting (and literary) tradition that preceded him. It is a book less about any real place than about crafted color lines and the perpetuation of myth. Explored, questioned, and eventually abandoned in a story like "The Battler," the mythos of Anglo-as-great-man in his many incarnations thus becomes Hemingway's point of focus in his early African writings. The African safari book in general, and *Green Hills* in particular, seeks to reestablish roots in this dying tradition and to resurrect that great man.

The short fiction springing from the 1933 safari ultimately reverts in more express fashion to this tried-and-true racial formula. We certainly see this greater adherence and loyalty to the established model in "The Snows of Kilimanjaro." Harry and his wife, Helen, travel many miles to hunt, take pictures, and write, only to have Harry face down death and a mountain of regrets as he looks at a life that could have been. While Harry in "Snows" embraces the apparent simplicity and honesty of life lived in Africa, this sublimation of Africa as site of regeneration and rebirth is itself a validation of the notion of the noble savage and the Anglo myth Hemingway visited early on in the Indian stories.

Assessing his life as a man, and especially as a writer, Harry indicts civilization's trappings (i.e., money, comfort, and convenience), his wife, and finally himself in his aesthetic undoing, for the complacency that comes with money, and for all his unproductive years. As Jeffrey Meyers suggests in his discussion of the African stories, Harry's own moral weakness "condemns him" (*Hemingway: A Biography* 270). To be sure, and by his own admission, he is a flawed (white) man; however, following a pattern established by Hemingway in *Green Hills,* this flawed man is also potentially redeemable. Africa, Harry insists, becomes a place of renewal: "Africa was where he had been happiest in the good time of his life, so he had come out here to start again. They had made this safari with the minimum of comfort. There was no hardship; but there was no luxury and he had thought he could get back into training that way. That in some way he could work the fat off his soul the way a fighter went into the mountains to work and train in order to burn it out of his body" (11). And go to the mountain he does, for clarity, for wholeness, for himself.

At the tale's heart sits neither Africa nor the African but a clarity-craving and self-seeking Harry. And as our white male representative, he is the essence of grace under pressure; after all, he bravely and truthfully faces certain death as infection seizes upon his gangrenous body. A minor scratch turns into a monstrous infection, and that monstrous infection gives Harry much cause to reflect on a life of wasted opportunity and wasted talent. Hemingway's depictions of

Harry's gangrenous leg and contemplative moments, replete with references to rotting flesh and circling vultures, are as close as we get to anything Gothic in this work; however, Hemingway maintains his ties to gross incongruity in this tale as well. Harry is this work's grotesque, and all truths funnel through him. Significantly, half of Harry's narrative invokes European and American memories, not African experience, as he lies dying, talking to his wife: "'Where did we stay in Paris?' he asked the woman who was sitting by him in a canvas chair, now in Africa" (8). Like Papa's gaze in *Green Hills of Africa,* Harry's is intense and focused westward.

Reflecting on his life and all the experiences he has lived but about which he has never written, Harry, self-professed writer, remembers warring against the Austrians, skiing in Vorarlberg and Arlberg, and whoring in Constantinople. He recalls his grandfather's quiet agony after losing his cabin to fire. He remembers Paris. And he laments not having written about *any* of it: "No, he had never written about Paris. Not the Paris that he cared about. But what about the rest that he had never written?" (22). Hemingway gives us a man whose stories, like his body, lie flaccid and quietly dying. Like Dr. Adams, Ad, and Steve Ketchel before him, Harry is our questionably great man. However, Hemingway seems to suggest, unlike those men, Harry may in fact retain some semblance of greatness.

To be sure, only the mountain, Kilimanjaro, seems to stand majestic in this work. The Harry we initially meet is a deeply flawed man corrupted by that which he supposedly despises: Western decadence. And like Dr. Adams of the Indian stories and perhaps even Ad of "The Battler," this white man realizes his own fallibility, his lost greatness. But Hemingway shows us that in Africa, the broken can be made whole again and one can sometimes restore greatness simply by being there, white among black, "Bwana" among boys. Underscoring her husband's reverence for the African continent, Helen (for still other reasons) declares her *love* for Africa, and her love for "the country." Harry's fatalism gives his wife pause, and she gives voice to the glee she too feels there in Africa, shooting game. And, true enough, wildlife and the countryside, as part of some idyllic geographic space, themselves take precedence over *anything* and *everything* else.

Moreover, a story named for the glorious, awe-inspiring African mountain becomes more a symbolic aesthetic ideal than a committed exploration of a country and its people. It becomes more an American moment than an African one. Instead, we get nameless dark bodies in the act of service underscoring one Western man's moment of self-realization, and Harry's central moment is a diminishing moment for those in his presence ("the boys lighting a fire" [47]). Our protagonist becomes "Bwana," his wife and traveling companion "Memsahib"; both are titles of respect, of reverence, of whiteness. The narrative succeeds in stripping name, age, and other markers of individuality from the Natives who prepare food orders for the couple ("I'll have them mash some potatoes with the Klim" [46], "Molo, *letti dui* whiskey-soda!" [47]), allow for the missus's "fun" as she hunts ("The two boys had a Tommy and they were coming along behind her" [47], "He saw . . . the other boy with the dishes" [49]), and tend to the white man's ailing gangrenous leg ("Did Molo change the dressings?" [44]). "Does Bwana want?"—a refrain implicitly lacing every East-West exchange—becomes representative of this narrative's entirety and of Hemingway's later, more extensive, encounters with the African continent.

Harry's African experience in "The Snows of Kilimanjaro" is, metaphorically, one of reversion and reflection. If Hemingway's Indian stories and his black-and-white tales are largely forward-looking exercises and an angst-laden inquiry into a racial totem, then the safari stories (including *Green Hills*) are very much a literal ordering for our protagonist, wherein Hemingway makes Africa his chosen site of white reconstruction. These narratives always succeed in reinscribing that all-important color line with some degree of certainty and in restoring whiteness to some degree of prominence, as Hemingway gives us narratives in which irrefutable authority always ultimately rests in white hands.

Unlike all the other texts featured in this examination, the African short stories ("The Short Happy Life of Francis Macomber" and "The Snows of Kilimanjaro" especially) never fully realize a subverted social order, nor do they feature a marginal figure of consequence truly threatening to cross the color line. But what we do have in the characters of Harry in "Snows" and Macomber and even Wilson in "The Short Happy Life" are flawed figures, white men with greatness that must be reconstituted, greatness that *can* be reconstituted. And through the binary game he plays, Hemingway at least partially complies here in the first African stories and, to a greater extent, in *Green Hills of Africa,* in reinstating white primacy. Moreover, within these texts, in each social space, the color line's transgression becomes *exclusively* a white prerogative.

Yet another work that does to some degree conform to this paradigm of a floating color line and illusive/elusive racial identity is "The Short Happy Life of Francis Macomber." Like *Green Hills* and its short companion piece, "The Snows of Kilimanjaro," this story also suggests an author looking for racial stasis. With its fallen white protagonist and his red-skinned nemesis, "The Short Happy Life" too becomes emblematic of Hemingway's attempted movement *not away from* but *toward* racial stability and definition. It may be but a fleeting moment in those formative years of the 1930s, but it is a notable moment nonetheless, and like the two other aforementioned African works, "The Short Happy Life" records that moment.

On holiday in Africa with his wife, Francis Macomber—a young, wealthy white American—hunts big game as part of his safari package. A moment of cowardice while shooting lions gives rise to a narrative push for redemption and costs him the already tenuous respect of his wife—and ultimately his life. Significantly, Macomber's cowardly moment becomes a heroic moment for their hired guide and gun. Tested, tried, and true to form, Wilson is this story's featured code hero. And significantly, while Hemingway repeatedly describes Wilson as "red," and while his hands are said to be brown, ultimately the senior hunter is a conflation of white masculine ideology; time and again, he stands simply as the white hunter.

Admittedly, Hemingway openly toys with the color line as he imagines his hunter in shades of red. Correspondingly, both Macomber and Wilson are faulted men, the young man a coward who has hidden behind his money his entire life, the older hunter a man hardened by years of violence and uncompromising self-service. (Money speaks most loudly to him, and he bunks on a double cot in the hopes of bedding the wives of his hunting clientele.) Macomber's cowardice makes him yellow; his shame makes him red. Not until the end, when he stares down a charging buffalo, unafraid for the first time in his life, does he become great. Always cool, calculating, and very much in control of himself and those around him, Wilson is the story's great white hunter from the outset. Yet Hemingway plays with identity boundaries—if only momentarily—in making Wilson's complexion an issue. He is a composite of color, always the "white hunter" with "cold blue eyes," a "baked red" face, and "big brown hands." In fact, Hemingway makes repeated references to his red face throughout the narrative. Further complicating this is Wilson's initially illusive but ultimately blunt response to a clearly intrigued Margaret Macomber, who questions the hunter about it:

> "You know you have a very red face, Mr. Wilson," she told him and smiled again.
>
> "Drink," said Wilson.
>
> "I don't think so," she said. "Francis drinks a great deal, but his face is never red."

> "It's red today," Macomber tried to joke.
>
> "No," said Margaret. "It's mine that's red today. But Mr. Wilson's is always red."
>
> "Must be racial," said Wilson. "I say, you wouldn't like to drop my beauty as a topic, would you?" (6)

In this sense, Wilson is a bit like Dick Boulton, who neighbors swear is really a white man masquerading behind red skin. Like Boulton, Wilson commands language; he speaks Swahili to the Natives in Macomber's employ, significantly translating for the utterly dependent American. However, in the end, "The Short Happy Life of Francis Macomber" is exclusively the story of the great white hunter and one of white primacy, the mythos of whiteness reverberating throughout the text: "no white man ever bolts" (8).

Years before, in "The Doctor and the Doctor's Wife," Hemingway challenged this purported truism in Dr. Adams's retreat from Dick Boulton. However, "The Short Happy Life" is arguably a redemptive narrative, with Macomber making good on the racial aphorism. His final moments as he stares down the charging buffalo do just that. His final moments are more than moments of self-realization; they are moments of racial fulfillment ("no white man ever bolts"). Moreover, they are moments of white privilege, moments that separate him from those (dark bodies) around him, and as Hemingway has shown us many times before, privilege is predicated upon assumptions of difference and superiority, a superiority ontologically rooted in whiteness.

White privilege unabashedly governs Macomber's narrative. In "The Short Happy Life of Francis Macomber," Hemingway strips the minority figure of all maturity, humanity, and semblance of individuality. We see racial diminution almost immediately in the opening sequence's master-servant dynamic. As the story unfolds, we learn that Francis Macomber is on holiday hunting game with Margaret, his aging trophy wife, in the wilds of Africa. Spooked by a lion they are tracking, the would-be hunter grapples with the aftermath of his cowardice and public humiliation and the consequences of his exceptional behavior, of being the white man bolting.

We are privy to the post-debacle discussion among Macomber, his wife, and the hired hunting guide, Robert Wilson, whose heroics saved the young man. Yet while so much seems to separate coward from (code) hero as Macomber and Wilson exchange glances, what the two men *do* share is unmistakably clear from the tale's outset: their whiteness. And that alone, Hemingway suggests, gives the young American, even in his diminished state, a distinct advantage. Here in Africa, white among black, he *can* redeem himself; he can make himself whole again.

Macomber's initial racial presence in the story manifests itself via an order from a white man to those blacks in his service: "Tell him to make three gimlets," he says as he and his wife and Wilson try to forget his act of cowardice earlier in the day (5). Anticipating his command in Pavlovian fashion, the nameless (African) cook assumes a purely perfunctory, responsive role ("The mess boy had started them already" [5]). From this point on, Hemingway's narrative relegates various members of the Macomber wait staff to the status of "boy" ("mess boy," "native boy," or simply "boy"). While the use of the pejorative may accurately reflect a racist era, the narrative itself does little to exonerate itself from this prejudiced worldview. Unlike "The Battler" or "Light of the World," this tale is exclusively the white man's. If DeVoto heaped praise upon Papa for his "splendid creations" in *Green Hills,* what could he possibly suggest of the dark figures peopling *this* fictional landscape?

We don't *know* Kongoni, the old gun bearer who aids Wilson and Macomber as they stalk game, nor do we get to know *any* of the countless nameless "boys" in the party's service. In most instances, the dark diminutive becomes the type, the label, and the function, with Native workers assuming job titles and little else along the way. The group includes gun bearers, skinners, cooks, and personal servants. The narrative's active stripping away of individuality approaches absurdity as it reduces even the dark body itself to constituent parts or erases it altogether. During a conversation after the botched lion kill, as the three principals (Macomber, his wife, and Wilson) sit for lunch, the black man becomes a phantom presence, denied both a voice and a body:

> "Oh no," she said. "It's been charming. And tomorrow. You don't know how I look forward to tomorrow."
>
> "That's eland he's offering you," Wilson said.

In this instance, the narrative summarily erases the servant's humanity altogether, removing all but the faintest signs of his existence. A bit later, a victory celebration in honor of Macomber's lion killing becomes a literal montage of arms and shoulders as the cook, the personal "boys," the skinner, and the porter bear the weight of our illustrious white hunter as he is carried into camp. Hemingway's strategy is clearly one of deliberate and effective erasure. Filling the void is white mythos.

Macomber's personal attendants are, according to the narrator, dumbstruck after Macomber's initial public defeat and humiliation by the lion: "Wilson could tell that the boys all knew about it now and when he saw Macomber's personal boy looking curiously at his master while he was putting dishes on the table he snapped at him in Swahili. The boy turned away with his face blank" (7). Hemingway takes great care to underscore the myth of the white hunter's invulnerability and Macomber's rather *exceptional* fallen status. Underscoring the order of the day is Wilson's threat to the awe-struck servant in question:

> "What were you telling him?" Macomber asked.
> "Nothing. Told him to look alive or I'd see he got about fifteen of the best."
> "What's that? Lashes?"
> "It's quite illegal," Wilson said. "You're supposed to fine them."
> "Do you still have them whipped?"
> "Oh, yes. They could raise a row if they chose to complain. But they don't. They prefer it to the fines." (7)

Gone are the days of slavery, but remnants of the old order endure. Underlying Wilson's whip and personal threats are authority, mastery, and the myth of white primacy.

Hemingway shows us that that protective racial umbrella even extends to the fallen. Even when diminished, Macomber retains his privileged position within the African sociopolitical space. Ironically, even his fallen-ness itself, as a purported quasi anomaly, underscores Anglo grandeur. Macomber's inherent glow extends to the other principal (white) figures as well, as Margaret never loses her social footing. She is always "Memsahib," or "lady" to those others in her presence. Hemingway emphatically points to her inclusion in this racial mythmaking as Wilson assures her cowardly husband that professional protocol guarantees that his faltering moments will remain in the bush, and that the embarrassment will remain between the two of them: "'Don't worry about me talking,' he said. 'I have a living to make. You know in Africa no woman ever misses her lion and no white man ever bolts'" (8).

Native complicity in this myth's maintenance ensures this confidentiality. A servant stares, post-debacle, at Macomber and is summarily chastised for it by Wilson. As an interesting, but I think significant, aside, James Mellow suggests that Hemingway tinkered with the Macomber character as he sketched him and conflated fact and fiction, replacing a fleeing Ben Fourie—Hemingway's white driver—with a nameless Native gun bearer in the story's final scene

(445). Such a conscious change only underscores Hemingway's awareness of the power inherent in color, and the power inherent in his planted motto: "no white man ever bolts." This all becomes paramount in crafting a narrative whose principal purpose is to reconstruct whiteness. "The Short Happy Life of Francis Macomber," like its complementary pieces, is not really about Africa or the African; this story is the great white hunter's story, and as Morrison would suggest, it is ultimately a story of white affirmation.

Questionable character and nebulous color aside, no figure shines brighter (or whiter) in this story than the great white hunter himself. As the tale's master hunter, Wilson becomes the white paragon on these African game trails; with his steely blue eyes, his rough-hewn weathered exterior, and his hunting expertise now legendary, he is the epitome of Hemingway's code hero. He is, after all, the one who shoots the lion that frightens Macomber, and later it is he who finishes off the rhino that has been slightly wounded but not killed by the cowardly hunter. Significantly, like his creator's hero, Teddy Roosevelt, Wilson earns his reverential code-hero status on the African game trails. His hunting heroics trump personal foibles every time. Even his defeated client, Francis Macomber, chooses the rifle as a tool to redeem himself; treading the game trail, it seems, is the first important step toward recapturing greatness. Thus, while Hemingway tinges all three of his key figures in the African stories—Wilson, Macomber, and Harry in "Snows"—with ambiguity, racial demarcation and re-entrenchment become the order of the day in his 1930s safari texts. Interestingly, Hemingway's chosen site of racial reconstitution would, in the years following, become for him a site of subversion as well as an ever-so-slight shift in attitude and focus.

In the works inspired by his last safari in 1953, Hemingway goes well beyond the simple paradigm of the early African texts. We can see again an artist looking for complexity in his attention to both the trope of white masculinity and his reintegration of that liminal racial figure of indeterminate status, missing for so long and alluded to but never realized in "The Short Happy Life." The difference, though, between the nebulous figure previously examined and those of the African text is one of both degree and kind. In the stories of Africa, gone are the transgressive *marginalized* figures we saw in the American tales—the Dick Boultons and the Bugses, who metaphorically and aggressively encroach on Anglo authority and the civilized world. In the African works, we see no others supplanting white authority. But in those final writings, what we do see is an artist willing to erase, if only momentarily, a color line he knows to be impermanent.

Some twenty years after his first safari, Hemingway returns to that narrative space—that space in which Harry sought to reconstitute himself as the great white man in "Snows"—to push the boundaries of aesthetics and identity once more, as he did so many years before. Hemingway's return to Africa and the works generated from it are a return to aesthetic form for an artist whose interest in racial construction arose in his youth. What Hemingway gives us in those final African texts is a complex narrator who himself acts as an amalgam of worlds on both sides of the color line. And that nebulous amalgam—that gray space between black and white—is where Hemingway gleefully lives as he revisits the African continent in the flesh in 1953, and in his writings again and again in the decade before his death.

CHAPTER SIX

The First Shall Be Last, the Last Shall Be First

Erasing and Retracing the Color Line in "The Good Lion," *True at First Light,* and *Under Kilimanjaro*

> During the past three centuries the spread of the English-speaking peoples over the world's waste spaces has been not only the most striking feature in the world's history, but also the event of all others most far-reaching in its effects and its importance.
>
> —Theodore Roosevelt, *The Winning of the West*

"... Almost nothing was true and especially not in Africa": so begins Hemingway's *True at First Light,* the first incarnation of his final African safari memories. But the very opposite is correct too; for the experimental aesthete, almost *everything* is true, it seems, and especially in Africa. In his last fictionalized memoir, Hemingway explores familiar ground—identity construction—but considerably older, perhaps wiser, certainly refocused since his first trip, he reaches deep into his old bag of tricks, and for a brief moment, he raises the stakes considerably.

To be sure, his trip of 1933–34 was very much about staying change, at least momentarily, and reifying a white truth; his sociological experiment ended there with the reconstitution. And although his last African safari literally and figuratively marks a return of sorts to (white) greatness—to a place where, it seems, whiteness is always great, it is also a slight return to form as he revisits an interrogative space he occupied as a boy and young man surveying his own country. In one of those final writings he pushes racial boundaries as he himself becomes the liminal figure. As his story's own transgressor, seemingly erasing the color line at will, he gleefully reconfigures ideas of race and identity, something he had done all those years earlier as he began his writing career. And he does so against a backdrop of political unrest and a shifting social climate.

The Hemingways—Ernest and his fourth wife, Mary—spent the summer of 1953 in Spain, priming themselves for their African adventure. In truth, Hemingway had been preparing himself for this return for some twenty years. Sightseeing in Burgos, taking in the bullfights in Pamplona, just enjoying the beauty of San Sebastian, the party immersed itself in the Spanish country. It was a cultural baptism for Mary and a welcome return for Ernest. An active campaign to visit the African continent on the part of his son Patrick laid the foundation, at least in part, for the safari of 1953–54. This time, Philip Percival and Hemingway were the sole familiar faces; replacing his hunting companion of the first trip, Charles Thompson, was Cuban friend Mayito Menocal, and *Look* photographer Earl Theisen helped round out the party.

That African trip in the winter of 1953–54, which would in fact be the author's last, would inspire parts of *The Garden of Eden* and something splintered and vaguely referred to as "The African Journal" in *Look* and in the 1972 editions of *Sports Illustrated.*[1] These segments would become Hemingway's second fictionalized memoir, *True at First Ligh*t (posthumously published in 1999). It would be published in a more complete form as 2005's *Under Kilimanjaro.*[2]

However, a curious thing happened in 1951. Anticipating his overseas excursion and related aesthetic experimentation by some three years, Hemingway published a short piece heavily invested in Africa and, arguably, all things racial. That piece, "The Good Lion," is a little-discussed and oft-forgotten fablesque short story that deserves attention, and one that fits our critical model well. First published alongside a complementary piece called "The Faithful Bull" in *Holiday* magazine in March of 1951, "The Good Lion" leaves behind the racially nebulous Dick Boultons of America and brings to the shores of Africa new figures of ambiguity with similar questions involving blood-mixing and identity construction. What remains consistent—a staple, really, from the earliest American and African tales—are the questions of racial construction (without ever expressly mentioning race) and the grotesques spurring those questions. To be sure, the incongruous figures of yesteryear people this new African landscape as well.

Part fairy tale, part fable, "The Good Lion" represents a pivot point of sorts for an author both seeking to retain some semblance of his former (clearly defined) self and set on again stretching the boundaries of identity. Like Harry in "Snows," Hemingway returned to the African continent a second time to "work the fat off his soul" (44). Life imitated art, as Hemingway, like Papa, had grown fat, comfortable, and complacent, a literary explorer now satisfied with retracing his own steps; by some accounts, he had become a grand example of self-parody. Michael Reynolds suggests in *Hemingway: The Final Years* that Hemingway was very much intent on recapturing from his celebrity some semblance of his former self, of simplifying his life. And simplification meant painting in shades of black and white (and gray).

However unlikely the comparison may seem, "The Good Lion," like "The Doctor and the Doctor's Wife" and "The Battler," gives us a narrator in flux, a storyteller caught between a desperate embrace of racial borderlands and the wonder inherent in their erasure. To that end, "The Short Happy Life of Francis Macomber" to some degree and, to a much greater degree, "The Snows of Kilimanjaro" reestablish those missing racial borders and bring us closer to the realities of white affirmation. Conversely, only with the African texts do we get a Hemingway narrative brimming with that oft-faded racially defined (self-) confidence. We saw this most especially in *Green Hills of Africa*—a narrative of racial fixity—two decades before, and, at least on the surface, we see it played out again, to some degree, in the memoir material engendered by the second trip.

To be sure, Hemingway toys with racial marginality in *True at First Light / Under Kilimanjaro;* however, he uses this flirtation ultimately to reinscribe and reconstruct a shattered whiteness. His early and late African excursions share this point of commonality. *Green Hills* was also very much about white affirmation. However, both in 1933 and in 1953, his redemption lay in his very deliberate construction of self, even as this self is consciously racialized and made expressly white. In his dissection of identity, then in its dissolution, and ultimately even in its reassembly in these final African texts, Hemingway debunks racial essentiality, hands us a grand complication, and smiles.

Further complicating matters though, in his last fictionalized memoir, Hemingway himself *becomes* what I call the new liminal figure, a figure that transgresses, blurs, or altogether erases the color line. *Green Hills* gives us no such character; even Kandisky, whose world has been inverted to some degree, is ultimately never anything but white, and Papa, in that text, underscores the color line and crafts himself as *ultra*-white. In his final African book, though, an older Hemingway, assuming the role of Papa, stands, temporarily, *between* the races; for a moment, perhaps reflecting his own ambivalence, he is, like Dick Boulton some twenty years earlier, racially ambiguous. And Hemingway explored this ambiguity already in 1951 as he looked toward Africa again and constructed his fable.

Following his own model established years earlier, Hemingway colors the entirety of "The Good Lion" with marked difference. The tale demonstrates

Hemingway's splintered racial conception going into his final safari of East Africa in 1953 (Trogdon). Years after the challenges of Dick Boulton and white authority's questioning in the Indian stories, a generation after his exploration of Bugs and the color line defining black-white relations in America, Hemingway's fascination with racial construction remained intact, unabated, possibly even stronger. Even his early African tales reconstructing and lionizing the white hunter attest to his fealty. And, as always, this fixation begins and ends with both an emphatic enunciation of difference and ultimately a fundamental questioning of the dialectic.

Hemingway splits the setting of "The Good Lion" between the heart of deepest Africa and southern Europe. The setting is at once foreign and familiar, and the narrative perpetually toys with lightness and darkness (both literal and metaphorical). In the midst of this darkness Hemingway strategically places the monstrous. In a sense, with its not-so-deeply imbedded racial truth lurking in the darkness among its beasts, this brief tale continues our author's engagement with the unspoken and with the Gothic begun decades earlier in his Indian stories. More importantly, it continues his lifelong dialogue about race.

Within the first couple of pages, the mini-fable shows us Hemingway's racial experimentation in its rawest, most direct, and least ornate form to date. Its language is like that of a fairy tale, and the story itself smacks of parable. Hemingway reaches for a morality-entrenched tradition as he spins his yarn of a flying lion who wishes for nothing more than to fit in:

> Once upon a time there was a lion that lived in Africa with all the other lions. The other lions were all bad lions and every day they ate zebras and wildebeests and every kind of antelope. Sometimes the bad lions ate people too. They ate Swahilis, Umbulus and Wandorobos and they especially liked to eat Hindu traders. All Hindu traders are very fat and delicious to a lion. But this lion, that we love because he was so good, had wings on his back. Because he had wings on his back the other lions all made fun of him. "Look at him with the wings on his back," they would say and then they would all roar with laughter. "Look at what he eats," they would say because the good lion only ate pasta and scampi because he was so good. (482)

This opening segment establishes the rubric of warring ideologies at work both here and throughout his oeuvre of race-centered texts. In it, Hemingway lays out, within the matrix of an African landscape, both his paradoxical conception of race and the uncertainties of boundaries.

The moral universe of "The Good Lion" is simple: goodness is the refined, the literate, the European (associated with foods, wines, and particular metropolitan locales); all else is evil. Hemingway strategically makes Africa the backdrop for a Manichaean showdown between apparent good and evil—or, in this case, good and bad. As readers, we identify with the story's protagonist, the good lion. We love the lion, the narrator tells us, because he is good. Thus early on, Hemingway seems to wage an essentialist's argument. By tale's end, though, we are a bit unsettled, uncertain as to just how good this good lion is, and just how implicitly different he is from those around him. We are also left to consider just how good, by implication, we are as champions for this good lion. And polarize is exactly what this text does.

The bad lions, the narrative insists, eat zebras and wildebeests as well as Swahilis and Umbulus, indiscriminately feasting upon beasts and man alike. They are consumers of the flesh; more particularly, they are man-eaters. We see in the chief lioness's taunting address to our protagonist that they are also accusatory, menacing, and petty: "'You are a worthless liar and the son of a griffon,' the wickedest of all the lionesses said. 'And now I think I shall kill you and eat you, wings and all'" (483). While she speaks, the other lions snarl, snap, and roar at one another and laugh at our protagonist: "They only stopped to growl with laughter or to roar with laughter at the good lion and to snarl at his wings. They were very bad and wicked lions indeed" (482). The bad lions do much to underscore difference (exteriority and physical markers do this initially), and, crafting a virtual catalog of unsavory qualities, Hemingway goes to great pains to have us read what is bad. These are his requisite grotesque figures facilitating our discovery of a greater (racial) truth.

The narrative tells us that like monstrous vampires, the bad lions feast upon their victims' blood. Aptly, the evil lioness has "blood caked on her whiskers" and "her breath . . . [is] very bad because she never brushed her teeth ever" (483). As such, these bad lions are the essence of savagery. They even roar in "African lion dialect," further distancing themselves from all things good (483). And this is what the good lion takes with him as he departs for Europe. When asked about his time in Africa by his father, the good lion responds very simply: "Very savage, father" (483).

Conversely, our (good) protagonist is meant to be the picture of gentility. Unlike his nefarious peers, our titular lion speaks "exemplary French" and converses "beautifully" in Spanish (483). Following in the footsteps of Dick Boulton, our protagonist is, significantly, this work's *master* of language. And, importantly, he hails not from the African bush but from Italy's shores. We can sense reverberations of George's praise of young Jimmy's father in "The Porter"—wherein

Jimmy's father was suggestively labeled a "noble Christian gentleman"—in the good lion's proud assertion that *his* father is "a noble lion." His father, he boasts, "lives in a city where he stands under the clock tower and looks down on a thousand pigeons, all of whom are his subjects." Speaking of his father's wealth, the good lion says, "There are more palaces in my father's city than in all of Africa and there are four great bronze horses that face him and they all have one foot in the air because they fear him. In my father's city men go on foot or in boats and no real horse would enter the city for fear of my father" (483). Emphasis here is on an Africa bereft of riches, glory, *culture*. Conversely, Venice has night lighting that counters the African continent's darkness.

While all the contrasting images and connotations make for a wonderful juxtaposition within our differential paradigm, the closing segment of the fable also proves problematic and most useful when we examine the story's deliberately racialized construction. Even as his paws tread European soil, the good lion, the narrative reminds us, is a changed lion, and his change is a sea change. In his marked descent to the ground and in his taking to all fours as he makes his way to Harry's Bar, the good lion is a fallen angel forced to terra firma. The narrator expressly tells us that "In Cipriani's nothing was changed. . . . But he was a little changed himself from being in Africa" (484). He is the site of change, and Africa the catalyst.

The good lion's bar order confirms his corruption: he orders not pasta and scampi but "Hindu trader sandwiches" (484). The narrative's insistence that Africa has changed him becomes a grand declaration that illuminates the lion's surprising transformation. It also suggests more than some superficial primitive embrace; it implies a fearful possession and supplanting of one's essence. It implies change on an ontological level. Civilization does not just *embrace* savage as spectacle; it *becomes* savage. Here Hemingway reconstructs the Conradian conception of the continent's "darkness" as an affective agent; the good lion's essential change recalls Kurtz's horror.

As with every other text examined here, though, simple polarity is only the first layer of Hemingway's greater interrogation. As the fable closes, the clear lines of demarcation between good and evil, civilized and savage, seem to fade away. At tale's end, our good lion is a special hybrid. The other lions label him a griffin; in truth, he is a lion with wings, whereas in Greek myth, the griffin is a lion with an eagle's head, forepart, and wings. As such, Hemingway infuses him with an implicit nobility. However, as a confused creature, the good lion is also an emphatic blending of blood. He is this text's "half-breed," and the narrative equivalent of Dick Boulton of the Indian stories (recall that Boulton was both an Indian and a white man). As the product of a union of civilized and savage, the good lion becomes the latest in a long line of indeterminate figures who defy label and category and therefore inspire fear.

Thus, when we add Hemingway's African fable to "The Short Happy Life of Francis Macomber" and "The Snows of Kilimanjaro," "The Good Lion" works wonderfully on one level as part of Hemingway mythological vision of Africa: these stories and his African book are an integral part of a Western romancing of the African continent. Initially, "The Good Lion" brings us closer to the space inhabited by Harry in "Snows," where we see Hemingway's truer loyalty to models of disparity. Harry's indictment of civilization and all its trappings, his embrace of Africa's apparent simplicity, and his sublimation of the African continent as a regenerative site are ultimately themselves savage romance and another example of white typology. So, like "Snows" and "The Short Happy Life," "The Good Lion" ultimately points to an essential (Anglo) truth that pervades and will not altogether wilt in the face of such questioning. Also, like its sister (African) stories, the fable, on the surface, does more to substantiate and perpetuate a Western Manichean model (of Western righteousness and Eastern fallibility and nefariousness) than to question or negate it. However, labeling these works as romantic requires the supposition that we stop with the surface reading.

On another level, Hemingway daringly pushes, tests, and redefines boundaries in "The Good Lion," well beyond what we get in the other aforementioned African stories; his experimental sensibility in the fable is reminiscent of what we saw in his earlier American stories. In it, he gives us—on the eve of his final African safari—closing images of a subverted order where associated notions of black and white, of East and West, conflate. Not at all a simple tale, "The Good Lion," from its inception, is a study in contradictions.

Thus, a narrative intention to simply build on the dark-light, good-evil, civil-savage polarities strongly underscores underlying assumptions and simultaneously (and most importantly) interrogates the paradigm's inherent veracity. Why do we label the good lion good? Just how good is our good protagonist? And why is this goodness not unassailable? So, while the racial spaces previously encountered do not exist in this fablesque world, "other"-induced anxieties do, and in them we can read Hemingway's racial ambivalence much in the same way we were able to do so in "Fathers and Sons." We can almost sense reverberations of young Nick Adams's uncharacteristically violent tirade against Eddie Gilby in the good lion's ordering of Hindu trader sandwiches. It would hardly be a stretch for us to imagine in that story an adult Nick suggesting to his son that his time spent with the Indians long ago *changed him.* However, Hemingway ultimately questions such reductive thinking. Perhaps his greater suggestion at fable's end is that these lions, good and bad, are actually one and the same, and that differences are ultimately imposed constructions. While "The Good Lion" apparently reverts in the end to the tried-and-true formula of an East-West *essentiality* (and a return of sorts for the [white] beleaguered self-seeker), it also seems to suggest—as does the narrative complexity of "Fathers and Sons"—the fallibility of absolutes and the folly inherent in the polarity of race. And for that we must commend Hemingway.

To be sure, our author begins and ends each of his African tales—and "The Good Lion" is no exception—in that narrative space of relative definitional certainty. But where he takes us in the interim should be our primary focus. Again, in his initial straying from the beaten path, and even as he brings us back to that comfort zone of absolutes, Hemingway dons the garb of explorer, ventures into relatively uncharted territory, and exposes the malleability of (racial) identity. Therein lies the exercise's greater import. The fable, written prior to the second safari, forecasts future aesthetic exploration and ultimately brings us back to the question that began this examination: *Is race essential?* In the end, Hemingway seemingly makes telling concessions to the traditionalist approach in suggesting that the "primitive" African continent, in all its ignobility, has infected our protagonist: "Africa had changed him" (484). But had it really? Or did it just expose him for what he truly was? "The Good Lion" reveals the same ambivalence and complexity we encounter in *True at First Light / Under Kilimanjaro,* the African book that would consume his imagination for the remaining years of his life.

While the importance of this ambivalence, this gray space, cannot be overstated, ultimately, the established racial totem with whiteness at its pinnacle remains intact. And if maintaining the racial hegemony is at least part of Hemingway's aesthetic agenda in his last African book—even as he interrogates it—then the fictional memoir is something both expressly liberal and notably conservative. It is in fact the perfect amalgam of all things experimental and constructive. Hemingway's open and deliberate recognition of race as a transmutable entity, his transgression of the color line, and his exploitation of this secret knowledge are what push this second safari narrative beyond the bounds of anything found in *Green Hills,* written two decades before.

Geographic (and psychic) distance and age (and wisdom?) allowed Hemingway's imagination to roam freely across the color line this second time around. The author, for a fleeting moment, *becomes* the Native. In *True at First Light / Under Kilimanjaro,* Hemingway inverts his interrogative model somewhat, working hard to initially *reduce* and *eliminate* disparity, to build a narrative of *equality,* not inequity. These moments show us an artist deconstructing, if not altogether erasing, the color line and racial typology. However, Hemingway's liberal moments are fleeting and his reversion to colonial discourse works to subvert any new world order he creates.

Just as quickly as he tears down barriers, he warily reconstructs them; just as quickly as he erases the color line, he redraws it. In the end, his Africa remains an imaginative space within which white masculine agency reigns supreme, and even in light of East Africa's imminent political and social change, Hemingway assures his reader (and himself) that ultimate authority rests in white hands. Contrary to what he suggests in several of the tales set in America early on in his career, white authority in this crafted African space is never in any real jeopardy. This Hemingway landscape, significantly, has no Bugs or Dick Boulton lurking in the shadows to expose white fallibility.

Casting himself as both protagonist and antagonist, Hemingway deftly ensures whiteness's preservation. Africa then, at least in part, becomes the tabula rasa upon which Hemingway rewrites the world according to white literary imagination. In Africa, he can erase and redraw the color line with the confidence that (white) order will prevail. To that end, Hemingway's African reality is more than Carlos Baker's conscious, *effects-driven* restructuring of *history,* his architectonics.[3] I would amend Baker's aesthetic definition and label this *imagination.*

In Africa, imagination would allow Hemingway to roam freely across the color line and back; moreover, imagination would allow him briefly to inhabit blackness and then to reconstitute his own white body. In its final iteration, Hemingway's fictional memoir works hard to initially reduce and eliminate disparity; Papa works hard to build a narrative of sameness between the Natives and himself. This is Hemingway employing what socio-linguist Norman Fairclough calls "false egalitarianism."[4] "False" may be too strong an indictment here, as these momentary lapses show us a Hemingway arguably seeking a true parity, momentarily delving into Wakamba skin. But Hemingway's reversion to colonial discourse undercuts his new world order, and it repairs the totemic tapestry unraveling an ocean away in America. In the end, like Francis Macomber, Hemingway's white narrator redeems himself.

True at First Light's entire opening sequence, with Hemingway engaged in personal reflection, reveals his narrative strategy. This sequence encapsulates in two paragraphs what transpires over the following several hundred pages of the published manuscript. The grand conclusion? Change was proving to be a curious animal:

> Things were not too simple in this safari because things had changed very much in East Africa. The white hunter had been a close friend of mine for many years. I respected him as I had never respected my father and he trusted me, which was more than I deserved. It was, however, something to try to merit. He had taught me by putting me on my own and correcting me when I made mistakes. When I made a mistake he would explain it. Then if I did not make the same mistake again he would explain a little more. But he was nomadic and he was finally leaving us because it was necessary for him to be at his farm, which is what they called a twenty-thousand-acre cattle ranch in Kenya. He was a very complicated man compounded of absolute courage, all the good human weaknesses and a strangely subtle and very critical understanding of people. (13)

Things had indeed changed very much since the last time Hemingway stalked lion and sat camp-side exchanging stories with Philip Percival, his lead hunter, friend, and mentor. Back then, Percival epitomized the great white professional hunter. He had stalked the jungles with a recently retired Theodore Roosevelt, and he helped popularize the safari among the West's wealthier set. By the 1950s, though, poaching was a new plague, conservation movements were afoot, and the professional white hunter was a dying breed (Steinhart).[5] Cameras slowly replaced guns as the accepted civilized means of subduing Africa's wilderness. Our author's own implied picture-taking mission the second time around attests to this. Moreover, Hemingway's final safari comes during a time of great upheaval as the race for Africa, with its attendant claim-making by Western nations, became the race to save a crumbling empire. Change was indeed a curious animal.

Under Kilimanjaro deliberately frames the narrative with references to this change in the form of the Mau Mau revolutionary movement. Robert W. Lewis and Robert E. Fleming, the text's editors, give us repeated allusions to the revolution-minded Mau Mau in the work's opening and concluding segments. Threats loom large and suspicions run high as the narrative opens. "'No. They will not do that,' the old man said. 'They would not do anything so stupid. These are the Wakamba Mau Mau'" (1). And the piece closes with Hemingway sharing some foreboding news from Loitokitok regarding an impending "operation." In between, the narrative gives us moments of waiting. Beginning as small pockets of isolated violence sparked by the Kikuyu in the late 1940s, Mau Mau activity became synonymous with anti-colonial and anti-British insurgency all across Kenya. Like disease, the rumblings of revolution infected and spread throughout the camps of the Wakamba and Masai. Rumors spread as the attendant fears increased among imperial loyalists.[6]

A decade after Hemingway's final African trip, lands formerly stalked and surveyed as safari country slipped out of German and British hands. For example, Tanganyika gained political independence in 1961, and Mozambique began a long and arduous road toward freedom three years later. France would lose control of its holdings in Algeria during these years as well. And Kenya, home to Hemingway's much-beloved Rift Valley and to much of his narrative, would declare its independence from Great Britain in 1963 after seven decades of colonial rule. Empire's roots were deep, its history long.

Commercial ventures became more overtly political at the turn of the century as the East Indian Company ceded control to the British government. And, of course, the succession was not without incident; in the nineteenth century's waning years, the clamor for rebellion accompanied the transition as Swahili Mazrui and Mijikenda warred in cities like Mombasa. A booming railroad project and the marketing of newly acquired lands defined the new geopolitical landscape and further added to colonial strife in the century's first decade (see Gellar, Keller, and Gordon). And the conflict in those early years would reverberate decades later, most fully realized among the Mau Mau and in the ever-attendant fear of rebellion.

As for Hemingway's reference to the white hunter, its purpose is multifaceted. In it, we get Hemingway's prescription for his "coded" heroic loner figure: he is observant, quietly skilled, and self-reliant. Hemingway paints Philip Percival as complicated, but he *expressly,* repeatedly, and simply labels him "the white hunter." Whiteness as an adjective necessarily conjures an understood and subservient phantom black presence in the text too. We saw in chapters 3 and 4 how Hemingway used this connotative tactic to great effect years earlier in "The Light of the World" and again in "The Porter." The "white" tag also quite significantly places Hemingway *outside* the colonial circle, which creates the semblance of space between narrator and empire. Hemingway effectively opens the work by momentarily linking himself with the nonwhite.

But Hemingway's work offers a grand complication. While he stands outside empire in one instance, he stands within it the next. The white hunter, Hemingway assures us, deserves our respect and trust. As Edward I. Steinhart suggests, "Whiteness would be worn as a badge of honor, distinguishing sporting gentlemen from the lesser breeds outside the law and custom of the hunt" (132). The white hunter's integrity was legendary, and his authority inherently paternal. And even as Hemingway, in *Under Kilimanjaro,* consciously separates himself from and speaks of "protected royalty" and "spoiled rich American children," "great and serious collectors of dead animals," and, ironically much like himself, the "many people who had hoped to come to East Africa during most of their lives and who devoted themselves diligently to killing the necessary beasts that represented, in big-game hunting, so many academic degrees" (20), he relates in rich detail, and with great approval, the love and devotion of Keiti (Percival's longtime safari headman) to his master. Witnessing the ravages of a world war and the machinations of revolution, and tending to his master's ailments in between, the old Kamba devotee loved and served "a very great white hunter for forty-three years" (1). In such an account, Hemingway demonstrates his own investment in the ideology underlying this relationship.

Like the plantation's master in America's Old South, Percival necessarily becomes a surrogate father to Keiti; he becomes "Pop." Pop in turn passes the baton to Papa. And Hemingway, as Papa, soon enough becomes that same great white hunter and mentor trusted, respected, and revered by the next generation. With lessons to give to a mature but still-learning Hemingway, this white hunter takes on the role of teacher as well, and this is a role Hemingway himself assumes with great relish as he interacts with others, most especially his wives and his hunting crew's Native "boys."

Immediately following his homage to the white hunter, Hemingway succinctly describes an underlying tension driving the entire narrative: "There are people who love command and in their eagerness to assume it they are impatient at the formalities of taking over from someone else. I love command since it is the ideal welding of freedom and slavery" (*Under Kilimanjaro* 4, *True at First Light* 14). In *Playing in the Dark: Whiteness and the Literary Imagination,* Toni Morrison points to such binary oppositions, subterfuge and sublimation, and projection as American romance's trademarks.[7] Power and authority are themes that reverberate throughout the American canon, as are freedom and newness. Hemingway's texts certainly benefit from such a critical reading. His rather candid admission regarding the nature of command underscores Morrison's assertions that twentieth-century documentarians and artists alike were driven to explore and define freedom's boundaries through the tropes of bondage and the dark body. Interestingly, Hemingway draws as his central thematic concerns here freedom and slavery, binaries necessarily tethered to race. In so doing, he too expresses his nation's latent racial anxieties. And as an interstitial figure in his own work, Hemingway as character assumes the roles of both master and servant as he explores these anxieties.

But Hemingway straddles the line and dons multiple costumes only for a moment. While his African narrative opens on a note of uncertainty, and even as he verbalizes his apparent cultural maturity, he also begins with a reversion to tried-and-true racial division. Standing in white greatness's shadows are the text's darker figures. In speaking of Pop's almost intuitive racial divisiveness, Hemingway says: "It was always they. They were the people, the watu. Once they had been the boys. They still were to Pop. . . . Twenty years ago I had called them boys too and neither they nor I had any thought that I had no right to" (*True at First Light* 16). While this enlightened Hemingway does make an effort to learn his attendants' names, the fact remains that those closest to him are always kept at a personal distance.

Arap Meina, for example, is our author's latest fool, who is given to histrionics, an ardent European supporter, and entrenched in the mythos of whitewashed Africa. Purveyor of gossip, Meina is the self-proclaimed camp "Informer" and, Hemingway tells us, he is one of Papa's "closest friends" (*True at First Light* 30). We quickly see, though, that he is nothing more than a type. In truth, the Informer is a lowly game scout; this, notes Patrick Hemingway in his commentary to *True at First Light,* was "the lowest ranked game law enforcement officer in Kenya. There were no white game scouts" (315). Meina's predictable histrionics and pork-pie hat do nothing to push him beyond caricature. They certainly do little to bring him any closer to the reader. Always there is distance.

Hemingway employs his divisive strategies in private quarters as well. Papa's first morning sans Mary—our narrator tells us she is shopping for Christmas gifts and in Nairobi after battling illness—is emblematic of this ordering. The exchange never rises above one between master and servant:

> When Mwindi brought the tea in the morning, I was up and dressed sitting by the ashes of the fire with two sweaters and a wool jacket on. . . .
>
> "Want fire?" Mwindi asked.
>
> "Small fire for one man." (235)

The remainder of the dialogue is a catalog of requests regarding clothing selection and meal preparation. Mwindi's dedication is arguably unrivaled. Papa was more than familiar with this kind of fealty, taking the trusted "uncle" figure of America and transplanting him to Africa. Although they share an intimate space, the two men never cross the color line separating master from servant.

Hemingway's tenure as master begins and ends with the hunt, and his prowess with the rifle undergirds the authority inherent in his white skin. Our narrator gives us one of our first instances of narrator acting as mythmaker as he, Mary, and the crew stalk a lion. The African natives call Hemingway "mchawi," ("witch") for his hunting prowess, reminiscent of Clarence Hemingway's nickname of "Eagle Eye" among northern Michigan's Indians. Papa uses the hunt to expand the breadth of the white hunter's celebrity and legend, demonstrating his skills for onlooker and reader alike.

Time and again Hemingway becomes the (white) code hero of his own narrative, gallantly donning the garb of camp protector. When threatened by a roving band of baboons, for example, the community seeks out the white man's protection. Not one to disappoint, Hemingway summarily dispatches the primate troop. In the process, our white hunter garners the gratitude of the mother of his Kamba bride-to-be, Debba, as well as the admiration of the Informer. However, the greatest admiration of this new incarnation of code hero comes from Debba herself, who conspicuously reifies the fantastic (and white fantasy) as she insists on holding our hero's rifle after his show.[8]

The gallantry Hemingway displays in this affair works wonderfully as a precursor to the slaying of bigger beasts in the days and weeks following. Soon after, neighboring farmers being terrorized by a rogue leopard summon Hemingway for assistance. While he later conveys a marked reticence to embrace his celebrity—his face soon glosses the cover of *Look* magazine—his eventual concession and his related running commentary throughout prove this lament specious.[9] Two shots severely wound the cat, and anticipating a third to finish him, Hemingway tells us, "I knew the drill now having learned it from Pop but every wounded leopard in thick bush is a new wounded leopard. No two will ever act the same except that they will always come and they will come for keeps" (*True at First Light* 238). The narrative's instructional impulse smacks of safari-book convention, and we can almost sense reverberations of Theodore Roosevelt's *African Game Trails* throughout: "The dangerous game of Africa are the lion, the buffalo, elephant, rhinoceros, and leopard. The hunter who follows any of these animals always does so at a certain risk to life or limb; a risk which it is his business to minimize by coolness, caution, good judgment, and straight shooting. The leopard is in point of pluck and ferocity more than the equal of the other four; but his small size always renders it likely that he will merely maul, and not kill, a man" (58). Like his boyhood hero, Hemingway sports the vestments of the experienced sage and he slays the spotted beast with a deathblow both precise and unparalleled. Of such stuff legends are made.[10]

Great white hunter is only the first of Hemingway's several assumed roles as he actively crafts a white mythos. Throughout much of the narrative, we also see multiple appearances by Hemingway as teacher. If skill necessarily undergirds the white hunter's authority, then knowledge underscores the teacher's. Hemingway conveys *special* knowledge in each recounted conversation, memory, and tangential aside, and an unbalanced economy of knowledge marks his relationships with village folk as he rations and doles out his expertise at will. A mission-schooled Native man trained in many languages seeks out knowledge from our white master hunter: "I could tutor you to speak proper Swahili and you could teach me hunting and the language of animals" (*True at First Light* 182). Offering a rather expansive curriculum, Hemingway even offers boxing lessons to neighboring Natives as well.

When not slaying beasts or teaching, Hemingway also dons the physician's mantle, playing doctor to the surrounding village. Always there is the chasm separating white from black, knowledgeable from ignorant, powerful from powerless. While Hemingway makes no claims to specific medical knowledge, Native ignorance and deficiency afford him much privilege and authority.[11] This leap therefore seems only natural.[12]

Early on, we see Papa tending to a young Masai villager's fight wounds. Hemingway's racial pejorative ("boy") underscores his status as white paternal figure and as *the* possessor of unquestioned expertise: "The medical chest had been brought from the dining tent and I dressed the boy's wounds. . . . I cleaned them out, poured peroxide into them for the magic bubbling effect and to kill any grubs, cleaned them again, especially the neck wound, painted the edges with Mercurochrome, which gave a much admired and serious color effect, and then sifted them full of sulfa and put a gauze dressing and plaster across each wound" (*True at First Light* 29). Ever eager to please his awe-struck (black) audience, Papa infuses his doctoring with magic and showmanship.

Before his safari days came to an end, Hemingway would tend to both the Informer and Mary. Papa responds to the Informer's complaints with a prescription of rest and aspirin and the promise of better health. As the keeper of healing agents, he is also the possessor of power: "I'll give you medicine" (*True at First Light* 103). As for Mary, the Natives see her illness as a curse for slaying her lion. Hemingway carefully juxtaposes Native beliefs with his own more professional conclusion (his diagnosis: malaria), craftily engaging this divide with talk of secrets and power: "I was delighted with how the Terramycin had acted and that she had no bad reactions from it and told Mwindi, touching the wood of my gun butt, that I had cured Miss Mary with a powerful and secret dawa but that I was sending her into Nairobi tomorrow in the ndege in order that a European doctor might confirm my cure" (*True at First Light* 222). Once again, Papa deliberately juxtaposes superstition and logic, savagery and civilization, East and West, and he does so to great effect. Always, he gives us the divide; always he is the possessor of power.

That power translates most effectively in his donning of badge and judge's robe. We learn early on that Hemingway wields a mighty gavel for Kenya's Game Department, which has bestowed upon him the title of honorary game warden. This title serves to underscore the rights and privileges that his white skin already affords him. As Patrick Hemingway notes in his "Cast of Characters" at the end of *True at First Light,* there were no black game rangers. There were certainly no black game wardens. Hemingway's persistent implied egalitarian push and proclamation ("We are all Kamba," he seems to say) only goes so far.

Papa's open pursuit of Debba, the woman he would soon call his second wife, demonstrates the expanse of white power in a land where Native custom formerly ruled. The Informer, Arap Meina, acts as translator and go-between for Hemingway in his romance.[13] We learn very early on of Debba's wish to marry her American admirer, a topic of great significance here.[14] Talk of dowry (or its absence) and of tribal customs prompts Hemingway to suppress any and all desire and defer to legal ordinance, tribal or otherwise. He is, he tells us, subject to the law first. This makes his exchange with Arap Meina worthy of closer examination:

> "I cannot break the law if we are here to enforce the law."
>
> "Brother, you do not understand. There is no law. This Shamba is here illegally. It is not in Kamba country. For thirty-five years it has been ordered removed and it has never happened. There is not even customary law. There are only variations."
>
> "Go on," I said.
>
> "Thank you, brother. Let me tell you that for the people of this Shamba you and Bwana Game are the law." (*True at First Light* 37)

Hemingway gives us only a slight deference ("I cannot break the law") as he solidifies two inseparable tropes—whiteness and the law—each bolstering the other and working toward the same end: underscoring white authority. "You and Bwana Game are the law," Arap Meina reminds Papa (and us) at the exchange's conclusion.[15]

In this African space, whiteness is more than mere legal representative; whiteness *is* law. The implicit associations are of judge, jury, and executioner. The Informer suggests with much earnestness to Papa the strength and value inherent in this imperative to stay within the parameters of this law, and here Papa's dictates are law. When others momentarily question his own loyalty,

Meina attempts to prove himself one of empire's most devoted servants. In response to the Mau Mau insurgency's threat brewing in neighboring camps, Meina insists, "I truly love and believe in the Bwanas. . . . Thinking of these great dead Bwanas fills me with the resolution to lead a better and finer life" (*True at First Light* 38).[16] Reinforcing the Anglo-as-father trope, Meina insists on Hemingway's metaphorical paternal role. We can almost hear echoes of Peroxide's worshipful praise of Ketchel in "The Light of the World" in the Informer's laudatory claims; he all but deifies whiteness as he insists that Papa *is* the law. Even the local police defer to our hero (they also call him "Bwana") and enlist his services. Like a god, Bwana is, apparently, all things to all people; such is the power of whiteness.

Later, in what ostensibly is a moment of comic relief meant to offset the lion hunt's dramatic tension, the Informer once again becomes Bwana's greatest champion and most faithful devotee—at his own expense, of course. Conscious of this fact, Hemingway relates to him a dream he's had (about the Informer) in which he aptly exercises a kind of divine right:

> "Brother, what is this of the dream that I am hanged?"
>
> "It is a dream that I had but I should not tell it to you before I have eaten breakfast."
>
> "But others have heard it before."
>
> "It is better that you do not hear it. It was not an official dream."
>
> "I could not bear to be hanged," the Informer said.
>
> "I will never hang you." (*True at First Light* 104)

In his playful assertion that "I will never hang you," Bwana is the ultimate arbiter. And in his ready assurance, we can read choice's inherent power, wrapped like a plum in pudding. While the white man *could* have his black compatriot hanged (at a time when insurrectional fears ran rampant), he chooses not to. Through the choice itself, Hemingway unabashedly maintains that imaginary line between white and black and guards the space between them.

This same authority that either denies or spares life defines the scope and depth of black-white relationships in this final African narrative as well. For much of it, white maintenance of the color line is a matter of course. We saw this in Papa's interaction with his staff, and his reification of white grandeur—as hunter, teacher, healer—does much to underscore the racial divide. Papa's imperative becomes that of everyone else. Everywhere there are markers of propriety and racial protocol. Even the most innocent of interactions—for example, Charo's admiration of Mary—are, arguably, about racial politics. For example, after she downs a wildebeest with Charo, Mary is quite affectionate in her postmortem celebration; however, she carefully observes the color line where socially mandated: "I'd like to kiss Charo," she tells us, "but I know I shouldn't" (134). Racial protocol and social mores suggest that she refrain. Mary's reaction to her husband's playful pursuit of Debba is equally revealing: "You don't love anybody else, do you? White I mean?" (99). Her choice of words is particularly important. Papa's narrative gives us a woman whose concerns are arguably less about marital fidelity and more about racial taboo.

Hemingway demonstrates to us that the fear of miscegenation (I use the term loosely to suggest an intimate racial commingling) extends well beyond his marital circle. G.C., Hemingway's friend, campsite neighbor, and fellow Bwana, is most adamant in his refusal to cross racial lines. Of G.C.'s aversion to racial mixing Hemingway says: "Because he had a career as well as because he had been brought up *properly* he could have nothing to do with African women. He did not think they were beautiful either nor attractive" (*True at First Light* 140). Still, the greater significance lies in whiteness's latent power. Hemingway makes clear that while his friend refuses to act as a matter of personal taste, he could, if his tastes dictated as much; G.C.'s white skin, his very whiteness, affords him both choice and opportunity.

And it's an opportunity Hemingway himself relishes. Where G.C. dares not go, Hemingway eagerly and boldly does. While he actively builds barriers throughout the narrative—and those barriers do abound—Hemingway also momentarily but repeatedly puts aside difference, erases the color line, and communes with the country. Things *had* changed since his first foray into those green hills years earlier. While we saw the same white aggrandizement and reification some twenty years earlier, we did not see the same willingness to jettison the very markers he works so hard to craft, and to plunge headfirst across the color line, even if only momentarily. This safari, unlike the first, has Papa tearing away a brick for each several laid, and while the associated accumulation may be—relatively speaking—small, the narrative builds nicely to several grand, racially transgressive moments.

Seen in this light then, Hemingway's apparent egalitarian moments, though few and fleeting, are potentially meaningful. Aptly, where G.C. and others fear to go, Hemingway, liberated by his wild surroundings, treads mightily, and gleefully. Mary sees as much, suggesting that in her husband's newly crafted mythology, "neither Papa nor I are white. . . . We tolerate the whites and wish to live in harmony with them as I understand it. But on our own terms" (*True at First Light* 79). With deliberate language, Hemingway effectively washes Western culture free of its racial markers to establish a colorless culture rooted in an African essentiality.[17] Whether sucking on a piece of shattered leopard bone or hunting by moonlight with only his moccasins and a spear, Hemingway deliberately utilizes the African space to cross racial lines. But his full-on savage holiday experiences are more than a series of fetishized moments (see Eby). Mary corroborates her husband's apparent earnestness, suggesting in her memoir that Papa expresses a wish to become "blood brothers" (450) with his Wakamba staff. Hemingway does not just go Native, then; he, for a fleeting moment, *becomes* Native. These Native moments in turn validate years of aesthetic experimentation and decades-old ideas regarding (racial) identity's tenuous nature. In *True at First Light / Under Kilimanjaro,* Hemingway momentarily merges black and white and he himself *becomes* the liminal figure we have seen many times through the years.

We experience these gray moments with Hemingway most vividly as he stalks the brush with his Wakamba brethren. As he and Ngui engage in the infamous leopard hunt, Hemingway again enters the skin of the African: "We were both very serious now and there was no White Man to speak softly and knowingly from his great knowledge, nor any White Man to give violent orders astonished at the stupidity of his 'boys' and cursing them on like reluctant hounds" (*True at First Light* 239). With the leopard's slaying, Hemingway suggests, "He was a good leopard and we had hunted him well and cheerfully and like brothers with no White Hunters nor Game Rangers and no Game Scouts and he was a Kamba leopard condemned for useless killing on an illegal Kamba Shamba and we were all Wakamba and all thirsty" (*True at First Light* 241). Within this new cosmos, Papa insists that a hunting brotherhood replaces all authoritative privilege, along with labels like ranger, scout, and white hunter. Of course, an irony laces this and other similar accounts: Hemingway tinges most, if not all, of his hunting recollections with the soft-spoken yet knowing white-man knowledge he openly mocks. But, for the moment at least, Papa enters that third space and wishes (us) temporarily to forget his whiteness.

Here in this third space—where he is neither wholly white nor wholly black, but both—Hemingway emphasizes whiteness's absence and celebrates all things Wakamba. Wakamba becomes for Papa a free-roaming space for his imagination. In the aforementioned sequence, a shared primordial passion works as a leveling device. But whiteness's marked absence works to further emphasize its latent presence. Within the third space, whiteness also temporarily becomes a menacing phantom presence, something obtrusive Hemingway must work to erase—and work he does as he openly criticizes a white totemic ideology and embraces Wakamba ontology.

Later, Hemingway bolsters this communal conception, considering the plight of his Wakamba kitchen servant, Msembi, in the process:

> At this time I called Msembi, the good rough boy who served as mess steward and was a hunting, not a crop-raising Kamba but was not a skilled hunter and was reduced, since the war, to servant status. We were all servants since I served the government, through the Game Department, and I also served Miss Mary and a magazine named *Look*. . . . But neither Msembi nor I minded serving in the least and neither of us had served our God nor our King too well to be stuffy about it. (*True at First Light* 264)

Though colored by that unflappable Hemingway humor, this segment strives to bring two divided worlds together. Working in the interstitial shadows, Hemingway embraces his African brother and this newly created third space and raises a communal flag of shared service and duty. But all the while, an irony persists and insists that the transgressor has in fact not ventured too far from home. This irony also suggests a man wrestling with his own ambivalence about race as only an artist can.

Mary's return from Nairobi—where she convalesces after an illness and shops for gifts—marks Hemingway's narrative recrossing of the color line and his final return to whiteness. After subsuming himself in his new brotherhood, Hemingway returns to himself as inconspicuously and as easily as he left, with Mary acting as the narrative trigger: "She was slim and shiny in her khakis and hard inside them and she smelled very good and her hair was silver gold, cropped close, and I rejoined the white or European race as easily as a mercenary of Henry IV saying Paris was worth a mass" (*True at First Light* 290). Their shared embrace is a celebration of the return of both flaxen-haired figures: Bwana and Memsahib.

And Mary's homecoming is a deity's, complementing her husband's own brand of exaggerated self-aggrandizement (she is always "shining"). Early on, Willie, the camp's pilot and the couple's friend, overtly enunciates what the later recurring images only imply. This strategy proves most effective in crafting a powerful picture. Commenting on Mary's role in Hemingway's new "religion," Willie posits: "You must be something along the lines of the White Goddess" (*True at First Light* 79). While Mary insists that her husband has renounced racial ties as a part of this new creation, racial markers litter the narrative scene.

With hair that's both silver and gold, and standing before us in her crisp, clean khakis, Mary is absolute radiance. Appropriately, Memsahib shines again. She becomes the European princess of her husband's earlier allusions. Most importantly, though, Mary's return, the couple's embrace, and Hemingway's visceral response all mark the temporal Wakamba's formal return to the white race. In each instance, reminiscent of his creations in "The Light of the World," Hemingway extols the glow and radiance of whiteness (without the push toward absurdity). Notably, this racial return is effortless, as "eas[y] as a mercenary of Henry IV saying Paris was worth a mass." It demonstrates for the final time the fluidity of racial conception and the power inherent in white privilege.

Even as he stands before us—head shaven, face painted, extolling an egalitarian sensibility—Hemingway is, through the narrative's entirety, the privileged Occidental tourist. While he speaks apologetically of Pop's use of racist pejoratives, or later of G.C.'s blatant bigotry, and as he speaks admiringly of changes wrought by a "modern" African people, Papa himself owns one four-letter word throughout: "boys." And whether he is openly enjoying playing master to a staff of many or reading Western literature by firelight and hunting big game by day with a contingent of specialists bought with Western money, his ties to (white) privilege cannot be undone.[18] Most importantly, Hemingway reserves the right to do such things, while retaining all other rights afforded the white in Africa.

With Mwindi to draw his bath for him and to dress him ("Dress me as you wish, . . . but put the boots on very easy" [*True at First Light* 244]) and with Msembi and Nguili to prepare his meals ("We're having Tommy chops, mashed potatoes and a salad. And it will be here right away," "He called to Nguili to bring drinks and I read the operation orders" [*True at First Light* 78]), Hemingway bears all the markers of transplanted royalty. Each such instance undercuts the egalitarian rhetoric, exposes whiteness in all its (vain) glory, and reconstitutes a dissolving social order. Such becomes the ultimate function and purpose of the African space for our artist in residence: to test boundaries, but also to reify a new world order predicated on old world ideas. Africa provided a formative space within which Hemingway could work out racial anxieties and still take comfort in the security of his own (white) skin.

However, the greater import here lies in what undergirds the entire exercise: Hemingway's recognition of both the color line's inherent fragility and its potential power. In Africa, white supplants black; in Hemingway's Africa, white *becomes* black. Clearly, for Papa, all things are possible in Africa. For both the young dreamer and the old man, Africa was a blank slate upon which new stories could be written, old ideas and theories could be tested, and myths could be created and perpetuated. What would allow for this, in each and every instance, was a keen understanding of identity's constructive nature.

Even as he made his way home from Africa for the final time, with revolution's rumblings in his ear, Hemingway was fully aware that change is inevitable, that change is perpetual, and that perhaps the last bastion of unquestioned white privilege lies within the confines of paragraph, page, and the literary imagination. Most importantly, though, Hemingway's final African works show us an artist self-aware, a man recognizing identity's constructed nature and the word's potency. And it is within the confines of paragraph and page that Hemingway, as a young artist dreaming of Africa and as an old man writing about it, pushed the boundaries of race, identity, and self-understanding.

EPILOGUE

Contextualizing Hemingway's Grand Complication

Hemingway once said that a writer's job is not to *say* what is on his mind but to write it (Nobel Prize in Literature Banquet Speech 1954). His oeuvre stands as a clear testament to his investment in this credo and as a fantastic example of what was on his mind for much of his literary career: masculinity, nationality, and race. But in looking at past and present criticism, and the dearth of related commentary, one would never know the extent of this man's entanglement with the issue of race. To be fair, by and large, Hemingway's classic novels—those novels read by students and casual readers alike—are not novels about race. For example, *A Farewell to Arms* is not, on its face, a book about race. In fact, in that novel and in his other most prominent titles, Hemingway's eyes and mind seem focused elsewhere. I would argue, however, that even there in those prominent spaces where our author seems least connected to what Du Bois anticipated would be the then-new century's principle hounding issue, race is very present; one need only look. I spent the better part of my examination forging connections among many works with express racial moments—including several that have received scant attention, and a couple that have been altogether overlooked—to demonstrate Hemingway's lifelong racial cognizance. Perhaps, then, that warrants a reassessment of the works we know, or think we know, so well, and perhaps when *these* texts are subjected to such scrutiny, conversation will follow. In what directions might our questions carry us if we interrogated such texts for their racial content (or for its apparent absence)? A brief revisit might show us.

Two of his most classic works, *A Farewell to Arms* and *The Sun Also Rises,* would certainly benefit from such a reading. *A Farewell to Arms*'s Frederic Henry is a man very much bent on crafting meaning for himself. His world is shaped by the Great War, by his love affair with Catherine Barkley, and by a faith that's tested in the midst of everything. *A Farewell to Arms* is a novel about love, about war, about death, and about faith, or its apparent absence. Given the current parameters and criteria engaged in assessing the novel, most readers would assuredly, comfortably even, assert that this is *not* a novel about race. However, given the parameters set forth by this examination, we could easily make this a novel about race. And the leap is an easy one to make. We need only look to the story's protagonist. Henry is young, he is American; he is also clearly white. Yet never in the text are we told this. This is a text operating on reader assumptions. Moreover, Hemingway need not offer an express homage to whiteness here for us to appreciate his (and Frederic's) investment in the racial medium.

A critical point in the narrative demonstrates this well. As Frederic's love for Catherine becomes most apparent to her, to the reader, and most importantly to Frederic himself, Catherine exposes her lover's growing dependency and insecurity; as such, she mocks his apparent jealousy of all things that consume her time and keep her from him. In doing so, she compares him to the Moor Othello in Shakespeare's play of the same name, and he clearly resents the comparison, as his retort evinces; a solitary line carries with it all the racial angst of a generation. While the general and Frederic may share common geographic space (Italy) and a uniform, "Othello," Frederic declares, "was a nigger" (257). Never again is blackness mentioned in the text, but to the wary eye, the potential effect is great. Although it is but a single line in over three hundred pages of text, its implications are several and its weight is grand, given our knowledge of Hemingway's lifelong racial investment. Like Jack Johnson in "The Porter" or in "The Light of the World," Othello's function here is that of phantom; like Iago's whispered counsel in Shakespeare's play, mention of the Moor here is a planted seed meant to grow in the reader's mind and serve as an apt dialogic reminder of a binary world in flux. It is a world, Hemingway reminds us, that falls apart at the seams, lest we consciously forge meaning for ourselves. And like Nick Adams before him, Frederic Henry, in part, relies upon a racialized world reading to construct that meaning for himself.

The mere mention of the Moor is enough to trigger the racial dialectic and help craft that meaning (for Frederic and contemporary readers alike). Fanon's postcolonial equation immediately comes to mind as black and white are wedged apart through binary association. Othello was "niggerly": he was jealous and led by his passions, he was the barbaric Turk, he was black. With Frederic's reminder to Catherine (and the reader) that "Othello was a nigger," Othello quickly becomes the "other." Had Hemingway stymied his usual impulse toward economy of language, he would have completed Frederic's assertion as follows: "Othello was a nigger; I am not." The connotative potency cannot be overstated. Frederic, who is white, becomes all things opposite the Moor. He is, after all, the tale's code hero: a man stirred not by unbridled passion but by self-conviction, a man led ultimately only by himself. He is the epitome of grace under pressure, and he is white. Perhaps the reference is meant to aid Frederic—an extension of Hemingway and the reader—a man unattached to family, country, God, and to remind him of who (or what) he is, to help him retain his moorings in a world quickly dissipating before his eyes.

Jake Barnes arguably suffers from this same extreme dispossession in *The Sun Also Rises,* another classic and, some would argue, another novel seemingly not about race (examinations that do interrogate "otherness" typically stop with Cohn and the Jewish question) whose treatment of race, more specifically blackness, also deserves another glance, given what we know of Hemingway's preoccupation with the color line in the years preceding *Sun*'s publication. For example, he had already published "The Doctor and the Doctor's Wife" and "The Battler" as a part of *In Our Time.* Blackness in particular intrigued him; immersing himself, ever so slightly, in its mystique, he crafted the character of Bugs, trying to convey, through a reliance on physicality and connotation, a black sensibility. He would try to replicate this with dialect in the years ahead in stories and in *The Sun Also Rises.* We know from Michael Reynolds's catalog of Hemingway readings that not only did Hemingway possess a copy of Edward Adams's *Nigger to Nigger,* but that he read it. Further, a letter in which he thanks his longtime editor, Max Perkins, for sending it to him and notes that he "enjoyed it greatly" suggests that the work had an impact (Reynolds, *Hemingway's Reading*). While its publication comes too late (1928) for it to have been an inspirational source for *The Sun Also Rises,* might such a work have informed his creation of George the porter—whose personality is as full and rich as any white character he has drawn—featured in his ill-fated novel manuscript "A New Slain Knight"?

Adams's *Congaree Sketches* (1927), a collection of poems, stories, and dialogues recorded and reordered by a white man and touted as a recounting of black southern life by blacks for blacks, was among the most celebrated racially representational works in print, and wildly popular in its day. With an intention to record African American dialect accurately, its primary aim was veracity, and it is exceptional for the degree of honesty captured by an unobtrusive observer as his subjects share more than quaint folktales, speaking candidly on such topics as the lynching bee, chain gangs, and a system stacked markedly against them. We can almost hear these moments being replayed in

George's solemn didacticism and in his quiet allusions to the stifled vigor of Jack Johnson and Tiger Flowers in "The Porter." Incidentally, and I think quite significantly, Tiger Flowers, as a (wrongfully) defeated figure, is mentioned in *The Sun Also Rises* as well. The allusions are brief but potentially meaningful.

Clearly Tiger Flowers's import should not be confined to the boxing ring, and Hemingway's deliberation suggests as much. Why has traditional scholarship missed this altogether? In *The Sun Also Rises,* the mention of Flowers comes as Bill Gorton gets reacquainted with his longtime friend and our protagonist, Jake Barnes. Barnes strains to recall the details of a marquee boxing match, and initially he fails miserably, save for his memory that it was an "enormous Vienna Prize fight." Immediately, though, he amends his declaration, adding, quite significantly, that it featured a fighter who resembled Tiger Flowers. It "had a nigger in it," he says. "Remember the nigger perfectly" (77). Blackness here, it seems, is that same divisive (and self-defining) marker it is in the works we have explored. Blackness is the "not me" Frederic Henry so adamantly insists it is in *A Farewell to Arms.*

But, arguably, as per his own prescriptive, Hemingway conveys a double-storied reality in this blackness. Imbued in this trope, too, is the same tragedy alluded to in "The Light of the World," in which "white hope" obscures any true sense of justice as a system takes down Jack Johnson. (Recall Ketchel's notoriety.) Of *this* nameless black man's trials, Gorton says: "Nigger'd just knocked local boy down. Nigger put up his glove. Wanted to make a speech. Awful noble-looking nigger. Started to make a speech. Then local white boy hit him. Then he knocked white boy cold. Then everybody commenced to throw chairs" (77). Gorton's apt encapsulation of the entire fiasco, a curt "Injustice everywhere," suggests a depth to the subtext seldom if ever discussed; instead, this racial moment remains one unexplored in Hemingway scholarship.

Moreover, we could extend the inquiry beyond the ring, beyond this moment, and ask what we are to make of the nameless black drummer we meet early on, a man whose drum play and shouts seem to echo the unspoken tension between Jake and Brett Ashley as they dance at a local nightclub. Brett apparently knows this drummer well, and connotation suggests that, like several other of her male companions we meet along the way, he enjoys an intimate knowledge of *her;* Brett curiously calls him her "good friend." Given Brett's dubious nature (she is a self-assured, sexually liberated woman sporting a bob and bearing a man's first name), can we make something of this potential complication? Hemingway's minimalist approach is most pronounced. Like the "noble-looking nigger" resembling Tiger Flowers (77), the drummer is nameless and defined only by his body: "He was all teeth and lips" (69). In this way, like Bugs before him—who crouches on "long nigger legs," and whose pink palms and gait make him "negro" (100), this black male, with drumsticks in hand, is pure type. Or is he? Might he, like his African American counterparts featured in other texts, have a more complicated story to tell were he given the chance to speak? (What of his relationship with Brett?) Only time will tell. The first step, though, will be to acknowledge his presence.

These two textual examples—two seemingly thoroughly examined works treated in brief here—demonstrate the untapped potential in Hemingway scholarship for those who know to look for it. If nothing else, I would like this examination to spawn additional questions, to spur further discussion, and to help take Hemingway scholarship in new directions as we enter the new millennium's second decade. Our doing so will depend much on our ability to see things as Hemingway saw them, to be able to look "at words as though . . . seeing them for the first time" (*Selected Letters* 583).

NOTES

Introduction

1. His nebulous ethnicity as a white man of "black blood" and the generally obsessive need to know, says Alwyn Berland in his *Light in August: A Study in Black and White,* inform Christmas's "rootlessness, homelessness, and loneliness" (37).

2. By "absolute identity" I mean identity that is free of confusion and that allows for easy and clear definition. It is, in a purist's sense, identity that is unencumbered, unobscure, unambiguous.

3. Carlos Baker's *Hemingway: The Writer as Artist* provides excellent insight into Hemingway's aesthetic aims. See also Nakjavani, "The Aesthetics of the Visible and the Invisible: Hemingway and Cezanne," for a fine correlative between the writer and the painter and modes of expressionism.

4. See Philip Young's biographical *Ernest Hemingway: A Reconsideration* or his reading of Nick Adams through the lens of initiation in "'*Big World Out There*': The Nick Adams Stories." For a rather thorough account of young Nick's coming to terms with that "big world," also see Joseph Flora, *Hemingway's Nick Adams.*

5. See Kinnamon, who in "Hemingway, the Corrida, and Spain" deals expressly with Hemingway's entrenchment in and reliance on Spanish culture, which he would use to inform many of his narratives. See also Wilentz, "(Re)teaching Hemingway: Anti-Semitism as a Thematic Device in *The Sun Also Rises.*" Wilentz asserts, along lines similar to my own examination, that Hemingway's novel manifests a marked fear of the foreign in the form of Robert Cohn. Cohn, Wilentz argues, is representative of the immigrant sea encroaching upon American shores during the first decades of the new century. In "Liberty and Just(us): Gender and Race in Hemingway's *To Have and Have Not,*" Prescott explores, among other things, Hemingway's augmentation of the white hero in *To Have and Have Not,* expanding upon Toni Morrison's assertions regarding Hemingway's need for what she terms an "Africanist presence" in defining that white hero and white masculinity. See also Meyers, "Hemingway's Primitivism and 'Indian

Camp'"; Monteiro, "'This Is My Pal Bugs': Ernest Hemingway's 'The Battler'"; and Lewis, "'Long Time Ago Good, Now No Good': Hemingway's Indian Stories." In addition, see Hemingway's employment of cultural typology in his treatment of all things Spanish (the Rousseauian conception of "primitive man" as innocent, for example), as explored in Angel Capellan's *Hemingway and the Hispanic World.* These works represent a fair percentage of the meager work that has been done on Hemingway and race. While some scholarship has been done in relation to individual stories, very few scholars have taken a look at Hemingway's textual dealings with race as a whole. However, for a very recent and more thorough exploration of early twentieth-century American popular culture (literature) and issues of race, see Nies, *Eugenic Fantasies: Racial Ideology in the Literature and Popular Culture of the 1920s.* Providing a fine complement to my own thesis, Nies suggests the presence of a pervasive American fixation on an Anglo ideal during the twentieth century's first decades, something demonstrated quite markedly in some of the day's literature, most especially in the works of Fitzgerald and Hemingway. Nies's examination is exceptional in its comprehensiveness. See also Whalan, *Race, Manhood and Modernism in America: The Short Story Cycles of Sherwood Anderson and Jean Toomer.*

6. Toni Morrison's *Playing in the Dark* serves as a critical framing device for my examination as I seek to demonstrate the import of reading the racialized "shadow" figures surrounding the Hemingway protagonist as a means of correctly reading that protagonist and, in turn, Hemingway himself.

7. Hemingway's 1953–54 safari narrative would initially receive piecemeal publication in periodical form. It would take decades for the incomplete manuscript Hemingway had been working on up until his death to see the true light of day. *True at First Light* would be edited by Hemingway's son Patrick and posthumously published in 1999. However, in 2005, Kent State University Press would publish a more complete version of Hemingway's African sojourn. Because of its more comprehensive nature, some feel it is a text more faithful to the author's original intent. Edited by renowned Hemingway scholars Robert Lewis and Robert Fleming, *Under Kilimanjaro* offers over one hundred pages of additional text not included in any prior iteration.

8. See Gallagher, *Rethinking the Color Line: Readings in Race and Ethnicity,* for an especially comprehensive look at the essentialist-constructivist debate and race-based argument in recent decades.

9. Because of the intricacies inherent in an exploration of simply any single race-centered Hemingway text, I deliberately limit the scope of my examination to a few of the short stories and the two African safari memoirs. I have not included "An African Story," or its later fully evolved narrative *The Garden of Eden* or the Cuban-based *To Have and Have Not.* Nor have I written extensively on *The Torrents of Spring,* a work I came to late in this manuscript's development, and a work definitely deserving of its own treatment elsewhere.

10. See Strong, *Race and Identity in Hemingway's Fiction.* Strong is correct in her assertion that Hemingway's treatment of race has often been overlooked by critics old

and new who assess the writer's canon within the parameters of established notions of modernity.

11. For an extensive examination of the traveling Western show, see Reddin's *Wild West Shows*. Reddin posits that these road show dramas, which flourished during the later nineteenth and early twentieth century, helped to forge and reinforce popular conceptions of the Indian in relation to our nation's western expansion and settlement. Purporting to be historical documentation, Wild West shows helped to define an America caught between a fading pastoral past and industrial progress's uncertainty. The Native American figure became the necessary physical fixture onto which the developing American imagination, searching for some tactile remnant of its past, could attach itself. The Wild West show became a means of social-historical validation. Each reenactment brought new opportunities to define "the Indian" and therefore to further define the American ideal of Manifest Destiny. Thomas Dixon's *The Clansman: A Historical Romance of the Ku Klux Klan* was more than instrumental in romanticizing and literally (re)constructing the Old South mythology and its greatest proponents, the Ku Klux Klan. Hemingway noted similarities between the film and the imagery of Willa Cather (see *Selected Letters* 105).

12. Madison Grant's *The Passing of the Great Race* and B. L. Putnam Weale's *The Conflict of Colour: The Threatened Upheaval throughout the World* became the Anglo's cry of encroachment against the "foreigner."

13. In fact, *The Torrents of Spring* is in some ways a reaction to such texts as Madison Grant's *The Passing of the Great Race* (actually spoofed in one of the novella's closing segments—"The Passing of a Great Race and the Marring of Americans").

14. For an especially illuminating study of American Western expansion through the decades, see Limerick.

15. William Unrau's *White Man's Wicked Water* presents an in-depth examination of white-Indian relations within the context of an oft-sanctioned alcohol trade between national governmental constituents and tribal members. It was a relationship, Unrau argues, overwhelmingly marked by loss (of land, money, and self-respect) on the part of the engaged tribes. Unrau also suggests, in discussing the nineteenth-century conception and perpetuation of race-based propaganda, that "immoderate, antisocial consumption was then viewed more as evidence of savage deficiency than as an individual malady or community pathology afflicting humans irrespective of social, ethnic, or racial boundaries" (118).

16. Unhappy with the mediocre sales of *In Our Time,* Hemingway pointed an accusatory finger at the publishing house of Boni and Liveright. He shrewdly escaped his contractual obligations to them by quickly producing a work he deemed bad and a text he knew would be passed on by the house editors. Hemingway was correct in his assumptions and the gamble and partnered next with the house of Charles Scribner, a relationship that would endure for the rest of his days. While noted for its absurdity and humor, and while deemed bad by both Hemingway and Boni, *Torrents* is actually very sharp satire. It also frames quite nicely Hemingway's career-long sociological concerns.

17. See Toni Morrison's essay of the same name, "Unspeakable Things Unspoken: The Afro-American Presence in American Literature," which would ostensibly give rise to *Playing in the Dark*, her longer treatment of America's literary canon and race.

18. See William M. Tuttle Jr., *Race Riot*, for a comprehensive examination of the city's darkest days of racial strife.

19. Certainly those fears were only heightened by claims from various minority circles that anywhere from 5,000 to 10,000 blacks crossed the color line each year in search of equality and better lives. Such assertions only grew in number during the later 1920s and early 1930s. These numbers work well as a rough estimate of those willingly crossing the color line and assuming white identities. In a December 1931 article in the *Afro-American*, an anonymous contributor asserts that, in Philadelphia alone, some 75,000 blacks were masking their blackness, most having come from southern towns. See Hahn, "Crossing the Color Line." See also Johnson, "Crossing the Color Line."

20. See the anonymous editorial in the *Independent*, March 2, 1911, rpt. in Larson 105–7.

21. *In Darkest Africa* was published in 1890, and *African Game Trails* in 1910, and both clearly played on young Hemingway's imagination.

22. Hemingway scholarship is indebted to Michael Reynolds for, among other things, cataloging the author's readings from childhood through midlife. *Hemingway's Reading, 1910–1940: An Inventory* demonstrates Hemingway's lifelong interest in wilderness taming and in the African continent; items in his possession included fictional texts by James Fenimore Cooper and Joseph Conrad and African travel literature by Sir Henry Morton Stanley and Theodore Roosevelt (as representatives of the better-known set). Christopher Isherwood's *Lions and Shadows*, Chauncey Stigand's *Game of British East Africa* and *Hunting the Elephant in Africa*, Prince Akiki Nyabongo's *Story of an African Chief*, and Richard Lydekker's *The Game Animals of Africa* are but a handful of lesser-known texts in Hemingway's possession as he mused about Africa. Further, Geoffrey Gorer's *Africa Dances: A Book about West African Negroes*, Edward C. L. Adams's *Nigger to Nigger*, and George Washington Lee's *Beale Street: Where the Blues Began*, a text that Hemingway actually special ordered, show a young man framing a journey (both literal and metaphorical) within the strictures of race.

23. See Annette Kolodny, *The Lay of the Land: Metaphor as Experience and History in American Life and Letters*. Kolodny engages the frontier trope of land as woman and as something to be "conquered," an image that, she suggests, permeates much of Western—and, more specifically, American—literature.

1. "Indian Camp" and "The Doctor and the Doctor's Wife"

1. A young Ernest Hemingway would make a sojourn with various family members to a private cottage on Walloon Lake every year through his early adulthood. Ojibwa Indians lived and worked nearby doing tanning and mill work, and Hemingway's father, Clarence, was, for a time, the only doctor available to them. This connection virtually guaranteed the young Hemingway intimate contact with Native Americans.

2. For a most informative and comprehensive look at Native American representation through the years from America's inception to the present, see Bird. This collection explores the crafting of Native history and image-making in literature, advertising, and film.

3. Goddu takes the reader from the Gothic tradition's inception as a primarily white aesthetic domain, as seen in the writings of Charles Brockden Brown, and later Hawthorne and Poe, to its subversion and appropriation (as an exclusively white art form) in American letters by contemporary African American writers like Toni Morrison.

4. *The White Man's Indian* has become the standard critical point of reference within the context of Native American representation and the cultural trappings of typology.

5. Babb's focus on a crafted "legacy" of (white) commonality is especially relevant as we explore a Hemingway narrative within the context of history and its apparent absence for the marginalized textual figures.

6. Clearly, Hemingway's recollections of his mother inform this scenario; Grace Hemingway, a devout Christian Scientist, complained about acute light sensitivity stemming from a childhood illness, so much so that drawn blinds became a fixture in the Hemingway house. Once again, though, the facts themselves become secondary to emphasis as Hemingway paints the scene (not the *what,* but the *how*).

7. In Johnson's classic work, the nameless protagonist, a mulatto, actively transgresses racial and therefore social lines in an emphatic example of the traditionally marginalized figure's realized self-volition. For a brief time, he literally is the "secret agent."

8. Demonstrating Hemingway's own ambivalence regarding racial matters, a 1925 letter to his father underscores prejudicial assumptions and their investment in the author's fiction. They also demonstrate the author's aesthetic license and power. In a written response to his father's review of "The Doctor and the Doctor's Wife," Hemingway rather cavalierly explains that he "put in Dick Boulton and Billy Tabeshaw as real people with their real names because it was pretty sure that they would never read the Transatlantic Review. I've written a number of stories about the Michigan country—the country is always true—what happens in the stories is fiction" (*Selected Letters* 153).

2. Beyond the Camp, Behind the Myth

1. Aside from his sister Ursula, whom he admired most during his early years, no one woman would command Hemingway's imagination more than Prudence Boulton. Prudence would also appear as Trudy Boulton in his fiction.

2. See, for example, Flora's *Hemingway's Nick Adams* or Young's "'*Big World Out There.*'" Both examine Nick's initiation into matters concerning love and sex. Flora takes the initiation a step further in suggesting that this is very much a father-and-son story as well, asserting that in a story such as "Ten Indians" Nick begins his journey toward "guides" outside himself and outside his old familial circle. I would suggest that the lessons learned are also markedly racial.

3. Once again, Joseph Flora makes mention of this date's import, but he does not elaborate. Flora's assertion is key and deserves follow-up for all of the holiday's implicit investment in matters of race, ethnicity, and (national) identity: "Whereas the American Indian has no special cause to rejoice over the Fourth, for most Americans it is the important holiday of the summer. In Nick's time in the early years of the century it was, next to Christmas, the greatest holiday of community goodwill and decidedly a family day" (*Hemingway's Nick Adams* 44).

4. Hemingway's original title, which was changed before publication, demonstrates the significance of the allusive date. The initial proposed title for "Ten Indians" was "After the Fourth." See Hemingway's letter to Maxwell Perkins, dated May 1927, in *Selected Letters* (250).

5. Hemingway exploits a truth here, as both men and women wore leggings, often uniform in style and color. But what the Garner boy chooses to ignore is that the style, stitching, and color of their moccasins differentiated the Ojibwa from other tribes, and color was often a marker of individuality within a single tribe.

6. For an especially enlightening look at American governmental relations with Indian tribes through the years, see Unrau, who demonstrates that Native American "degeneracy" is, in many respects, a creation of the American imagination, as well as, in some cases, a product of governmental greed.

7. All the more ironic is Hemingway's choice of name for the Indian girl, who briefly becomes the apple of young Nickie's eye. The character of Prudence Mitchell is based on his recollection of an actual childhood friend, Prudence Boulton, but perhaps this is also Hemingway's joke. (His tales are rife with the unexplained.) Her name, Prudence, denotes discretion, caution, wisdom. Even more fruitful and germane to our investigation is the old French (*prude femme*), which is suggestive of a woman's worthy respectability (see "Prudence"). A prude is one whose sensibilities are easily shocked, especially when it comes to matters concerning sex. We soon find out that none of these associations and definitions apply to young Prudence Mitchell. See Baker's *Ernest Hemingway: A Life Story* and Reynolds's *The Young Hemingway* for details of the story's factual investment.

8. I find the exchange equally interesting for Hemingway's diction and play on pejoratives. The narrative not only negates Prudy's humanity in drawing a correlation between her and the animal, but it also anticipates the reader's prejudice in its choice of representation. "Coon" is a racial pejorative for the African American, a racial slur Hemingway himself used (see his letter to John Dos Passos in *Selected Letters* 157). In this sense, with coon indistinguishable from skunk, the marginal figure becomes an almost amorphous entity.

9. Hemingway's memorializing of Prudence Boulton (as Prudence Mitchell) is significant in this instance in that it demonstrates his own personal investment in fetish and racial typology. Despite his claim that Prudy "did first what no one has ever done better," Hemingway, in reality, began his sexual experimentation much later and was crafting memory here, according to Meyers in *Hemingway: A Biography* (375).

10. I think it rather significant that we never see or hear from Prudence herself in this story. Like Jack Johnson in "The Light of the World," Prudence is a phantom presence.

11. Once more, Hemingway sets up reader expectation with hints of white grandeur as he delves into his very real memories of his own father's hunting prowess and his quasi legend. Adept with a rifle, he was nicknamed "Eagle Eye" by the Ojibwa locals. Placed symbolically at the forefront of Ojibwa tribal totems, the eagle classification stands significantly as the grandest of compliments. Those of the bird clan often became spiritual leaders of the nation, and according to his son, Clarence Hemingway held that distinction among the Ojibwa of northern Michigan. Ernest fittingly juxtaposes this phantom greatness with young Nickie's less-than-laudable, terrified defense of his sister against the encroaching so-called red scare (see Benton-Bania).

12. Note that the Indian's reckless pillaging is necessitated by a system put into place by the white male subject. This realization haunts the American psyche, and Hemingway proves a shrewd observer.

13. Berkhofer's suggestion is applicable to a twentieth-century model as well, as he posits that "most romantic of all was the impression of the Indian as rapidly passing away before the onslaught of civilization. The nostalgia and pity aroused by the dying race produced the best romantic sentiments and gave that sense of fleeting time beloved of romantic sensibilities. The tragedy of the dying Indian, especially as portrayed by the last living member of a tribe, became a staple of American literature, beginning with Philip Freneau's poems in the 1780s" (88).

14. As Abby Ferber suggests in *White Man Falling: Race, Gender, and White Supremacy,* the importance of race and gender to the white hegemony cannot be overstated: "From the moment the concept of race was invented, interracial sexuality became a concern" (34). Ferber offers an interesting account of racial construction in America and the importance of white supremacist conceptions and notions of difference to the maintenance of American identity through the years.

15. Ferber notes a series of laws passed in 1681 that mandated, among other things, the banishment of "white women engaging in miscegenation . . . from the colony." The import here, again, is the "violation" of white womanhood, not just a deviation from the color line. As Ferber suggests, "Interracial sexual relations between white women and black men . . . were not tolerated. . . . A mulatto child born to a white woman . . . was a threat to the entire system of slavery and white supremacy. Because it was assumed that the child of a white woman would remain with its mother, racial segregations would be breached" (35). With such a breach, gone is any power formerly held by the white hand.

16. Unrau notes the representative tenor of nineteenth-century sociopolitical opinion of the Indian figure in the testimony of one agent working on behalf of the United States government as liaison to the Shawnee prior to the Civil War: Agent James B. Abbot's words demonstrate both a sincere concern for the Indian and a condescension steeped in racial typology: "It [is a] well known fact that there are between thirty and forty places within and near the Shawnee settlements where spirituous liquors can

be obtained, and it is also a well established fact that the moral development of the Indians is not sufficient to protect them against the temptations and sources which are set for them by the unscrupulous liquor vendors, and being possessive with a natural appetite for strong drinks, the consequences are that a very large portion of the Shawnees are either habitual or occasional drunkards, and they and their families have to suffer the ruinous effects, which naturally follow" (98).

17. The demise of Simon Green and his people become Goddu's Gothic metaphor of "cultural contradictions that undermine the nation's claim to purity and equality" (10). The Native devolution demonstrates a marked narrative divisiveness and insistence on typological formation, and, as the narrative engages a cultural romance—that of the dying race—it admits culpability.

18. For example, the Bureau of Indian Affairs called for the removal of all Ojibwa west of the Mississippi to Minnesota, resulting in the Sandy Lake Tragedy. See Warren's *History of the Ojibway People* for a comprehensive accounting of major happenings among the Ojibwa people.

19. Thus questions posited generations before by the Reverend William H. Goode, minister to Natives in Kansas during the height of governmental trade with the Natives and a prominent white representative, continue to reverberate in Hemingway's depiction of middle America. Goode served as a special minister to Native Americans, who were affected by governmental trade and liquor sales. His testament is not uncommon. Goode's observations in the wake of an 1864 visit inform my own reading of Hemingway's stories and underscore this notion of blurring (racial) identities and the emphasis on (white) selfhood: "Our guide informed us that . . . about thirty barrels and several jugs of whiskey had been discovered in the vicinity of the Council Ground . . . a large portion of it the property of a white man. I have seen, I feel, the deep degradation of our Indian tribes; but often I have been compelled to ask myself, 'Who is the civilized and who is the savage?' Their principal vices are emphatically our vices. If they get drunk it is upon our whiskey. . . . And yet we claim to be 'civilized' and freely deal out to them the epithet 'savage'" (quoted in Unrau 124).

3. The Truth's in the Shadows

1. Hemingway drew from contemporary headlines in composing his cast of characters. Ad Francis and Bugs were based on Ad Wolgast and Jack Doyle, both white men (see Baker, *Ernest Hemingway: A Life Story* 141).

2. In *Hemingway's Fetishism: Psychoanalysis and the Mirror of Manhood*, Eby rightly posits that Hemingway came to represent the psychosocial dilemmas of his age—an age in which many of his white male compatriots felt challenged by the rising power of racial and sexual others.

3. For a thorough exploration of early twentieth-century American popular culture and its racial politics, see Nies, who uses Hemingway as a cultural lens through which to read the era's racial concerns and the efforts of a nation to reaffirm white masculin-

ity. Perhaps Amy L. Strong, in her *Race and Identity in Hemingway's Fiction,* comes closest to a comprehensive vision of Hemingway's racial awareness and to my own vision of race within the author's oeuvre. While Strong also rightly pairs the two featured boxing stories ("The Light of the World" and "The Battler"), her focus remains on white racial cognizance of racial construction, not on a growing black awareness and recognition of the color line's artificial nature.

4. In *Playing in the Dark,* Morrison suggests that much of the American literary canon, even texts seemingly devoid of a minority presence, has at its core a dependency on some (often phantom) minority presence to help define itself. In "The World and the Jug," Ralph Ellison seems to anticipate, some thirty years earlier, Morrison's assertions, as he suggests that "Southern whites cannot walk, talk, sing, conceive of laws or justice, think of sex, love, the family or freedom without responding to the presence of Negroes" (*Shadow and Act* 116).

5. In a letter to his friend and fellow expatriate John Dos Passos dated April 25, 1925, Hemingway describes the story as "a swell new Nick story about a busted down pug and a *coon* called The Battler" (*Selected Letters* 157). Race clearly marks the story. However, Hemingway's epithets, littering both the printed page and private conversation, demonstrate a marked struggle with and ambivalence toward matters of race and certainly complicate and cloud the picture of modernity.

6. Flora suggests that the initial encounter between the boy and the ex-prizefighter produces no "communal fellowship," and later that the real connection is between Nick and Bugs (88).

7. In *Tuxedo Junction: Essays on American Culture,* Early underscores the importance of the sport's Anglo roots in tracing the history of its apparent "appropriation" by nonwhites. Hemingway's entrenchment within such an ideological framework becomes apparent in Carlos Baker's account of the author fresh on the heels of his first African safari. A 1935 trip to the Bahamas found Hemingway passing the time with fishing excursions (with shark in his sights) and, according to lore, boxing sessions with local toughs. Baker notes that during an interruption of his fishing, Hemingway "took advantage of the interval to issue a challenge. He would pay $250 to any Negro who could stay in the ring with him for three three-minute rounds, using six-ounce gloves. He had no fears about losing." According to Baker in *Hemingway: A Life Story,* the white man won every time, even when goaded into going gloveless and fighting bare-knuckle style (274–75). Hemingway's challenge, its specifics, and the resulting lore all demonstrate the writer's own investment in the rhetoric of the day and in some ways sharply contrast his liberal conclusions regarding the race question and the construction of identity.

8. Hemingway's working title, as he negotiated his contract with Horace Liveright in March of 1925 and put the finishing touches on the collection that would become *In Our Time,* was "The Great Little Fighting Machine." Clearly notions of greatness were something Hemingway wished to explore, define, and challenge as he honed this work.

9. Bugs represents that spectacle of wonderment and fear: the willful minority figure. Hemingway's narrative works to demonstrate how Bugs astutely exposes the Anglo's

vulnerabilities and effectively beats him at his own game, referencing the Anglo rule book. This is the essence of social subversion. Miscegenation, as a general racial commingling in its broadest sense, becomes a black supplanting of white as the African American literally looms large over a prostrate "little white man" (101). Bugs's general facility, coupled with his white comrade's inability to operate within this same framework, becomes the greater horror and the point of greater significance. And it all begins with a smile.

10. See Hine, Hine, and Harrold as well as Franklin, for excellent histories of the nation's racial tenor during these years.

11. Philip Young, in *The Nick Adams Stories,* was the first to situate this story within the Nick Adams paradigm. While the narrator is in fact nameless, because of the attendant similarities to Nick and Nick's world, scholarship has followed Young's lead.

12. In a cautionary statement published in the *Paris Review,* Hemingway notes that "The Light of the World" "is about many things and you would be ill-advised to think it is a simple tale" (see Trogdon 314).

13. In "The Light of Alice's World," Maloy offers Lewis Carroll's Alice as a means of reading Hemingway's text and its narrative experimentation with notions of reality and illusion (what we know to be true). Joseph Flora's explication of the text, while providing a useful alternative intertextual reading of "The Light of the World" and pointing to Hawthorne as a possible influence, only glosses over the racial subtext informing the story. More recently, Hannum has extended a reading by Matthew Bruccoli and looks to religion and the need for something redemptive as a means of reading this seemingly simple story. Gregory Green actually does what few critics have done before or since its publication in his treatment (albeit slight) of race as a lens through which to read the story. Framed within an inquiry of Hemingway's narrative technique of omission, Green's article explores the Ketchel figure within the parameters of history and the Hemingway story and the idea of the unspoken. Here that unspoken suggestion becomes the absurdity inherent in the idea of what Green calls the "promise of a redeemer" (32) in the Johnson boxing era. America would call this redeemer its great (white) hope. Green seems to read Hemingway as more of a racial sympathizer than an unsettled initiate himself.

14. While Steve Ketchel was indeed an active contemporary fighter, it was Stanley Ketchel who fought Jack Johnson.

15. See also Sammons for a fine study of the cultural meaning and impact of the sport. For exceptional histories, see Bert R. Sugar's *100 Years of Boxing* and A. J. Liebling's *The Sweet Science,* a classic point of reference for the pugilistic historian.

16. While Johnson openly transgressed divisional lines, D. W. Griffith's *Birth of a Nation* broke all attendance records and galvanized white fear. Hemingway recollects in a letter to friend and noted art historian Bernard Berenson his memories of seeing the film with his paternal grandfather when he was a boy (see *Selected Letters* 811).

17. Lindsay provides an interesting examination of the shifting racial dynamic of the sport through the years.

18. In *Bad Nigger! The National Impact of Jack Johnson,* Gilmore provides excellent insight into the furor that the larger-than-life figure of Jack Johnson unleashed on America in the early twentieth century. With a litany of threats to Johnson's person at his disposal, Gilmore demonstrates the visceral hatred purveyed by national newspapers in response to Johnson's open cavorting with white women and the accusations and rumors that followed such relationships. Gilmore asserts that "many Southerners, who normally lynched, murdered, or maligned blacks upon the slightest intimation of their being even remotely associated with white women, wished that Johnson was in their area of the country" so that they could exact a brand of justice fit for such "crimes" (96).

19. Jack Johnson took the heavyweight title from then-champion Tommy Burns in Sydney, Australia, in December of 1908. Johnson would lose the title seven years later to Jess Willard in 1915, also on foreign soil, this time in Havana, Cuba. In *Saga of the Fist: The 9,000 Year Story of Boxing in Text and Pictures,* John Grombach offers a concise but thorough overview of the sport's major happenings.

20. In his autobiography, Johnson himself recognizes the full significance of this bout as he recalls all that surrounded the fight of the century: "Rumors had come to me that there actually was talk of a chance shot at me if I whipped Jeffries. It was hinted that gunmen had been hidden in the crowd and that if my boxing opponent did not dispose of me a bullet would" (56). As perhaps his own greatest cheerleader, Jeffries echoes the popular sentiment in his own predictions and thoughts before the fight in the *Reno Daily Telegraph* dated July 5, 1910: "I'll lick this black man so badly he'll never want to see a boxing glove again. . . . No matter what my condition is, or what it isn't, I'm going to lick Johnson. . . . It's no fun for a man of my inclinations to have to deny himself everything, to knuckle down and work his blamed head off just on account of a coon" (quoted in Johnson, *Jack Johnson* 3).

21. Significantly, Hemingway himself referred to Johnson, in a rare instance where he speaks of the champion at all, as "the smoke." In a friendly letter to former fellow ambulance driver and friend Howell Jenkins in March of 1922, Hemingway touts the virtues of Ketchel and never mentions the heavyweight champion by name. Curiously, none of the letters in the published collection directly address Jack Johnson or his reign as champion (see *Selected Letters* 64).

22. Fanon's text and theoretical approach inform my reading of Hemingway and his narrative strategies of omission.

23. Ketchel's notoriety had played on young Hemingway's imagination years earlier in "A Matter of Colour." Written in high school, in 1916, that short story anticipates a mature Hemingway's challenge to race essentiality in "The Light of the World" and constructs a narrative in which a fixed fight ends with the white cheater on the canvas and the racial other victorious because of the color-blindness of one of the conspirators.

4. Killin' 'Em with Kindness

1. Strong's study is exceptional in its comprehensive examination of the author's body of work through the racial lens. Few scholars have taken her lead. Strong also notes Hemingway's recognition of race's part in identity construction.

2. The novel, with the working title of "A New Slain Knight," also spawned "The Train Trip," another fragmentary piece included in *The Complete Short Stories of Ernest Hemingway.*

3. Hemingway originally conceived of a novel told from a first-person point of view but increasingly questioned that strategy as the narrative languished in familial conversations. Even more vexing, apparently, was the question of whose narrative, ultimately, this was to be: that of the young naïf or his revolutionist father. The extended father-son conversation did nothing to help clarify things for its author.

4. The race riot that rocked Chicago began on July 27, 1919, when Eugene Williams, a black teenage boy playing with several others on a sweltering summer day, decided to go swimming in an area reserved for whites only. Perhaps as a taunt, perhaps as a mean prank, a white man standing ashore threw rocks at the teenagers. One struck and killed Williams. When pleas for justice went unanswered, and amid rumors of apparent police corruption, vigilantism prevailed and retaliatory shots were fired. White gangs, particularly in the packing district, seized the opportunity to realize long-held fantasies of racial violence. The beach skirmish was just the beginning. As Tuttle rightly suggests, "the battle that ensued was frightening in its violence, but it merely anticipated Chicago's long-feared race war" (5). This series of events touched off five days of nearly unabated street warfare. Stretched thin and, in some cases, all but sympathetic to the white community, a force of 3,500 police was ineffective in stemming the mayhem; some blacks charged collusion and corruption. Only after major bloodshed did Chicago's mayor, William H. Thompson, engage a National Guard force of 6,200 to enforce peace, and only then did the violence abate. When the dust settled, 38 had lost their lives, more than 500 were injured, and countless homes had been burned. With such material very present in his mind, Hemingway imbues the porter's tale with the explosiveness of those days and nights.

5. Originally, as a part of the proposed plot trajectory of "A New Slain Knight," young Jimmy traveled with his father from northern Michigan to Chicago and then New York. As things stand in "The Porter," father and son travel to some unnamed destination, and this significantly shifts the emphasis from place to character, dialogue, and the action aboard the train.

6. See Franklin, *From Slavery to Freedom,* as well as Hine, Hine, and Harrold, *The African-American Odyssey,* for wonderful general histories of American segregationist practices. While black Pullman porters certainly wore their uniforms with pride, as they were celebrated among the African American community for their cosmopolitan

lifestyle and (relatively speaking) apparent financial comfort, that status came with an extremely high price: a 400-hour, 11,000-mile work month (before unionization during the 1920s) left little time for sleep, let alone leisure. For decades, overtime pay was an abstract concept. The ability to master multiple jobs (that of chef/cook, steward, even conductor, although that title itself belonged exclusively to whites) increased a porter's tip-earning potential and therefore his worth aboard the train. This became almost a necessity as the porter saw his base pay, his fair living wage, being chipped away by extraordinarily long hours and work-related expenses that would include meals and boarding (porters lived aboard their vessels) and, in some instances, payments for broken, lost, and stolen company provisions. Supplementing one's income became an art of the resourceful, notes Perata in *Those Pullman Blues.* George Smock, who, along with his brother and father, worked as a Pullman porter, is quick to dispel the myth of the porter's high life, recalling, "The Pullman Company took advantage of the employee. Everybody made more money than the Pullman porter. You could go to some people in the yards and find that they made more money than the actual pay from the Pullman Company because they took advantage of the passenger—the passenger would take care of and give them or pay them the salary that they should have been paying" (quoted in Perata 6). Also see Bates, *Pullman Porters and the Rise of Protest Politics in Black America, 1925–1945,* for a comprehensive account of the trials of America's Pullman porter and his push for economic and social justice.

7. *Plessy v. Ferguson* upheld the predominantly southern Jim Crow tradition of public segregation of the races, significantly via the medium of the train. Additionally, as John Hope Franklin notes in *From Slavery to Freedom,* during the first two years of the new century, the occurrence of over two hundred lynchings underscored the hyper-contentious relationship between the races, especially in the South (342). However, with rioting in cities to the west and north during the first two decades of the new century, we see that racial strife was not an exclusively southern phenomenon.

8. The Pullman Strike of 1894 began as a heated conflict over the company's proposed wage decreases. The company's actions smacked of self-preservation, as the nation was experiencing a crippling economic downturn. Wages would be decreased while rent in Pullman's model town was not. As a result, in early July of 1894, over 3,000 Pullman workers, beginning in and around Chicago, refused to work. The stakes were certainly high; while the boycott was centered in Chicago, it would have national implications as thousands more railroad workers in various capacities, in various areas outside Chicago, joined in just days later. Many blacks looking for work seized the opportunity and crossed the picket line, adding a racial element to the tension. These tensions escalated as President Cleveland, anticipating a crippling ripple effect nationally and using the federal mail dispersal as leverage, issued a federal injunction and ordered some 12,000 troops to break the strike. Fires were set, strike breakers were threatened, and lives were lost. By late July, over thirty were dead. In the years following, the Pullman Sleeping Car Company organized its own union to meet (and control) the challenge of rising discontent within its ranks. Pullman's wrangling with its increasingly dissatisfied (primarily

African American) employee base continued long after the initial strike and rioting of 1994; the threat of violence loomed for decades, and continued developments during the 1920s most certainly provided fodder for Hemingway. In July of 1919 (the same year as the infamous race riot), A. Phillip Randolph began laying the foundation for what would become the Brotherhood of Sleeping Car Porters (officially recognized in August of 1925), the Pullman porters' official organized labor union and the nation's first African American labor union. By the end of the decade, Pullman porters had solidified their credibility as professional laborers, now "railroad employees," on a national and then world stage, gaining acceptance into the American Federation of Labor's fold. But the great company would not concede anything without a fight; several arbitrated meetings garnered very little in the way of actual gains and reports of threats to Pullman employees were rampant as dissidents were bullied, and many fired, for supporting union activity and an agenda that included a push for fewer hours. The next ten years saw minimal concessions; marked gains would not be seen for a decade, when, during Franklin Roosevelt's presidency, the 240-hour work month was finally realized. See Perata, *Those Pullman Blues.*

9. As a student of history (both documented and living), Hemingway would have been familiar with the porter's reality as well. Many porters slept where they could, when they could. For most, there were no designated sleeping quarters, so a makeshift bed of this type would have been commonplace (see Perata). As an artist, Hemingway craftily exploits this truth.

10. Hemingway's interest in history, specifically American histories of war, social history, and the West, is well known. He owned multiple historical volumes along with several titles by Wyndam Lewis, as well as several of Roosevelt's books (most importantly, his hunting accounts). See Reynolds, *Hemingway's Reading.*

11. I must emphasize that while Dr. Adams paints himself in a glowing manner for his makeshift operative skill, Nick's Uncle George questions the good doctor's "greatness." By implication, the reader is meant to do the same, especially in light of his apparent callousness toward the ailing Native American woman's plight (her screams, he tells Nick, are "not important"). The treatment has been the subject of some debate. See Strong, "Screaming through Silence."

12. In *Benito Cereno,* Melville gives us Babo, the seemingly devoted black manservant to Spanish ship captain Don Benito Cereno. We encounter Cereno, captain of a slaver, and the Senegalese Babo, through the eyes of the tale's American protagonist, Captain Amasa Delano. Delano picks up Cereno upon hearing from the captain himself that the Spaniard's crew has reportedly been depleted by killer storms and disease. However, Babo's apparently hopeful smile throughout belies a shrewdness (and a tragic series of events) that is revealed as we learn that he has not only engaged in but orchestrated a full-blown revolt aboard the slaver. Smile notwithstanding, he is a murderer of men. Tempering his violence with a smile, though, and posturing for a white audience, Babo slyly becomes master of the ship and of himself and effectively subverts the known order. The ease of such subversion becomes the thing that haunts

Captain Delano long after his experiences aboard the *San Dominick*, and Babo's tempered violence and knowing smile are a phantom presence here too, haunting the pages of Hemingway's fragmentary tale of George the porter.

13. Recall Bugs's admission in "The Battler" that his arrangement with the former boxer as caretaker allowed him to live like a gentleman.

14. In "Richard Wright's Blues," Ellison notes that "the blues is an impulse to keep the painful details and episodes of a brutal experience alive in one's aching consciousness, to finger its jagged grain, and to transcend it, not by the consolation of philosophy but by squeezing from it a near-tragic, near-comic lyricism" (*Shadow and Act* 59). We see that this sensibility colors the porter's relationship with his co-worker, the nameless chef.

15. While the boxing ring would continue to provide a livelihood for blacks and other men of color (this would change following the reign of Jack Johnson), baseball closed its doors to African Americans in 1887. In an official dictum, the International League capitulated to individual white player requests that black players no longer be signed and altogether barred African Americans from the game. This move prompted blacks to form a league of their own, and interracial play would not return to America's pastime for another sixty years. See Hine, Hine, and Harrold, *The African-American Odyssey* (255–57).

16. A seemingly simple task such as making up and breaking down beds could potentially take hours aboard a standard train, sometimes leaving time for little else before one had to do it all over again, substantially jeopardizing one's tip-making potential. Indeed, any one of the porter's standard duties could be exhaustive; standard practice often meant the porter truly did put the passenger (and the company) before himself. George McLain, Pullman porter for the Southern Pacific line for over forty years, remembers the rigors of being a porter for the company early on, noting, "It used to be that in the dining car those men [porters] had to get up early enough to put away their beds, roll up their beds, and put 'em down the hole in the possum belly and clean up and set up the dining room, 'cause the railroad wasn't thinkin' 'bout gettin' no dormitory for those men. They wasn't gonna pull no extra car there for that dining car help. So they made 'em sleep in the diner, and I just tell ya, that was something awful, but they did it—sleep on them chairs and those slats and different things" (quoted in Perata 131).

17. For example, of America's contentious engagement with immigration, and more specifically a growing Asian immigrant population, Lothrop Stoddard suggests in his *The Rising Tide of Color against White World-Supremacy*, "Unless some such understanding is arrived at, the world will drift into a gigantic race-war—and genuine race-war means war to the knife. Such a hideous catastrophe should be abhorrent to both sides" (308). Polarity and a sense of urgency underscore Stoddard's prescription. More germane to my thesis regarding white fears of blacks is B. L. Putnam Weale's *The Conflict of Colour: The Threatened Upheaval throughout the World*, which examines the threat of a burgeoning revolt against empire, even in wake of perceived progress. Weale asserts, "But though a steady cultural improvement is increasingly the order of

the day, it must not be supposed that this means any diminution of the dangers of the black problem. . . . For [the black man] will finally constitute himself, or try to constitute himself, an imperium in imperio, wherever he lives among the large communities of other men; and he may even demand as his right that just as he is restricted in many ways by the white man, so shall he restrict the white man in certain other ways. . . . In other words, the negro will not only demand his own reservations, his own lands, his own communities, but he will clamour for a policy of retaliation" (245). Echoes of these concerns can be heard years later in the pages of *True at First Light / Under Kilimanjaro* and the drumming of the Mau Mau.

18. From that fateful summer of 1908, when Johnson took America's heavyweight boxing title from Tommy Burns, the search was on, nationally, for a "great white hope" to dethrone him. Lynchings, on the rise once more during the black man's reign, averaged five per month during his six years as champion (see Lindsay). See chapter 3 for further details.

19. For an especially insightful look at how the so-called science of eugenics shaped American cultural perception and its particularly timely popularity at the beginning of the last century, see Nies, *Eugenic Fantasies: Racial Ideology in the Literature and Popular Culture of the 1920s.* Nies suggests that eugenics, with its emphasis on such empirical applications as phrenology, served first and foremost to help reconstitute what she calls the "classical white male body," shattered by world war and displaced by shifting ethnic populations. Madison Grant led the charge on behalf of whites with such works as *The Passing of the Great Race,* in which Grant, speaking from a privileged position and touting ideas of progress, posits: "Mankind emerged from savagery and barbarism under the leadership of selected individuals whose personal prowess, capacity or wisdom gave them the right to lead and the power to compel obedience" (6). While Nies correctly suggests that writers like Hemingway both publicly and privately ridiculed racist eugenic ideology (see Hemingway's *The Torrents of Spring*), I argue that Hemingway's collective work demonstrates, at the very least, an ambivalence about matters of race, and that he too at times fell prey to this attempt at white corporeal reconstitution. His first African works seem to suggest as much.

20. This is a good example of the black boxer's self-awareness and his cognizance of his very precarious position as he defended his title in the highly anticipated fight with Jim Jeffries some two years after assuming the boxer's throne. Johnson was well aware of the price on his head before the "fight of the century": "Rumors had come to me that there actually was talk of a chance shot at me if I whipped Jeffries. It was hinted that gunmen had been hidden in the crowd and that if my boxing opponent did not dispose of me a bullet would" (56). Johnson's boldness and his penchant for all things white, including women, made him a target for many, including legislators eager to take him down. The Mann Act of 1910 eventually did just that, as it set its sights on men who ran with prostitutes, making it illegal to "transport women across state lines for immoral purposes." Johnson's flagrant fraternization with white prostitutes (he ran

with several and even married one) earned him the general rancor of the white community as well as a year in prison at Leavenworth, which he reluctantly served after several years overseas on the run from American authorities. See chapter 3.

21. Curiously, none of the letters in the *Selected Letters* directly address Jack Johnson or his reign as champion. In rare instances where he speaks of the champion at all, Hemingway himself refers to Johnson as "the smoke." See his letter dated March of 1922 to former fellow ambulance driver and friend Howell Jenkins in *Selected Letters* (64). Clearly, though, Hemingway's crafting of the black man's story and George's sullen words stand in stark contrast to the epithets and the letter's projected bravado, and they demonstrate the author's hyper-cognizance of the color line, its impact, and all things racial.

22. Abby Ferber's argument regarding the driving force behind the white supremacist movement in America is easily transposable to my examination of Hemingway's African sojourn: "Every white supremacist organization desires the reestablishment of racial segregation, and in order to prevent future threats of integration, they desire some form of geographical separation" (132). Also see Tompkins, *West of Everything,* for an interesting account of white masculine identity construction.

5. "The Snows of Kilimanjaro," "The Short Happy Life of Francis Macomber," and *Green Hills of Africa*

1. Hemingway promises to "do pioneering or exploring work in the 3 last great frontiers [of] Africa, central south America or the country around and north of the Hudson Bay" (quoted in Reynolds, *The Young Hemingway* 29).

2. While the racial divide is still very much a presence in Hemingway's African experience, it is much less a haunting presence, or specter, and much more of a spectacle, or something to be seen. The racial divide alone drives Hemingway's early African narratives, but without the same attendant, seemingly burdensome historic complexities found in his Indian stories and his black-and-white tales. Moreover, this seeming simplicity, I would argue, is quite deliberate.

3. Hemingway's reading in the years leading up to and immediately after his first Africa trip included Theodore Roosevelt's *African Game Trails,* Lord Stanley's *How I Found Livingstone,* John Boyes's *The Company of Adventures,* Charles Curtis's *Hunting in Africa East and West,* and Carl Akeley's *In Brightest Africa,* just to name a few. Clearly, these had some influence on an eager and—at least in his youth—impressionable Hemingway (see Reynolds, *Hemingway's Reading*).

4. Constant violent rebellion in the 1880s made for difficult German rule early on, and resistance only increased as German economic policies grounded in the plantation tradition became more entrenched. Cotton, tea, and coffee exports came at a bloody cost to a resistant Native populace, who suffered well over 100,000 casualties during years of insurgency. With such a violent history behind it, the Great Rift Valley

in central Tanganyika (formerly composed of mainland Tanganyika and the island of Zanzibar) fittingly becomes the primary focus for the hunting party as Hemingway and friend Charles Thompson compete for big game.

5. In actuality, Kandisky is Hans Koritschoner, an Austrian transplant who surprises Hemingway with his ready awareness of the author and his relatively minor recent publication in *Der Dichter.* Kandisky serves as a ready and convenient sounding board for a man of letters critical of his American literary forebears and contemporaries.

6. Hemingway prefaces his first African book with an admonishment to the reader: "The writer has attempted to write an absolutely true book to see whether the shape of a country and the pattern of a month's action, can, if truly presented, compete with a work of the imagination" (*Green Hills* 7).

7. This reading of the body enjoyed considerable popularity in America and abroad during the nineteenth century and into the twentieth century. The supposed science of phrenology suggested a direct correlation between physiognomy and intellectual capacity, for example. The Fowler family led the movement and even established a national institute to promote their scholarship. See Fowler and Fowler, *The Illustrated Self-Instructor in Phrenology and Physiology with One Hundred Engravings, and a Chart of the Character.* Hemingway clearly walks in the Fowler shadow as he appraises the Masai character before him. This only bolsters the privilege already afforded them by their tribal designation. Seen as pure pastoralists by many, the Masai have cultivated a reputation through the generations of being a proud and valiant people, only hunting dangerous game, such as lion, that pose a threat to the tribe's well-being (see Steinhart). Hemingway too falls sway to this view, and he engages it in both *Green Hills* and in his final African book. He conflates the two conceptions in his treatment of P.O.M.'s lion hunt in *Green Hills.*

6. The First Shall Be Last, the Last Shall Be First

1. *Sports Illustrated* serialized segments of Hemingway's so-called African book in 1971 and 1972. Hoping to rejuvenate a languishing and now-sprawling manuscript, Hemingway planned a third trip to the continent in the closing months of 1956, but political strife over the Suez Canal's nationalization and its effects on travel in the region kept Hemingway away, and an African return remained an unfulfilled wish. His manuscript, too, was left, by most accounts, unfinished.

2. Hemingway would work on this text on and off until his death in 1961.The text was never completed. Before his death in 1961, the unpublished manuscript of the African book ran over eight hundred pages. This would become *True at First Light* in 1999 and *Under Kilimanjaro,* published in 2005. For a look at Hemingway's early African musings, see *The Garden of Eden.* Part of his African experience would be translated into fiction and posthumously published twenty-five years after his death as this novel.

3. In *Hemingway: The Writer as Artist,* Baker suggests that, like Twain in *The Adventures of Huckleberry Finn,* Hemingway relies on a unique blending of truth-telling,

an account of things "as they are," and time manipulation. Hemingway, says Baker, manipulates time, not truth, to craft drama. Truth, I would argue, is relative.

4. Every verbal exchange, says Fairclough, is colored by an inherent vying for narrative control. Fairclough's "false egalitarianism" can be read as a specious power equation in which parity is nonexistent.

5. Steinhart's argument that the English carried with them to the continent all the elitist baggage of class inherent in the hunt is especially compelling when one is examining the African safari as a political exercise. The complicated set of laws governing the hunt was established to conserve both game (for ecological concerns) and the political status quo. Within this framework, poaching, with its illegalities and attendant unethical associations, became an almost exclusively black act as indigenous tribes attempted to maintain age-old practices. As Steinhart notes, "The idea that hunting was the exclusive privilege of an upper class, that it betokened wealth and status denied to common folk, and that it conferred on the hunter exclusive membership in an aristocracy of blood and wealth would set them directly at odds with their African hunting counterparts" (68). At its heart sits the issue of ownership. African anti-poaching legislation then becomes the white hunter's last stand in keeping the hunt an exclusively white domain.

6. Suspicions ran so high among colonial sympathizers that, according to several sources, almost 100,000 Africans of various ethnic groups were arrested and some 12,000 more executed before the dust settled with the eventual imperial fall and Kenyan independence in 1963 (Appiah and Gates 1267).

7. Morrison would suggest that the tension between these two ontological states defines much of American literature.

8. In fact, Hemingway's phallic fixation and selective memory have Debba possessively fondling Hemingway's weapon here and elsewhere. The violence of the hunt is sexualized as he tells us repeatedly of her fondness for the sensation of his pistol and holster against her thighs. Additionally, we see Debba's sexualized hero worship in her wish to "experience" Hemingway's masculine show by holding the gun responsible for taking down the baboon threat: "The last one I had shot was screaming and I shot and finished him. The others were out of sight. I reloaded in the brush and Debba asked if she could hold the rifle" (*True at First Light* 144).

9. Hemingway's fictionalized safari recollections (*True at First Light*) were first published as "Hemingway Writes on Africa" in the pages of *Look* in January of 1954. The January issue featured some sixteen pages of text and never-before-seen pictures of the writer's African experience. Later incarnations of these reflections would be published in *Sports Illustrated* as "The African Journals" of 1971. For a fine account of these years, see Meyers, *Hemingway: A Biography.*

10. A young African mission-taught servant enlisted locally as interpreter indulges Papa as hero. Speaking publicly of the leopard incident, he asserts: "Everyone said you had fought him with your hands and killed him with the pistol" (*True at First Light* 253). We hear further echoes of an anecdotal Roosevelt in Singh's storytelling: "My friend, Carl Akeley, of Chicago, actually killed barehanded a leopard which sprang on him. . . . It

bit him in one arm . . . but Akeley threw it, holding its throat with the other hand, and flinging its body to one side" (Roosevelt 58). Like the placard on Singh's wall with its bare-fisted conqueror, the Interpreter's words indulge white lore and iconography.

11. Mudimbe underscores the idea of a Eurocentric privileging of knowledge during the colonial process, asserting of Africa's white explorer that "he concerned himself with mapping out the continent and, in the nineteenth century, compiling information and organizing complex bodies of knowledge, including medicine, geography, and anthropology" (47).

12. Mary's own account in her memoir includes a virtual catalog of ailing individuals, including an old woman plagued by a cough, a feverish old man, and a boy stricken with boils. In each instance, Mary tells us, "they seem to have acquired great faith in the white man's medicines, especially injections" (407).

13. Ironically, Hemingway would berate critics of his work for, according to him, reading too much into what he wrote, looking for things that were not there (at least not intentionally so). In a letter to *New York Times* correspondent and friend Harvey Breit a couple of years after his second safari, Hemingway jokingly asks if Carlos Baker could "con himself into thinking I would put a symbol into anything on purpose. . . . What sort of a symbol is Debba, my Wakamba fiancée? She must be a dark symbol" (*Selected Letters* 867). I would argue that she indeed does become a symbol of sorts for one bent on transgressing the color line and for a (white) man ultimately searching for a formal metaphoric reclamation of the black body and of whiteness.

14. While Debba's existence and her relationship with the writer are never in question, Mary Hemingway's personal notes and memoir, *How It Was,* fail to corroborate the degree of intimacy shared by the two. Mary's account *does* give the reader a greater sense of the African "character," outside Debba, exploring in greater detail the friendships they made and cultivated on that last safari. Mary's interest in and sense of admiration for those around her (she wishes to "learn more" [448]), given her attention to detail, ring true. (For instance, Mary's account gives us bits of Masai legend to counter Western lore's re-creation by Hemingway in his book.) Carlos Baker indulges the notion of a possible physical relationship (suggesting Hemingway showed "signs of wanting to go native" [*Ernest Hemingway* 517]), but his sources, which include interviews with camp friends, do not corroborate any Hemingway talk of a second marriage. While Mellow's *Hemingway: A Life without Consequences* quietly questions the veracity of the given accounts, in *Hemingway: A Biography,* Meyers expressly refuses to grant any credence to the couple's relative recounts (502).

15. The perpetuation of the ideal of black-sanctioned white superiority is something Hemingway would replicate from texts by geographic conquerors like Theodore Roosevelt. In his *African Game Trails,* Roosevelt perpetuates the happy notion of an embraced subservient self-conception by the black figure. According to Roosevelt, they "speedily christened each of the white men by some title of their own, using the ordinary Swahili title of Bwana (master) as a prefix," an action that comes as naturally to these Wakamba as it does "speedily" (102).

16. The Mau Mau were (largely indigenous) freedom fighters invested in the cause of Kenyan national liberation. While this movement had been afoot for decades (since the late nineteenth century), the Mau Mau movement proper did not become a real threat to British rule until the 1940s. By 1963, the British stronghold would be no more. For a fine comprehensive history of the politics that helped shape the African continent, see Mazrui, who couches his observations within the framework of Africa as (European) creation, beginning with its "discovery" by those in the West. See also O'Toole, "The Historical Context."

17. By "African essentiality," I mean an understood essence pervading day-to-day African life as the American Hemingway experienced it and knew it to be.

18. Both Meyers in *Hemingway: A Biography* and Mellow in *Hemingway: A Life without Consequences* note the exorbitant fees paid to Hemingway just prior to his second African excursion. *Look* reportedly paid the author over $25,000 for a January 1954 pictorial and article. The extravagant fees subsidized the costs of his formal return to the "simple" life and the "primitive."

WORKS CITED

Adams, Edward C. L. *Nigger to Nigger.* New York: Charles Scribner's Sons, 1928.

Anolik, Ruth, and Douglas L. Howard. *The Gothic Other: Racial and Social Constructions in the Literary Imagination.* Jefferson, NC: McFarland & Company, 2004.

Appiah, Kwame Anthony, and Henry Louis Gates Jr. *Africana: The Encyclopedia of the African and African American Experience.* New York: Basic Civitas Books, 1999.

Babb, Valerie. *Whiteness Visible: The Meaning of Whiteness in American Literature and Culture.* New York: New York University Press, 1998.

Baker, Carlos. *Ernest Hemingway: A Life Story.* New York: Charles Scribner's Sons, 1965.

———. *Hemingway: The Writer as Artist.* Princeton, N.J.: Princeton University Press, 1963.

Bates, Beth Thompkins. *Pullman Porters and the Rise of Protest Politics in Black America, 1925–1945.* Chapel Hill: University of North Carolina Press, 2001.

Benton-Bania, Edward. *The Mishomis Book: The Voice of the Ojibway.* St. Paul, Minn.: Indian Country Press, 1991.

Berkhofer, Richard F., Jr. *The White Man's Indian: Images of the American Indian from Columbus to the Present.* New York: Alfred A. Knopf, 1978.

Berland, Alwyn. *Light in August: A Study in Black and White.* New York: Twayne, 1992.

Bird, S. Elizabeth, ed. *Dressing in Feathers: The Construction of the Indian in American Popular Culture.* Boulder, Colo.: Westview Press, 1996.

Capellan, Angel. *Hemingway and the Hispanic World.* Ann Arbor, Mich.: UMI Research Press, 1985.

Derounian-Stodola, Kathryn Zabelle, and James A. Levernier. *The Indian Captivity Narrative, 1550–1900.* New York: Twayne, 1990.

Divine, Robert, T. H. Breen, George M. Fredrickson, and R. Hal Williams. *America: Past and Present.* New York: Longman, 1999.

Dixon, Thomas. *The Clansman: A Historical Romance of the Ku Klux Klan.* New York: Grosset & Dunlap, 1905.

Du Bois, W. E. B. "The Souls of Black Folk." *W. E. B. Du Bois: Writings*. New York: Library of America, 1986. 357–547.

Duran, Bonnie. "Indigenous versus Colonial Discourse: Alcohol and American Indian Identity." *Dressing in Feathers: The Construction of the Indian in American Popular Culture*. Ed. S. Elizabeth Bird. Boulder, Colo.: Westview Press, 1996. 111–29.

Eagleton, Terry. *The Ideology of the Aesthetic*. Oxford: Blackwell, 1991.

Early, Gerald. *Tuxedo Junction: Essays on American Culture*. Hopewell, N.J.: Ecco Press, 1989.

Eby, Carl. *Hemingway's Fetishism: Psychoanalysis and the Mirror of Manhood*. Albany: State University of New York Press, 1999.

Ellison, Ralph. *Shadow and Act*. New York: Quality Paperback Book Club, 1994.

Fairclough, Norman. *Language and Power*. New York: Longman, 1989.

Fanon, Frantz. *Black Skin, White Masks*. New York: Grove Weidenfeld, 1991.

Farnsworth, Robert M. Introduction to *The Marrow of Tradition*, by Charles W. Chesnutt. Ann Arbor: University of Michigan Press, 1995.

Faulkner, William. *Light in August*. New York: Vintage International, 1990.

Ferber, Abby. *White Man Falling: Race, Gender, and White Supremacy*. Lanham, Md.: Rowman & Littlefield, 1998.

Flora, Joseph. *Hemingway's Nick Adams*. Baton Rouge: Louisiana University State Press, 1982.

Fowler, Orson Squire, and Lorenzo Niles Fowler. *The Illustrated Self-Instructor in Phrenology and Physiology with One Hundred Engravings, and a Chart of the Character*. New York: Fowler and Wells, 1854. Excerpt in *Popular American Literature of the 19th Century*. Ed. Paul Gutjahr. New York: Oxford University Press, 2001. 436–72.

Franklin, John Hope. *From Slavery to Freedom: A History of American Negroes*. New York: Alfred A. Knopf, 1974.

Fredrickson, George. *The Black Image in the White Mind: The Debate on African American Character and Destiny, 1817–1914*. New York: Harper Collins, 1971.

Gallagher, Charles. *Rethinking the Color Line: Readings in Race and Ethnicity*. Mountain View, Calif.: Mayfield, 1999.

Gellar, Sheldon. "The Colonial Era." *Africa*. Ed. Phyllis M. Martin and Patrick O'Meara. Bloomington: Indiana University Press, 1995. 135–55.

Gilmore, Al-Tony. *Bad Nigger! The National Impact of Jack Johnson*. Port Washington, N.Y.: National University Publications, 1975.

Goddu, Teresa. *Gothic America: Narrative, History, and Nation*. New York: Columbia University Press, 1997.

Gordon, Donald L. "African Politics." *Understanding Contemporary Africa*. 2nd ed. Ed. April A. Gordon and Donald L. Gordon. Boulder, Colo.: Lynne Rienner, 1996. 53–93.

Gorer, Geoffrey. *Africa Dances: A Book about West African Negroes*. London: Faber and Faber, 1935.

Grant, Madison. *The Passing of the Great Race*. New York: Charles Scribner's Sons, 1922.

Green, Gregory. "A Matter of Color: Hemingway's Criticism of Race Prejudice." *Hemingway Review* 1 (Fall 1981): 26–32.

Greene, J. Lee. *Blacks in Eden: The African American Novel's First Century.* Charlottesville: University Press of Virginia, 1996.

Grombach, John. *Saga of the Fist: The 9,000 Year Story of Boxing in Text and Pictures.* South Brunswick, N.J.: Gazelle, 1977.

Hahn, Emilie. "Crossing the Color Line." *New York World,* July 28, 1929. Rpt. in Larson 117–20.

Hannum, Howard L. "Nick Adams and the Search for Light." *New Critical Approaches to the Short Stories of Ernest Hemingway: Critical Essays.* Ed. Jackson J. Benson. Durham, N.C.: Duke University Press, 1990. 321–30.

Hegel, G. W. F. *The Philosophy of History.* Trans. J. Jibree. New York: Dover, 1956.

Hemingway, Ernest. "The Battler." *The Complete Short Stories.* 95–104.

———. *The Complete Short Stories of Ernest Hemingway: The Finca Vigía Edition.* New York: Charles Scribner's Sons, 1987.

———. "The Doctor and the Doctor's Wife." *The Complete Short Stories.* 73–76.

———. "Fathers and Sons." *The Complete Short Stories.* 369–77.

———. *The Garden of Eden.* New York: Charles Scribner's Sons, 1986.

———. "The Good Lion." *The Complete Short Stories.* 482–84.

———. *Green Hills of Africa.* New York: Charles Scribner's Sons, 1935.

———. "Hemingway Writes on Africa." *Look,* Jan. 26, 1954.

———. "Indian Camp." *The Complete Short Stories.* 65–70.

———. "The Indians Moved Away." *The Nick Adams Stories.* Ed. Philip Young. New York: Bantam Books, 1973. 34–36.

———. "The Light of the World." *The Complete Short Stories.* 292–97.

———. "The Porter." *The Complete Short Stories.* 571–78.

———. *Selected Letters, 1917–1961.* Ed. Carlos Baker. New York: Charles Scribner's Sons, 1981.

———. "The Short Happy Life of Francis Macomber." *The Complete Short Stories.* 5–28.

———. "The Snows of Kilimanjaro." *The Complete Short Stories.* 39–56.

———. *The Sun Also Rises.* New York: Charles Scribner's Sons, 1926.

———. "Ten Indians." *The Complete Short Stories.* 253–57.

———. *The Torrents of Spring.* New York: Simon & Schuster, 1987.

———. *True at First Light.* New York: Charles Scribner's Sons, 1999.

———. *Under Kilimanjaro.* Ed. Robert Lewis and Robert Fleming. Kent, Ohio: Kent State University Press, 2005.

Hemingway, Mary. *How It Was.* New York: Alfred A. Knopf, 1976.

Hine, Darlene, William Hine, and Stanley Harrold, eds. *The African-American Odyssey.* Upper Saddle River, N.J.: Prentice Hall, 2000.

Isernhagen, Hartwig. "The Representation of 'the Indian' in the Federal Writer's Project and in Contemporary Native American Literature." *Native American Representations:*

First Encounters, Distorted Images, and Literary Appropriations. Ed. Gretchen M. Bataille. Lincoln: University of Nebraska Press, 2001. 168–97.

Isherwood, Christopher. *Lions and Shadows.* Minneapolis: University of Minnesota Press, 2000.

Johnson, Caleb. "Crossing the Color Line." *Outlook and Independent,* August 26, 1931. Rpt. in Larson 121–23.

Johnson, James Weldon. *The Autobiography of an Ex-coloured Man.* New York: Vintage Books, 1989.

Johnson, John Arthur. *Jack Johnson: In the Ring and Out.* London: Proteus, 1977.

Keller, Edmund J. "Decolonization, Independence, and the Failure of Politics." *Africa.* Ed. Phyllis M. Martin and Patrick O'Meara. Bloomington: Indiana University Press, 1995. 156–75.

Kevles, Daniel J. *In the Name of Eugenics: Genetics and the Uses of Human Heredity.* Berkeley: Univ. of California Press, 1985.

Kinnamon, Keneth. "Hemingway, the Corrida, and Spain." *Ernest Hemingway: Five Decades of Criticism.* Ed. Linda Wagner. East Lansing: Michigan State University Press, 1974. 57–74.

Kolodny, Annette. *The Lay of the Land: Metaphor as Experience and History in American Life and Letters.* Chapel Hill: University of North Carolina Press, 1975.

Lamothe, Daphne. "*Cane:* Jean Toomer's Gothic Black Modernism." *The Gothic Other: Racial and Social Constructions in the Literary Imagination.* Ed. Ruth Bienstock Anolik and Douglas L. Howard. Jefferson, N.C.: McFarland, 2004. 54–71.

Lardner, John. *White Hopes and Other Tigers.* Philadelphia: Lippincott, 1951.

Larson, Nella. *Passing: Authoritative Text, Backgrounds and Contexts, Criticism.* Ed. Carla Kaplan. New York: W. W. Norton, 2007.

Lee, George Washington. *Beale Street: Where the Blues Began.* New York: Ballou, 1934.

Lewis, Robert W. "'Long Time Ago Good, Now No Good': Hemingway's Indian Stories." *New Critical Approaches to the Short Stories of Ernest Hemingway.* Ed. Jackson J. Benson. Durham, N.C.: Duke University Press, 1990. 200–213.

Liebling, A. J. *The Sweet Science.* Westport, Conn.: Greenwood Press, 1973.

Limerick, Patricia N. *The Legacy of Conquest: The Unbroken Past of the American West.* New York: W. W. Norton, 1987.

Lindsay, Andrew. *Boxing in Black and White: A Statistical Study of Race in the Ring, 1949–83.* Jefferson, N.C.: McFarland, 2004.

Loomba, Ania. *Colonialism/Postcolonialism.* New York: Routledge, 1998.

Lounsberry, Barbara. "Green Hills of Africa: Hemingway's Celebration of Memory." *Hemingway Review* 12.2 (1987): 23–31.

Lynn, Kenneth. *Hemingway.* New York: Simon & Schuster, 1987.

Maloy, Barbara. "The Light of Alice's World." *Linguistics in Literature* 1 (Spring 1976): 74–86.

Mazrui, Ali A. *The Africans: A Triple Heritage.* Boston: Little, Brown, 1986.

Mellow, James R. *Hemingway: A Life without Consequences.* Boston: Houghton Mifflin, 1992.

Meyers, Jeffrey. *Hemingway: A Biography.* New York: Harper & Row, 1985.

———. "Hemingway's Primitivism and 'Indian Camp.'" *Twentieth Century Literature* 34 (Summer 1988): 211–22.

Monteiro, George. "'This Is My Pal Bugs': Ernest Hemingway's 'The Battler.'" *Studies in Short Fiction* 23.2 (1986): 179–83.

Morrison, Toni. *Playing in the Dark: Whiteness and the Literary Imagination.* Cambridge, Mass.: Harvard University Press, 1992.

———. "Unspeakable Things Unspoken: The Afro-American Presence in American Literature." *Michigan Quarterly Review* 28.1 (1989): 1–34.

Mudimbe, V. Y. *The Invention of Africa: Gnosis, Philosophy, and the Order of Knowledge.* Bloomington: Indiana University Press, 1988.

Nakjavani, Erik. "The Aesthetics of the Visible and the Invisible: Hemingway and Cezanne." *Hemingway Review* 5.2 (1991): 2–11.

Nies, Betsy L. *Eugenic Fantasies: Racial Ideology in the Literature and Popular Culture of the 1920s.* New York: Routledge, 2002.

O'Toole, Thomas. "The Historical Context." *Understanding Contemporary Africa.* Ed. April A. Gordon and Donald L. Gordon. Boulder, Colo.: Lynne Rienner, 1996. 23–51.

Perata, David D. *Those Pullman Blues: An Oral History of the African American Railroad Attendant.* New York: Twayne, 1996.

Plimpton, George. *Shadow Box.* New York: G. P. Putnam's Sons, 1977.

Prescott, Jeryl J. "Liberty and Just(us): Gender and Race in Hemingway's *To Have and Have Not.*" *CLA Journal* 37.2 (1993): 176–88.

"Prudence." *Random House Webster's College Dictionary.* New York: Random House, 2011.

Reddin, Paul. *Wild West Shows.* Urbana: University of Illinois Press, 1999.

Reynolds, Michael. *Hemingway: The American Homecoming.* Cambridge, Mass.: Blackwell, 1992.

———. *Hemingway: The Final Years.* New York: W. W. Norton, 1999.

———. *Hemingway's Reading, 1910–1940: An Inventory.* Princeton, N.J.: Princeton University Press, 1981.

———. *The Young Hemingway.* New York: W. W. Norton, 1986.

Roosevelt, Theodore. *African Game Trails: An Account of the African Wanderings of an American Hunter-Naturalist.* New York: Charles Scribner's Sons, 1909.

Said, Edward. *Orientalism.* New York: Random House, 1978.

Sammons, Jeffrey T. *Beyond the Ring: The Role of Boxing in American Society.* Urbana: University of Illinois Press, 1988.

Sandburg, Carl. *The Chicago Race Riots.* New York: Harcourt, Brace & Howe, 1919.

Santino, Jack. *Miles of Smiles, Years of Struggle: Stories of Black Pullman Porters.* Chicago: University of Illinois Press, 1989.

Shanley, Kathryn. "The Indians America Loves to Love and Read: American Indian Identity and Cultural Appropriation." *Native American Representations: First Encounters, Distorted Images, and Literary Appropriations.* Ed. Gretchen M. Bataille. Lincoln: University of Nebraska Press, 2001. 26–51.

Spurr, David. *The Rhetoric of Empire: Colonial Discourse in Journalism, Travel Writing, and Imperial Administration.* Durham, N.C.: Duke University Press, 1993.

Steinhart, Edward I. *Black Poachers, White Hunters: A Social History of Hunting in Colonial Kenya.* Oxford: Oxford University Press, 2006.

Stoddard, Lothrop. *The Rising Tide of Color against White World-Supremacy.* New York: Charles Scribner's Sons, 1922.

Strong, Amy L. *Race and Identity in Hemingway's Fiction.* New York: Palgrave Macmillan, 2008.

———. "Screaming through Silence: The Violence of Race in 'Indian Camp' and 'The Doctor and the Doctor's Wife.'" *Hemingway Review* 16.1 (1996): 18–32.

Sugar, Bert R. *100 Years of Boxing.* New York: Routledge Press, 1982.

Tompkins, Jane. *West of Everything: The Inner Life of Westerns.* New York: Oxford University Press, 1992.

Trogdon, Robert, ed. *Ernest Hemingway: A Literary Reference.* New York: Carroll & Graff, 1999.

Tuttle, William M., Jr. *Race Riot: Chicago in the Red Summer of 1919.* New York: Atheneum, 1980.

Unrau, William. *White Man's Wicked Water: The Alcohol Trade and Prohibition in Indian Country, 1802–1892.* Lawrence: University Press of Kansas, 1996.

Waisberg, Leo G., and Tim E. Holzkamm. "'A Tendency to Discourage Them from Cultivating': Ojibwa Agriculture and Indian Affairs Administration in Northwestern Ontario." 1984. Rpt. *Ethnohistory* 40.2 (1993): 175–211.

Warren, William. *History of the Ojibway People.* Ed. Theresa Schenk. St. Paul: Minnesota Historical Society, 2009.

Weale, B. L. Putnam. *The Conflict of Colour: The Threatened Upheaval throughout the World.* New York: Macmillan, 1910.

Whalan, Mark. *Race, Manhood and Modernism in America: The Short Story Cycles of Sherwood Anderson and Jean Toomer.* Knoxville: University of Tennessee Press, 2007.

Wilentz, Gay. "(Re)teaching Hemingway: Anti-Semitism as a Thematic Device in *The Sun Also Rises.*" *College English* 52.2 (1990): 186–93.

Williamson, Joe. *A Rage to Order: Black-White Relations in The American South since Emancipation.* Oxford: Oxford University Press, 1986.

Young, Philip. "*'Big World Out There'*: The Nick Adams Stories." *The Short Stories of Ernest Hemingway: Critical Essays.* Ed. Jackson J. Benson. Durham, N.C.: Duke University Press, 1975. 29–45.

———. *Ernest Hemingway.* London: G. Bell & Sons, 1952.

———. *Ernest Hemingway: A Reconsideration.* University Park: Pennsylvania State University Press, 1966.

INDEX